Additional Praise for *Business Blindspots*

"In *Business Blindspots*, Gilad teaches the art of surviving in the competitive environment, and provides a powerful competitive intelligence process to identify the corporate myths, beliefs and assumptions that hamper an effective competitive response. Using his trademark conversational style, Gilad informs, exhorts and challenges management to learn how to pick up and interpret market signals early enough to make strategies effective and prevent disasters. This is must reading for any business person who wishes to effectively compete in the 1990s."

> Bonnie Hohhof
> Editor
> *Competitive Intelligence Review*

"An extremely valuable book for any manager wanting to ensure sustainable competitive advantage in the '90s and beyond. I highly recommend *Business Blindspots*. It offers an enlightened look at the reasons for contemporary business failure. Sustainable competitive advantage in the '90s and beyond will depend on the rate at which competitive learning takes place. By implementing Professor Gilad's proposals and harnessing the collective learning power of employees, suppliers, customers and their networks, managers will ensure that the paradigms of the past don't become roadblocks to future success"

> Mark A. Sutton
> Business Unit Manager
> 3M/Commercial Office Supply Division

"Benjamin Gilad, one of the most qualified academics in the field of competitive intelligence (CI), blends academics and practicality in his approach to CI . . . A noted author in the field . . . Ben has been a thought-provoking speaker at SCIP conferences. Through his work with international audiences he has advanced the field of CI."

> From The Society for Competitor Intelligence
> Professionals' Award Ceremony for Fellows
> New Orleans, 1991

Additional Praise for *Business Blindspots*

"*Business Blindspots* provides an invaluable and well-tested recipe for challenging outdated business assumptions — and getting your company to change before it's too late."

> Mark Stott
> Manager, Strategic Business Research
> Corporate Strategy Office
> Motorola

"I thoroughly enjoyed reading Ben Gilad's book, *Business Blindspots*. Shifting the paradigm to better understand competitive intelligence, Benjamin Gilad challenges executives to remove the blinders. His book looks beyond fashionable management techniques into the soul of the marketplace, indispensable for sustaining competitive advantage. A revealing look into an often neglected yet critical dimension of management for the '90s."

> Tom Starr
> Associate Director, Business Management Planning/
> Sandoz Pharmaceuticals Corporation

"Further to his masterpiece, *Business Intelligence Systems*, Dr. Ben Gilad now makes another wonderful contribution to the advancement of business intelligence. Business executives including Japanese executives suffering the current severe recession shall derive much benefit from *Business Blindspots*. A must-have book for executives."

> Juro Nakagawa
> Associate Professor, International Marketing
> Aichi-Gakuin University, Nagoya, Japan

Additional Praise for *Business Blindspots*

"Ben Gilad's message is strong and clear to American corporations competing in today's global marketplace—heal thyself or perish! Ben's diagnosis of American executives is severe: they are affected by debilitating, often fatal, 'business blindspots,' exacerbated by ignorance about their competitors and arrogance concerning their own management capabilities. He prescribes his new competitive intelligence process, which he calls an 'immune system,' designed to cure the competitive sclerosis which he believes afflicts most American corporations. He—and I—hope it's not too late to learn and begin competing effectively. His book sounds both an alarm and school bell for American executives."

> Jan P. Herring
> Vice President
> Business Intelligence and Strategy
> The Futures Group, Inc.

BUSINESS
Blindspots

- **Replacing Your Company's Entrenched and Outdated Myths, Beliefs and Assumptions with the Realities of Today's Markets**

- **Benjamin Gilad**

PROBUS PUBLISHING COMPANY
Chicago, Illinois
Cambridge, England

ISBN 1-55738-536-X

Printed in the United States of America

BB

2 3 4 5 6 7 8 9 0

JB/BJS

To my gorgeous Shirly, who makes me laugh—and what is more important than that?—this book is for you, with a lot of love.

Table of Contents

Preface

Why do successful companies fail?
They fail because they no longer know how to read market signals.
Market signals are not easy to read: they are weak and ambiguous,
and they need *deciphering*.
Only a systematic and powerful process can decipher market signals
early enough to save a firm from decline.

"Oh, well," say you, the busy executive, "another book from another
management consultant heaping tons of trite statements on us."

To borrow a phrase from my friend Jeff, a manager of competitive
analysis at a hugely successful firm, "Bzzzzz, WRONG!"

First, I am an educator, not a consultant. I consult for fun. And when it
is not fun, as in running into the "I already know everything I need to know
about *my* industry"-type executive, I walk away. I can afford it.

I teach a course in strategic management and another in competitive
intelligence at Rutgers University, in Newark, New Jersey. Do you see a
connection between these two subjects? I see more than a mere connection;
I see an umbilical cord. And I have seen too many once-extremely-success-
ful firms that severed the cord and died.

I am an educator—I educate students, *and companies*, in the art of
surviving in a competitive environment. It is an art: the art of reading weak
market signals early enough to make a difference. It is amazing how many
companies do not have an effective process to recognize change signals
early and fight decline. Is decline inevitable?

Because I am not a strategy consultant, I *refuse* to advise managers on
strategy. Executives are responsible for charting strategies. They get paid
nicely for it. They are also the *only* ones close enough to the battlefield to do
the job right. Those who delegate this job to outside consulting firms are
either *not* close enough to their own markets or apparently have not learned

the lesson from the past two decades: Corporate America, by listening to the big consulting firms and paying a fortune to teams of MBAs, has lost its world status to the Japanese and Germans. Perhaps if we could convince the Japanese and Germans to employ the prestigious consulting firms as often as Americans, we could level the field again. But then, they are not as irresponsible, are they?

As an educator I firmly believe that executives, like managers, like workers, like *people*, need to learn *how* to make decisions, not *what* decisions to make. This is the role of education: Give people the tools to make the best decisions, and they will make them. I teach companies to *fight*.

This book is about why successful companies and executives stumble—about the blindspots that wreck their businesses and the way to fight them. This book offers companies an immune system, not an immunity. An immune system fights disease. "What disease?" you may ask. "Our company is netting 25 percent return on investment, we have been growing by 15 percent per year for the past five years. We lead the industry in . . . [fill in the blank]." Or, "Immune systems won't help us anymore. Man, we can't even afford to buy this book—I just borrowed it from a friend!"

An immune system for a corporation aims at fighting **competitive sclerosis**—a disease that takes executives who have been extremely successful for many years and turns them blind to reality. Why do these bright people lose touch with what's happening around them?

It is not their fault. It is a human tendency to develop specific blindspots and then, in turn, be blind to their existence. And if the company does not have a forceful way to marshal forces against this phenomenon, it can easily turn into another IBM, General Motors, Kodak, Sears, American Express, Citibank, Hoffman-La Roche, Chrysler, Digital, Xerox, and a host of other legends that are struggling to regain lost glamour. If it could happen to these almost indestructible giants, are you immune?

No, it is not size that causes all the problems for successful firms. Do not fall for cliches. Bureaucracy, complacence, and arrogance do not necessarily correlate to size (a Japanese keiretsu, for example, is huge yet still agile). Instead, it is the cumulative destructive power of Business Blindspots.

This book is for every senior executive who cares to keep his or her company successful—and for middle- and junior-level managers who care to make their next year's mortgage payments.

Benjamin Gilad

Acknowledgments

To Mark Stott, Tim Stone, Lera Chitwood, and their co-workers, who continue to prove that good decoders can keep a company a world leader.

To Stan Kaish, who made the first three chapters readable to the English-speaking world and encouraged me to write the next 14.

And to a special group of friends who suffered my company for a whole year while this book was being written: Gary, Carlos, Mike, Pat, Micki, and especially Jeff and Celeste. Your friendship means a lot to me.

Finally, to Shirly, who sustained me through the stress and deadlines without so much as one complaint. Your support made this book possible; your love made it worth writing.

CHAPTER ONE

Why Giants Fall

They fall because they no longer know how to read market signals.

Market signals are not easy to read: they are weak and ambiguous, and they need *deciphering*.

Only a systematic and powerful process can decipher market signals early enough to save a firm from decline.

Jack Welch, General Electric's CEO, once defined management as the task of "staring reality straight in the eye" and then having the courage to act. This is much easier said than done.

There are two basic problems with this definition. First, management must be *close* enough to reality to stare it in the eye. Second, it must not only stare but also *see* what is in front of its face.

This is a tall order. First, top management, through no fault of its own, is *never* close enough to the market. Second, some top executives can't see competitive reality staring at them.

One of the facts that amazed me the most over the past eight years, while helping American and European firms improve their ability to read their markets, was how insulated top executives were from competitive reality. This is because they secure their *competitive intelligence* (market signals regarding change) at best through a close circle of "trusted" personal sources, or at worst through those one-page news summary clippings. Top managers' information is *invariably* either biased, subjective, filtered, or *late*.

This is a repeated phenomenon. By the time *most* top executives get *firm* evidence regarding changes taking place in their markets, the company has lost touch with customers, technology, competitors, suppliers, government, and the other myriad forces operating to squeeze profits out of competitive markets. As Ben Rosen, the chairman of Compaq, lamented recently in describing Compaq's changing market, "We got hit in the head by a two-by-four."[1]

> **❝The question is not whether your company will lose touch with the competitive arena, but *when* it will lose touch.❞**

Indeed, many top managers face change only when it hits them in the head. They can never be close enough to the competitive arena to notice the signals of change early on. Moreover, early signals are never unequivocal: they are weak, ambiguous, deceptive. They need deciphering. Who has the time and access to continually and systematically identify signals early on? Who has the expertise to attempt to decode all of them? The $64 billion answer is: people who are in touch *daily* with the competitive arena—i.e., *lower*-level managers and employees.

But then there is always the problem that some top executives either fail or refuse to see reality, *even when they stare straight at it*. As Eckhard Pfeiffer, who replaced Rod Canion as Compaq's CEO, stated: "We had to overcome the denial before anything constructive could start."[2]

A Dangerous Malady

Denial, failure, or refusal to see reality are the biggest problems companies face. These problems wrecked IBM, Digital, General Motors, Sears, Hoffman-La Roche, Schwinn, American Express, Tandy, Citibank, Xerox, Kodak, and the list goes on and on. It stems from what I call "Business Blindspots." The three most devastating blindspots are *unchallenged assumptions, corporate myths,* and *corporate taboos.* Every company harbors blindspots, or is breeding some as you read these lines. The question is not whether your company will lose touch with the competitive arena, but *when* it will lose touch.

This is not a claim that one can do nothing about losing touch. It is a claim that if one does nothing, blindspots will *always* prevail. Without taking specific preventive measures, such as *ensuring* that top managers consider competitive information in making decisions, companies will be hit on the head by change time and again. And, as many managers already know, it hurts.

Consider the Case of Mercedes Benz . . .

For many years Mercedes Benz has been THE symbol of "Good Products Sell Themselves." After Mercedes' sales in the United States plunged 24 percent in 1991, its top management at last conceded that it had to change its strategy because of the competition (i.e., the Japanese). Until then, Mercedes' management refused to even acknowledge the *existence* of competition![3]

Ridiculous, you say? Yet even two decades of stiff competition have not completely uprooted the deep-seated belief, held by many companies throughout the United States and Europe, that it is enough to have a good, solid product and tight financial control to win the competitive game. The stronger this belief is, the ruder the eventual awakening. *Until 1980, Sears' internal position papers did not mention Wal-Mart!*[4] Since top management has many subtle, and not so subtle, ways of sending messages throughout its organization as to what really counts, this type of strongly held yet often unspoken belief affects the overall strategy as well as the daily operation of a company. It is just one small example of a business blindspot—in this case, a corporate myth that competitors don't count—that causes successful giants to fall from grace. Corporate taboos and a host of unchallenged assumptions do the rest.

Success as the Enemy

In the past two years or so, I haven't read one issue of *Fortune* or *Business Week* magazine in which there wasn't one executive or expert quoted as saying, "We have been too successful for too long, and now we are paying the price." It has become a joke: Every current management guru, former guru, or future hopeful is claiming that success leads to companies being arrogant, complacent, and a host of similar adjectives, depending on the guru or the audience or the management fad in vogue. When did success become the enemy? I ask you: Do you really need to pay $15,000 for a lecture by a famous "management consultant" to hear that? It reminds me of what Lou Gerstner, until recently RJR Nabisco's CEO, said in an interview in 1992: "Discounting is too easy. I don't need marketing people for that."[5]

Blaming success does not explain anything. If everyone knows that too much confidence is bad, and complacence is bad, and arrogance is bad, and *not listening to the market* is bad, how come successful companies still find themselves broke? How come Sears and IBM and American Express and Citibank and Hoffmann-La Roche and General Motors and Mercedes and USX and Procter & Gamble and Travelers and Southland and Westinghouse and U.S. Air and ITT and DuPont (have I missed some? Sorry, next book around) couldn't see competitive developments happening all around them?

Were they blind or something? The answer is: *exactly*. Success is wonderful. *Blindness* is not.

This book does not pretend to solve all the ills of corporations. It merely explores the reason success can turn "bad." It shows why it is almost inevitable that successful companies and executives fail to see changes around them. It takes away the blame from the managers who are hailed as geniuses one year and villains the next. More important, instead of throwing banalities around and then offering a miracle solution of restructuring, revitalizing, reengineering, reinventing, or some other re-something, it shows what should be done to prevent success from becoming a menace—not what can be done to prevent success, which seems to be the principal achievement behind the repeated restructuring of some giant corporations, like Kodak and IBM.

No List of Excellent Companies

The companies described in this book, the executives quoted, and the examples analyzed do not form a list of failures and successes. The essence of the tool I am giving you is the understanding that survival is tentative and success transitory, unless a company finds a way to keep its management alert. One of my favorite quotes is from Andrew Grove, the wise (at least for now) CEO of Intel:

> There is at least one point in the history of any company when you have to change dramatically to rise to the next performance level. *Miss the moment, and you start to decline.*[6] (emphasis added)

Unfortunately, without a focused, powerful process to track that moment, missing it is *guaranteed*. As Louis Hughes, president of General Motors' European operations, states, "You can fall very deep and very fast if you don't pay attention."[7] He should know. His company did not pay attention for years.

What does "pay attention" mean? It boils down to the seemingly obvious act of knowing how to pick up and interpret weak, ambiguous market signals early enough to make a difference for the future of the company. Obvious, perhaps, but not well practiced. By the time most senior executives receive such signals, they are loud enough for *everyone* to hear, and too late for meaningful proaction. It takes a powerful, systematic, patient, company-wide effort to practice this art well. This book describes a very old tool for doing just that.

This tool, which I call the competitive intelligence process, *is the most powerful and misunderstood managerial tool available today* to corporations. It has slowly gained in popularity and respect since the mid-1980s, as competition became global and Western firms found themselves at a growing disadvantage against agile competitors from the East who excelled in this area. In the 1990s, the need of Fortune 100 companies to emulate what other Fortune 100 companies do has led to another surge in interest, if not in effectiveness. The process has the capability, *if deployed right,* to keep companies alive and to extend success into the future. Alas, I can count on one hand the number of firms currently deploying it right. In fact, I *do* count them in this book.

Learning-Based Competitiveness

No, this is not another corporate buzzword, such as time-based competition, competency-based competition, capabilities-based competition, etc., etc., etc. It is much more fundamental and requires the oldest skill in the world— listening (yes, even the oldest profession needed to use this skill to become a *profession*). Consider the following example.

Bernard Marcus is the very successful executive founder of Home Depot, the enormously successful retail chain (10-year return to investors of 45.5 percent, 10-year growth in earnings per share of 42.5 percent on average).[8] In 14 years, Marcus built 224 stores in 21 states and reached sales of $7.1 billion in 1992. Impressive, wouldn't you say? What made Marcus so successful?

Take a deep breath. The list would probably go on for many pages, and each analyst and academic and leadership scholar would name different qualities. For me, though, it was one paragraph in the article describing Home Depot that screamed, this is it! In this little paragraph, *Fortune* magazine reported that a few years ago, while already *very* successful, Marcus visited Wal-Mart's Sam Walton and David Glass in Bentonville, Arkansas. They convinced him that offering everyday low prices was better than seasonal sales, which caused a run on the stores and ill feelings among customers.

How many successful executives do you know who visit other companies to *learn*? And how many *change their minds* about the right strategy after listening to some piece of competitive information? Competitiveness is based on learning, which is based on the ability to listen: to customers, to consumers, to partners such as suppliers, or to competitors, to industry experts, and, most important, to *one own's employees*. The essence of this philosophy is so simple it is embarrassing. The competitive environment sends messages all the time: signals about change, trends, prospects, threats, and weaknesses. Early on, these signals are weak, ambiguous, and hidden. Tapping them and then learning from them is an art that requires open eyes, ears, and *minds*. Companies that harness the power of learning, that develop a sonar system to listen to faint signals can fight decline. Companies that take learning for granted, or practice it haphazardly, or simply ignore early signals, charge blindly into Andy Grove's "miss the moment" trap.

Competitive learning is *not* learning only from competitors, although they are a very powerful source of learning. It is learning from *anyone in the competitive environment who has something to offer* that will enable the company to maintain its success: competitors, partners, suppliers, other companies, consumers, customers, government. American Express did not learn. Customers were sending signals that value was more important than prestige. AT&T listened, and came out with its no-fee Universal card, while CEO Robinson of American Express was forced to retire early.

Despite recent emphasis on empowerment and decision decentralization, competitive learning at the top of the organization is more crucial than competitive learning at the bottom. Kay R. Whitmore, Kodak's former CEO, masterminded the acquisition of Sterling, the drug company Kodak acquired in 1988 for $5.1 billion. In 1993, Kodak was in trouble in its core film business and carried a huge debt load of $9.5 billion. But Sterling was Whitmore's "pet" project—in other words, a blindspot. When an outsider brought in as chief financial officer suggested reducing the debt, which might have required selling Sterling, he had to quit after only 11 weeks.[9] One wonders how long it would have taken Whitmore to learn that Sterling was too costly, and the debt was too heavy, if he had not had to quit in 1993. Learning at the top is often painful but always crucial.

Learning to Learn

In this book I present a model of organizational learning that requires few resources but a lot of political courage. In its center is the creation of a new structure, the Office of the President, a cross-breeding of a Japanese design and an American organizational innovation aimed at supporting the heads of business units with competitive intelligence. "Business units" means companies, or divisions, or operating units, or subsidiaries, or whatever term is in use in your company to describe a unit that *actually engages in the competitive battle*. The model is then extended to cover corporate management as well, and the support a CEO needs in this area. It is clear, therefore, that one target market for this book is business leaders, from top division-level executives to top corporate executives, especially division presidents and corporate CEOs.

Sounds simple, doesn't it? When the reader who is a business unit's chief reads the next few chapters about blindspots and their horrendous consequences, I have no doubt that he or she will see immediately why the new structure makes perfect sense. Now all one needs to do is get the president to read this book, get the other top executives to accept the change as beneficial and nonthreatening to their standing, and get the rest of the organization to believe that this is not just one more "management fad." As I said, *sounds* simple.

When top management buys into this book's basic concept, the process of competitive learning makes *everyone* in the organization more in tune with competitive developments. But what if top management does not want or have the time to read this book? Or worse, what if top management is convinced that its own sources and personal collection of intelligence are sufficient to keep disaster away? The consequences of top executives being blind to a changing marketplace are often massive wealth destruction and layoffs. When there is no systematic, all-powerful, all-encompassing process at the organization to keep the top in tune with competitive reality at all times, who pays? Mostly middle management and workers. Consequently, this book is as much for middle- and junior-level managers as it is for top-level executives.

Responsibility at All Levels

The model in this book relies heavily on the voluntary cooperation of managers and workers in identifying early market signals and persisting in offering interpretations. The time when one could rely on the top four or five people in a division to be able to collect and interpret all the relevant signals is over. The environment is too complex, the executives too busy or, worse, wear too many blinders. Because of that, they are often the *last* ones to receive or decipher the signals. If middle management and plant workers and service technicians and salespeople and all the other employees *choose* to put their faith blindly in their top executives' limited ability to "pay attention," and are content to just "do their job," they should not be surprised if one sunny day they find themselves looking for a midlife career change.

The message of this book is that in today's competitive pressure-cooker, every manager and *every employee is responsible for ensuring that his or her job is there five years hence.* And if the manager is near retirement, it is his or her responsibility to keep the stock price up (assuming the company encouraged stock ownership). And if the manager has already retired, it is his or her responsibility to keep the company prosperous so that a grandchild may find summer employment when grandpa or grandma picks up the phone and calls good old Jim in personnel. Just shuffling papers from point X to point Y, or putting in the eight-hour shift at the plant, or convincing the retailers to stock more of the product won't do it. As story after story will prove, one cannot rely on top management to do all the "attention paying." It is time employees took that responsibility into their own hands.

And what if management does not want to listen to its own people? This is usually the same management that brings in the famous consulting firms and pays them millions to come up with ideas that everyone has tried for years to get management to adopt. What can the purchasing manager in room 213C, who complained for years that the relationship with supplier X was too relaxed, or the operation manager who knows of a better product development process at the competitor, do?

> **❝The time when one could rely on the top four or five people in a division to be able to collect and interpret all the relevant signals is over.❞**

The answer is, keep hammering it in. It does not matter, it *should* not matter, that some top executives lose the ability to listen to their own people, let alone listen to weak signals from the environment. It is up to the purchasing manager and the operating manager and the sales executive and the service representative and the tax specialist to scream and shout and nag and bug and, most of all, persist. *With the help of the new intelligence process introduced here, the operations manager may have a fighting chance to change things*, and his job may be there next year and his mortgage will be paid. If he gives up—disgusted, cynical, disheartened—he should not blame top management alone for the failure of the company. It was he who decided not to fight any more.

A Focus on Action

Finally, many information and intelligence professionals are going to read this book (or so I hope) because it deals with their jobs. To them I would like to offer an apology: Sorry if I fail to make the subtle distinction between competitive data, competitive information, and competitive intelligence. I am more focused on getting the division president to do *something* with the data, information, or intelligence.

One distinction I make very clearly is that competitIVE intelligence is not competiTOR intelligence. Concentrating on what your largest competitors are doing is only one aspect of competitIVE learning. It is not that competiTOR intelligence is reactive—a common confusion, since one must know what competitors' intentions and assumptions are in order to be *proactive* and outmaneuver them. It is that competitive learning can never be limited, or one will end up like General Motors, which paid $750 million just *not* to learn from a man named Ross Perot.[10]

Competitiveness starts at the division level and moves upward to corporate headquarters. The need to identify and decipher weak market signals early on starts with the division president and moves upward to the CEO. If they do it right, the entire organization will do it right. If they believe everyone else but them needs help in keeping up with the market, the organization will never become competitive.

Fighting competitive decline can take many forms. One way, exemplified by UPS's CEO, Kent Nelson, was to appoint four very senior executives to a task force to study the company's blindspots and formulate a better response to its competitors. That was back in 1990, after a two-year decline in profit margins.[11]

The solution offered in this book is *preventive*. It relies on a systematic process of reading market signals early on, and it starts with one manager, a telephone, a PC, and top management that is not ashamed to demand help.

That is not too expensive, is it? It can make the entire organization more attuned to the competitive reality. It can prevent the formation of deadly Business Blindspots. Give it a try.

PART ONE

A Theory of Blindspots and Bloodshed

"There is nothing more practical than the right theory."

Gen. (ret.) Ezer Weitzman
Former Israeli Air Force Chief

"Get your facts first, and then you are free to distort them as much as you please."

Mark Twain

● CHAPTER TWO

The Winner's Curse— Competitive Sclerosis

The winner's curse is a well-known phenomenon in research on bidding. The winner in an auction usually pays too much, since the winner is always the one with the most optimistic assumption about the value of the commodity under auction. Similarly, as the following examples show, overly optimistic assumptions take hold of successful companies. For companies that take the top position in their industries, the winner's curse seems to lead to an inevitable path: downward. Many managers I talked to believed that decline is a natural consequence of being number one. Is it really that inevitable?

Case Study 1

Question: Which company started as a small, mail-order outlet in Illinois and grew to be number one in gross sales in the United States, and if we don't count the state monopoly in the former U.S.S.R., number one in gross sales in its category in the *world*?

Answer: Sears, Roebuck & Co., of course.

Question: Which company lost 15 percent of its market share to its four competitors between 1971 and 1990, saw its earnings fall by an annual rate of 7.7 percent each year from 1984 to 1989, and sold its crown jewels (an insurance company and the largest real estate brokerage operation in the country) to finance a last-ditch effort to escape a buy-out?

Answer: Sears, Roebuck & Co., of course.

How could a company as powerful as Sears decline so peacefully without anyone crying "wolf"?

What Happened to Sears?

According to an article in the *Academy of Management Executive* analyzing Sears' decline,[12] three external developments precipitated the demise of the empire. The first was the rapid growth of discounters such as Wal-Mart, Kmart, and Target. These discounters carried name-brand merchandise at substantial reductions, purchased lower-priced import goods, and used lean methods of operations and distribution.

How did Sears react to these competitive developments? It didn't.

Sears' policy—or, more accurately, its basic philosophy, on which it was founded—was to buy domestically, sell at high prices, and run periodic sales. Customers flocked to Sears during these sales and to the discounters at all other times. Sears became the leader in . . . cost.

The second development was the appearance of the specialty chains, such as Home Depot. The specialty stores focused on a narrow line of products and, accordingly, put different pressures on different lines of products carried by Sears.

How did Sears react to these competitive developments? It didn't.

Sears' policy was to offer a full line of merchandise in the same general "Sears way." It continued with this policy even if a particular line came under pressure and required a different marketing approach. It continued with this strategy even as profits declined.

The third factor, according to the article, was the rapid development of specialty catalogues. These began operating through the 800-number system 24 hours a day, with operators "ready to assist you." Direct-mail sales have been, for several years, the fastest-growing segment of the retail market in the United States.

How did Sears react to this competitive development? It didn't.

Compared with the beautiful catalogues of Spiegel, L. L. Bean, and others, the Sears catalogue was antiquated and unappealing. Compared with the ease of ordering from the beautiful catalogues, the Sears ordering system was the most cumbersome marketing tool around. To order from it, one needed to take a course in Reading Obscure Instructions.

So what was the reason for Sears' lack of competitive response? The article identified two major causes:

1. Top management was out of touch with the reality of the competitive arena and unwilling to examine its own assumptions about competitors and customers.

2. Sears' internally promoted, conservative managers did not react for years.

The two problems are clearly related. When management lives in a world of its own creation, detached from what is really happening out there, managers have no reason to react. *Reaction always follows a change in the view of the marketplace.* If the view of the competitive environment is totally protected from a reality test, as it was at Sears, there is no reason to change course. The change then takes place only when a crisis hits home. Losses, especially at firms that never lost money before, serve as powerful stimuli to check the executives' basic view of the industry. Often the reexamination of basic beliefs is feasible only with the arrival of a new leader. In the case of Sears, the long-term decline eventually led to the ouster of top management and the nomination of Edward Brennan as chairman. Yet even Brennan, who grew up at Sears, resisted the need for a major overhaul in Sears' philosophy for two years. Only a loss and a restive board led to Brennan's agreeing to sell or spin off several divisions in 1992, paring Sears to its retail core. It is too early to tell whether this change came too late to save Sears. That the change came about *late* is easy to tell.

> **"Losses, especially at firms that never lost money before, serve as powerful stimuli to check the executives' basic view of the industry."**

Case Study 2

In the 1960s, Hoffmann-La Roche was the world's biggest drug company, with one of the industry's first megahits—Valium. By 1978 it was close to bankruptcy and ranked 17th in sales!

What Happened to Hoffmann-La Roche?

As its turnaround-CEO Fritz Gerber admits, HLR came to believe that it was immune to competition.[13] With Valium sales booming, it built research labs all over the world, staffed them with top scientists, and adopted the following three-pronged philosophy:

1. A drug that does not promise to be a megahit is not worth our attention.

2. New products will come from our own labs *only*.

3. We have nothing to learn from competitors' management (i.e., we don't hire top executives from competitors; we don't form joint ventures with them; we keep to ourselves).

HLR's top executives believed that its scientists would come up with another megahit. They did not. HLR's executives further believed that even after the expiration of patents on Valium, HLR's marketing muscle would be enough to protect its market position. As it turned out, that was a gross underestimation of competitors' strengths. Valium came off patent in 1985, and by 1987 HLR's pharmaceutical sales fell by almost 50 percent. HLR's management before Gerber arrived definitely suffered from the winner's curse of overly optimistic assumptions.

Gerber's remedy was radical: He forged nine strategic alliances in eight years, hired executives away from competitors, bought the rights to new products from competitors, and entered the biotechnology market earlier than any other major drug company. These bold steps reflected a radically different view of the *rules of the game* in Hoffmann-La Roche's industry.

Paranoia Can Save Your Company's Life

Sears Roebuck and Hoffmann-La Roche are clearly not the only cases of companies losing their competitive edge. They perfectly demonstrate, however, a simple lesson facing every American CEO tempted by the human tendency to rest on one's laurels:

What worked yesterday fitted yesterday's environment.

The statement does not imply that what worked yesterday will not work today, tomorrow, or the day after. In the early to mid-'80s, as Edward Land retired from active management of Polaroid and the new CEO, William McCune, faced severe competitive pressures, some analysts put Polaroid down as a "has-been." They urged management to seek its fortune through diversification into areas other than instant photography, such as magnetic media, video cameras, fiber optics, etc. Yet two years later Polaroid bounced back with the introduction of Spectra, and instant photography still provided the largest percentage of sales and profit.

The statement above does imply that managers must always treat present success as temporary, viewing it with the suspicion of a paranoid-schizophrenic. In line with the scientific tradition of Karl Popper, they should always look for contrary evidence, suggesting that what works now will soon *stop* working.

Roger's Law (dedicated to Roger Smith, General Motors' former CEO):

If you do not keep checking your view of the competitive arena and its basic rules of the game, and revise it constantly, there will always be at least one competitor who will be happy to do it for you.

If you are especially unlucky, there will be four such competitors— all Japanese.

Preaching this lesson to executive audiences on a tour in Israel last year, I was amazed by the depth of responses from a tough crowd of battle-seasoned CEOs. A typical response came from the CEO of a metal company, who approached me after the talk and said, "You know, under the tremendous pressure of reacting to daily problems, we really don't have the time to pause and check our view of what is really happening out there. I am always worried that one day I may wake up and find out the company is out of touch."

Is it inevitable that companies, upon reaching success or even leadership of their segments, will start losing their grip on competitive developments? Is there a winner's curse operating in the business world? Examining the cases of IBM, Citicorp, American Express, Compaq Computer, Digital Equipment, and endless other famous names, one gets the impression that indeed the eventual decline of successful organizations is inevitable. After all, even the Roman Empire (and any other empire) succumbed to the winner's curse. Yet Rome existed for 1,000 years, not a mere 50 or 100.

❝What worked yesterday fitted yesterday's environment.❞

Competitive Sclerosis

Let us look at Sears and Hoffmann-La Roche again. Sears declined because its top, middle, and junior executives insulated themselves from the market, like the Roman Empire's caesuras. Hoffman-La Roche, on the other hand, did not get that insular. Its decline can be compared to the surprise suffered by the Americans at Pearl Harbor. One just doesn't believe it can happen. In both cases, the organizations started to make unrealistic assumptions about the competition without questioning these assumptions. They underestimated the capabilities and intentions of the other players in the battlefield and overestimated their own strengths. Resting on one's laurels turns into blindspots. These blindspots are the causes for the disease I call *competitive sclerosis*.

In real arteriosclerosis (sclerosis of the arteries), the hardening of the walls of the arteries leads to diminished flow of blood to vital organs. In competitive sclerosis, success seems to restrict the flow of competitive updating information (blood) to the firm's top decision makers (heart), who then remain committed to an unchecked view of the competitive arena. This *hardening of assumptions* leads to a diminished ability to foresee competitive developments. In arteriosclerosis, psychological, physical, and lifestyle changes are recommended to prevent the progress of the disease. In competitive sclerosis, cultural, political, and organizational changes can prevent the decline and check the spread of blindspots.

Business blindspots are easy to recognize. Do you find any of the following expressions familiar? "This can't be true"; "That will never work in this industry"; "The decline is clearly recession-related"; "The consumer does not want radical change"; "We shouldn't tamper with what works"; "This is how things are done here." If you hear them around you, your company is suffering from blindspots. Blindspots on the collective corporate retina tend to spread like fire, until the entire company turns a completely blind eye to whole areas of its operations. At that point, no external signal of strategic significance registers on the radar of the company's top executives. Everything is fine, growth will continue forever, the formula that brought success yesterday is adhered to religiously. "We are number one!" booms the CEO, the great motivator, at the company's annual sales meeting in Orlando (or Phoenix, or Salt Lake City, or anyplace *sunny*).

Then a new and unexpected competitor turns up with a new process no one thought would work. Or the consumer, that fickle creature, switches to a cheaper/higher-quality/more convenient (circle the appropriate choice for your company) alternative. Or the technology takes an unexpected turn. The world caves in. All the unchecked assumptions about the rules of the game, the myths about how things should be done, the taboos that frustrated generations of junior managers come down with a big "Thud!" Reality is the best, the ultimate, and the most painful cure for blindspots on the corporate retina. Remember that as you go through the harrowing tales in the next chapter.

CHAPTER THREE
Business Blindspots

The underlying cause of competitive sclerosis—business blindspots—falls into three broad categories: *unchallenged assumptions, corporate myths* and *corporate taboos.*

Unchallenged assumptions are just that: incorrect assumptions about the competitive arena, typically about competitors, consumers, suppliers, or technology, that are taken for granted and allowed to go unchecked for long periods of time.

Corporate myths: a special class of assumptions that companies hold about themselves—their relative strengths, the way they do things, the value of some practices relative to competitors or the industry's "rules of the game." These assumptions can grow to the level of myths, partially or completely detached from the competitive reality.

Corporate taboos: Some incorrect assumptions survive attacks and contrary evidence to become untouchable. These typically enjoy strong support from the top.

Some companies suffer from one category's destructive effect more than another, and some are perfect examples of all three operating at full power.

To cure blindspots, we need to know what causes them. In this chapter, I lay the groundwork for a "theory" of blindspots. This is no claim to a rigorous scientific theory, but rather a first attempt at developing a *practical* framework for understanding the phenomenon in order to fight it. From the collection of anecdotes provided in the text, I derive a few fundamental laws that seem to describe the behavior of blindspots pretty well and are applicable to *many* organizations. Whenever possible, I also highlight the more frequently found characteristics of blindspots based on the included evidence and my personal experience with corporate America. Let us start with a mild case of mountain dizziness.

Unchallenged Assumptions

Cycling on Empty

The U.S. bicycle industry has gone through several phases during the past 30 years. After decades in which bicycles were mainly toys for kids, and adult choices were limited to heavy, single-speed, coaster-brake bikes with fat tires, the '50s saw a renaissance in the industry brought on by changing demographics, concern for health, and other macro factors. Then, in the '70s, lightweight, high-speed bikes appeared and pushed the demand to record heights. Bicycles became an adult product, cycling became a hobby, and cycling enthusiasts grew in numbers.

In these years, one company led the high end of the industry through its vision, quality, product development, and manufacturing technology. Schwinn, which led in selling through a chain of independent dealers, was the first American firm to recognize the change in consumers' characteristics and the product's image. It was somewhat surprising, therefore, that it was *another* company—Specialized Bicycle Components, a tiny company in Morgan Hill, California—that saw the potential in launching the first mass-produced mountain bike (the Stumpjumper) in 1981.

The irony, though, is not that Schwinn missed the opportunity to be the first on the market with the latest technology. Letting others test the water is a legitimate strategy. Rather, it was the fact that for the *next 10 years,* Schwinn continued to sell its traditional bicycles, ignoring the lesson it had taught everyone else: Many consumers have turned into enthusiasts, and enthusiasts are willing to pay a premium for the *latest* product. Specialized Bicycle Components grew to 6 percent of the world market (by value of shipments), expanding by 25 percent per year from 1986 to 1991.[14]

Schwinn's slowness in spotting the new trend in consumer preferences was the consequence of one type of competitive blindspot—*unchallenged assumptions.* Managers operate under a whole *set* of assumptions regarding the rules of the game in their industry: assumptions about themselves (treated later under the label corporate myths), the capabilities and weaknesses of competitors, the characteristics and tastes of customers, the barriers to entry to the industry, the strength of substitute products, the desired relationships with suppliers, the cyclical nature of demand, etc. Often these assumptions are summarized in the popular beliefs about the so-called "success factors" in the industry. As the Schwinn case demonstrates, many of those *fundamental* assumptions can become obsolete. Being fundamental, these unchecked assumptions behave according to the First Law of Business Blindspots:

● *First Law: Unchallenged assumptions underlie every corporate activity, from strategies to tactics to operating procedures.*

A Classic, and Rather Universal, Blindspot

Assumptions can be obvious or hidden. It is not always easy to uncover hidden assumptions. One classic example: Many top executives at large corporations assume that there is nothing worthwhile to learn from *smaller* competitors. Schwinn's attention was probably focused on Raleigh, on the Japanese, on Murray. Specialized Bicycle Components was too small to be significant. Or take Nike, which for years assumed that its main competitors were Puma and Adidas, the two big firms in the athletic shoe industry. When Reebok appeared out of nowhere with a stylish but technologically inferior aerobic shoe, Nike was not impressed. When Reebok took over the aerobic market, Nike's top managers began to realize that it was Reebok, not the larger competitors, that could teach them a thing or two about what the consumer actually wanted! This is a common competitive blindspot: *Large companies pay attention to large companies* (or to large consulting firms, which pay attention to *large* companies).

The reason for this universal blindspot is that small competitors are not considered as "professional" (a synonym for efficient and effective). Their leaders are not similar in background to the executives at a larger competitor. They are "not in the same league" as the manager who controls a billion-dollar-plus business. How can they teach him or her what the customer wants? Many managers pay lip service to the importance of monitoring all competitors, but it is the large rivals that elicit competitive response. The result is that developments coming out of smaller firms, which can often serve as *leading indicators* of things to come, are systematically ignored (until, inevitably, performance at the large company starts to decline).

Some executives pay dearly for this popular blindspot. Compaq's CEO Rod Canion lost his job in 1992 after his failure to pay attention to the little clone makers that eventually outflanked Compaq with cheaper machines. Compaq's chairman, Ben Rosen, admitted, "We were focused solely on IBM."[15] One commentator wondered "why so astute a man as Chairman Ben Rosen took so long to react to the changing market."[16] Elementary, my dear Watson; astuteness has nothing to do with it. Even the best of us develop a blindspot sooner or later.

Sometimes this blindspot reaches absurdity.[17] As problems at Westinghouse Credit Company mounted due to a bad real estate portfolio, Westinghouse executives, headed by then-chairman Paul Lego, looked for ways to rid themselves of the portfolio. But they did not trust the "real estate types." Lego rejected proposals from real estate developers who offered to buy the properties, calling them "bottom-fishers." Instead, Lego turned to General Electric for a deal. After all, large companies respect only large companies. GE made such a low offer that the talks collapsed. Later on, a second round of talks collapsed as well. Lego paid with his career. Westinghouse may pay with bankruptcy.

Flushing Out Assumptions

At times, the only way to flush out management's assumptions is to infer them from actual behavior, as opposed to asking managers "What are your assumptions about the industry?" This is especially helpful when a manager attempts to analyze a *competitor's* assumptions in order to identify *its* blindspots (see Chapter 6: Blindspots as a Competitive Weapon). It is unlikely that a competitor will give *any* answer, when asked about assumptions, let alone a truthful one. Analyzing overt strategy then becomes the method to infer assumptions. Take for example the case of Cramer Electronics.

> **❝The story told by Michael Porter is of a company that believed *success would come from being all things to all people,* in an industry that called for the opposite philosophy. ❞**

Once a major player in the electronic components distribution industry, Cramer Electronics' only claim to fame now is its inclusion in the seminal Competitive Strategy case book written by Michael Porter.[18] The story told by Porter is of a company that believed *success would come from being all things to all people*, in an industry that called for the opposite philosophy.

From its early days, the company adopted the following strategy: It carried the broadest line of electronic and other components with overlapping product lines, supported the largest sales force of nontechnical people in the industry, maintained a large number of warehouses across the country, and competed on *every* contract and in *every* segment, matching prices with *every* competitor. And competitors were abundant: The electronic component distribution industry at the time (the '70s) was fragmented, consisting of a few larger firms (Cramer among them), dozens of medium to small regional ones, and no clear industry leader—the quintessential characteristics of a fragmented industry.

Let's assume that you were Cramer's competitor trying to understand its strategic thinking. Analyzing Cramer's *overt* (i.e., observable) strategy, described above, would have led you to the conclusion that its management must have adhered to the following three tenets:

1. Every customer was a valuable customer—that would explain why it maintained such a large sales force, selling to every segment of the market including small, medium, and large customers.

2. Customers valued a "supermarket," one-stop shopping-type operation—that would explain why Cramer kept the broadest product line, even though most of the profit came from just a small fraction of the items in inventory.

3. Every deal was worth fighting for—that would explain why Cramer bid on every contract regardless of margins.

Why would a company strive so hard to please every customer? The most logical explanation is that its management held an even more basic "master-assumption": Volume was the name of the game. And why would any company strive so hard to achieve volume? Most likely because it *believed* that volume would lead to the wonderful world of economies of scale.

The strategy had tremendous cost in high and redundant inventory, excessive payroll, and low margins. The trouble was not the strategy, though. It might have been a wonderful strategy—*for a different industry*. In the electronic components distribution industry, however, *none* of the assumptions held true. The essence of a fragmented industry is that *it is unprofitable for the player to try to be all things to all people*. Rather, as Porter points out, focus is the road to competitive advantage. Worse yet is the fact that despite its efforts to achieve that incremental sale, there weren't any real economies of scale to be reaped! If anything, order processing caused *dis*economies of scale, since both small and large orders cost the same to process!

The case of Cramer Electronics clearly demonstrates that blindspots can kill. Despite mounting evidence to the contrary, Cramer's management stuck to its assumptions about the success factors in its industry until the company went broke and was liquidated in 1979. Throughout its decline, Cramer's top management attributed the continuing success of its number-one competitor, Hamilton/Avnet, more to luck than to brain. The moral is summarized in Business Blindspots' Second Law:

● *Second Law: Unless managers have the ability (cognitive, emotional, and organizational) to perceive and then question their implicit competitive assumptions, they are not going to perceive the value of learning from experience.*

Corporate Myths

The year 1991 was a bad year for the largest American tire manufacturer, Goodyear. It was its first money-losing year since the Great Depression. At the same time, its main competitors, Michelin and Bridgestone, were expanding their market share. The shock was severe enough for the board to bring in a new CEO, Stanley Gault, the former CEO of Rubbermaid.

Gault faced several "traditions" at Goodyear. First, Goodyear sold its tires *only* through its network of dealers. Second, Goodyear *always* sold its new products to the automakers first. Third was the tradition of introducing new products one at a time at regular intervals.

Traditions are practices that solidify through years of success. They may be wonderful and/or harmless, as long as they do not become corporate myths, out of touch with the changing competitive reality. While Goodyear sold through dealers only, American consumers were buying more of their tires at the big retail chains. Goodyear sold to the Original Equipment Manufacturers first, yet they were responsible for aggravating its problems by pressuring margins severely with volume discounts. The myth of introducing new products one at a time was just that: There was no rational reason to sustain it. It caused delays in product introductions and diluted the effect of significant technological advances.

Not to be outdone by Cramer from the previous example, Goodyear's executives also operated under the influence of a decade-old, *unchallenged assumption*: They were convinced that buyers would never buy an "ugly" tire, even if its ugliness was the result of a sophisticated feature! Stanley Gault had no respect for traditions. He launched four new tires at once, one of them the "ugly," technologically advanced Aquatred. He signed up Wal-Mart, Sears, Kmart, and other chains to distribute Goodyear tires and placated the Goodyear independent dealers by refusing to sell the Aquatred to the auto companies, limiting it only to the replacement market.

Gault broke every sacred tradition at Goodyear, and in the process Goodyear earned $97 million in 1991 and a new sales record in 1992. The "ugly" tire has been selling like hot cakes.[19] Goodyear has gained market share. A fairytale story with a happy ending? Time will tell. One clear moral is that *corporate myths are powerful enough to wreak havoc.* They must be subject to continuous testing. On occasion, challenging them *just to test their validity* may save a manager from losing his job!

Quite often, corporate myths grow out of the distinct character of a company. Compaq, the computer maker, was founded by a team of Texas Instruments engineers whose engineering mentality initially proved enormously successful. The character of the founders became the character of the whole company—an engineering-led company that almost had no choice but to become a prisoner of a myth that *technology was all that mattered.* Compaq's legacy was building technologically superior machines, concentrating on features and performance, and *never* undercutting prices (i.e., IBM's prices; Compaq did not believe in watching other competitors at all). Overengineering was a way of life. That was evident everywhere: Compaq built its own power supplies, designed extremely strong casings, and doubled the number of radiation shields actually necessary to protect against radiation, among other investments in quality and performance. The cost was appropriately high, and so was the price.

Because Compaq's philosophy worked so well, how could its managers have avoided developing a corporate myth? Since its creation in 1982, Compaq set growth records for a start-up in the '80s and by 1990 was considered a performance powerhouse. But then the roof fell in. In 1991 Compaq suffered a 17 percent revenue drop and its first loss.[20] What caused such a dramatic turn of fortunes?

Well, it was not really that dramatic, nor unexpected. The marketplace was changing under Compaq's nose, but its myth-captive managers could not really see it. Rod Canion, a cofounder, simply refused to believe customers would go for the cheaper clones made by Dell, AST, or Gateway 2000. So strong was the hold of this myth of technology over price (or, actually, over *value*) that even as sales dropped off and the market penetration of clones was growing by leaps and bounds, Canion continued to claim that Compaq's troubles were "recession-related." Compaq's culturally built momentum supported him wholeheartedly. Reality didn't.

Canion's successor, Eckhard Pfeiffer, who came from Europe and therefore was less a prisoner of the headquarters mentality, turned Compaq into a low-cost producer almost overnight. In his words, "We threw our pricing policy overboard." He also started marketing through catalogues, by telemarketing, and through discount "superstores"—strategies Compaq's old engineering culture would never have *dreamed* of using.

This is an important point to remember (recall Gault's at Goodyear):

If you want to shatter a truly sacred myth, shatter a few related ones as well. There is power in numbers, and you may never get a second chance.

Corporate Taboos

Corporate taboos are just like their social counterparts: acts or things which by general agreement are not to be "touched." Unlike unchallenged assumptions, taboos can withstand persistent questioning and attacks from within without as much as a scar. Often they can be traced to strong leaders and their personal convictions.

Consider the case of IBM. Many blame the centralized decision making—its "top-down" corporate culture—for IBM's troubles in the '90s.[21] An all-powerful management committee has been known to scrutinize every move and initiative at the giant's various business units. Critics claimed this bureaucracy slowed down decision making and product development at IBM. However, bureaucracy and centralized management are too easy a target for critics, and the criticism often misses the point. *Bureaucracy and centralized decision making are bad only when the top decision makers suffer from strong blindspots.* When this is the case, the lack of fresh views—the essence of decentralization—and the concentration of all decisions at the *blinded* top is a recipe for disaster.

In the case of IBM, its extremely strong culture served as a perfect petri dish for the germination of some of the most sacred competitive taboos. The most famous one was the complete domination of policy by the mainframe computer division. Products or initiatives that were even remotely competitive with the mainframe had no chance of getting anywhere.[22] The mainframe taboo is blamed for a whole set of strategic blunders at IBM: the botched entry into laptops; the insistence on developing compatibility among its different lines rather than letting its units follow open, industry-standard software, which the market clearly preferred; the enormous spending on the operating system OS/2 despite customer resistance; and the fact that IBM scientists pioneered the application of reduced instruction set computing technology (RISC), but IBM top executives squelched it to protect the mainframe business.[23] As a result, Sun Microsystems was the first to adopt the new technology and grow into a market leader in workstations. Moreover, a 1988 restructuring at IBM, which was supposed to speed up decisions (and presumably make them better), failed miserably. No wonder—the taboo of "don't dare touch the mainframe" remained as strong as ever. In 1992, as IBM worldwide market share tumbled to less than 19 percent and losses approached $900 million, John Akers, IBM's CEO, went for *another* restructuring—this one, at last, aimed specifically at reducing the dominance of mainframes. The clear lesson is that *restructuring that leaves people **thinking** the same way leaves them as blind as before.*

> **"Bureaucracy and centralized decision making are bad only when the top decision makers suffer from strong blindspots. "**

An Apple a Day Doesn't Do Much . . .[24]

In 1990, Apple announced a reversal of a six-year policy of charging premium prices for the Macintosh line. Apple then cut prices by 40 percent. Was the timing right? Should Apple have waited six long years to reverse its policy? The facts in this case, especially the Apple CEO's background, suggest a powerful taboo at work.

The history of the Macintosh is the history of John Sculley, the former PepsiCo executive who became Apple's CEO. Back in 1983, he figured a premium price would allow him to plow profits back into advertising to gain market share. *This was a classic brand-management strategy borrowed from the success of Pepsi Cola;* no wonder Sculley was stuck on it. Nevertheless, the strategy failed. After a strong opening, Macintosh sales nosedived. Sculley then decided that in addition to the aggressive advertising, he would use the high gross margin to finance a heavy R&D program. *The high prices remained, and the fat gross margins became a taboo.*

The technologically sophisticated Mac was a favorite of enthusiasts but was ignored by much of the market. Firms refused to switch from their simpler IBMs until prices dropped. Several proposals made by Apple employees in the late 1980s for a low-cost Macintosh were rejected. (Remember the definition of taboos: incorrect assumptions that withstand attacks.) By 1990, Apple's share of the market was so low (6.9 percent) that software houses stopped developing new products for the Macintosh. Then Windows 3.0 appeared, giving IBM-compatible machines advanced features that wiped out most of the Mac's technological advantage. Only then did Sculley succumb and reverse Apple's pricing policy.

The six-year pricing policy, which went against all market evidence and internal dissent, seems suspiciously like a corporate taboo. This impression gets stronger when one examines Sculley's background and the industry he came from. As you will see, a similar explanation accounts for certain taboos created by GM's Roger Smith and Chrysler's Lee Iacocca. This is a frequently found characteristic of taboos: *Taboos can often be traced to the executive's personal background.*

This characteristic can serve as a potent weapon for competitors, as is evident in the following development: When the pricing taboo at Apple was finally broken, sales exploded. By the third quarter of 1992, Apple passed IBM in PC shipments for the first time since 1981. Indeed, this is another frequently found characteristic of taboos: *Breaking them can be a profitable enterprise.*

Style by Any Other Name

Often, corporate myths and taboos go by the more elegant label of "style." Sears did not lower its everyday high prices, despite the inroads of discounters such as Wal-Mart, because it was not the "Sears way." Tandy Corporation found itself in a similar straitjacket. It built its fortunes on the basis of small stores (2,500-square-foot Radio Shacks) selling a limited product line at a high profit margin with slow inventory turnover. The formula worked in the '60s and '70s, but stumbled in the '80s with the appearance of giant consumer-electronics superstores that emphasized large selection at very low prices and thrived on volume. Because it was not Tandy's "style" to push volume, it took John V. Roach, its CEO, several years of decline (between 1989 and 1992, earnings plunged 43 percent!) to realize that the original Tandy concept was no longer practical. His solution was radical: In 1992 he entered the superstore race with two Incredible Universes, 160,000-square-foot stores. Some analysts predicted failure because the new direction was so removed from Tandy's style that its management lacked the expertise to deal with it. Whether that prediction comes true or not is less important than the realization that *having a strong corporate style often implies a whole bag of blindspots.*

A Live Laboratory for Blindspots

It seems reasonable to assume that the slower the change takes place in a given industry, the more entrenched the blindspots become, having had many decades to develop and set roots. While this might be true (I leave the empirical test of this assumption to future researchers), it is the computer industry, with its rapid change, that provides us with a live (and painful) laboratory for studying the modus operandi of business blindspots. In this rapidly evolving industry, if you are blinded, you run into a wall quickly—and with no safety belts!

No one will seriously dispute that the computer industry is a turbulent competitive arena. In PCs, for example, product cycles are down to as little as six months. In microchip technology, the computing power a dollar can buy doubles every 18 months. Compared to that, many industrial and even consumer industries are as stable as a rock.

The computer industry is an industry *in the making*: It is becoming more fragmented as you read these lines. This is a radical structural change from the way it was just few years ago—a concentrated industry dominated by a few vertically integrated giants. In the process of structural evolution, the fundamentals of competing in the industry are being redefined faster than one can say IBM.

In a rapidly changing environment, who has the time to entrench the wrong assumptions and build up corporate myths? Everybody, or so it seems. And if the affliction affects the computer companies, imagine what it does to your company!

Take for example the maxim that the profit potential in the industry was in the mainframes, the *big* machines. One would expect IBM and Digital to entertain this assumption based on their success at selling mainframes. Yet in a dynamic market such as theirs, one would also expect them to follow closely the developments of micro-based alternatives, and to be able to see the writing on the screen: Large machines have been increasingly threatened by flexible networks of powerful desktop machines. Instead, in July of 1992, Digital's board had to oust Ken Olsen, the chairman and founder, for "failure to tap trends toward more powerful microchips."[25]

As mentioned earlier, IBM announced an ambitious reorganization in 1992 aimed at freeing its business from the straitjacket of the mainframe mentality. A little late—its profit had been declining since 1984.[26] Regarding this trend toward powerful microchips and away from mainframes, Gilbert Williamson, president of NCR, is quoted as saying, "It has unfolded beyond our wildest imagination."[27] The only thing that constrained the big computer companies' imagination was this "size" blindspot.

An even more fundamental change in the industry has been the redistribution of profits. The makers of systems saw their profits disappear. Yet the belief that the key to success was to sell finished computer products was so entrenched that management in many companies assumed that the fall in hardware profits was due to economic recession. In fact, the decline in profit was due to a reallocation of profit from hardware makers to component suppliers, software writers and service providers—a fundamental change brought about by "open" systems that turned the market into a fully competitive one (buyers could mix different machines), and by the emergence of PCs as commodities. In a rare admission, James Unruh, CEO of Unisys, said, "A lot of people in our industry, including myself early on, didn't see that clearly . . . the economic model had changed and the cost structures of the past were obsolete."[28]

It is exactly *early on* that one must notice that one's assumptions have become obsolete. What prevented Unruh of Unisys, Akers of IBM, and Olsen of Digital from distinguishing the change from a mere cyclical downturn was the fact that years of high margins on systems had created a very powerful *business blindspot*. The fact is, most companies could survive cyclical downturns (recessions) but for the confounding effect of blindspots. *With blinders on, recessions become a scapegoat and fundamental market changes go unnoticed.*

One unexpected benefit of rapid and radical change is that it can make some players acutely aware, often not by choice, of the need to actively fight blindspots. In the computer industry, companies such as ICL, Hewlett Packard, and battle-scarred Unisys have used some radical strategies to combat blindspots. Since no industry today is truly stable, companies can learn from the experience of these firms (see Chapter 5). One clear lesson is that *no strategy is too radical to fight competitive sclerosis.*

An Anatomy of Unchallenged Assumptions, Myths, and Taboos: The Automobile Industry[29]

The history of the American automobile industry offers a striking opportunity for studying the anatomy of business blindspots. For an entire decade—the '80s—GM, Ford, and Chrysler exhibited almost every corporate myth, unchallenged assumption, and taboo in the book. On the other hand, the Japanese automakers offer a lesson in how difficult it is to compete with companies that already understand the essence of constantly fighting sclerosis. The most striking lessons are for those who tend to forget that ultimately, the fate of the firm is determined at the top. And therefore, ultimately, the blind eye turned by top management is the reason for corporate failure. Finally, the automobile industry offers us an opportunity to discover a few more fundamental laws of business blindspots.

Blindspots in the American car companies were readily apparent back in 1973, when the Japanese began their penetration of the American market. With the second gasoline crisis in 1979-1980, the Japanese gained a 20 percent market share from the Americans. One would think America would have learned its lesson regarding the astuteness of Japanese managerial talent. Yet in a 1992 interview, a top Chrysler executive said, "By the time we *woke up* to the fact that they were really chewing on us, they had 20 percent of the market. From that point on, they just chipped away." (emphasis added)

Well, they did not just chip away, they kept on *chewing*. In 1981, the industry got the Japanese to "agree" to voluntary import quotas. Then, over the next 10 years, the Japanese increased their market share by more than 10 points, restraint notwithstanding! The amazing fact is that the lesson of the '70s was heeded *not at all* as the competition moved into the '80s. Says one executive who worked for both Toyota and GM, "After 1978 or 1979, the Japanese did a better job of reading the market."

How could the American managers ignore the Japanese achievements in the '70s? Another executive's comment sheds light on the mechanism—the Americans simply created a *revised assumption* that went *unchallenged*:

> We gave the Japanese all kinds of credit for building reliable if somewhat boring automobiles. With the larger Honda Accord and the new Toyota Camry, and the whole movement up-market with Lexus and Infinity and Acura, we underestimated how quickly the Japanese were going to get really excellent in engines and transmissions and styling.

As the quote suggests, presented with indisputable evidence that the Japanese knew basic manufacturing, American executives simply revised *portions* of their blindspots regarding the Japanese abilities. Blindspots die hard, even in the face of clear evidence, unless there is a deliberate attempt to eradicate them. U.S. automobile companies were never known for deliberately fighting to stay tuned to their markets.

The corporate culture that allowed the above behavior can be glimpsed from the following anecdote. In 1985, a colleague of mine who was then the planning head for a big retailer was invited to tour the planning department at one of the Big Three. He spent three hours being presented with a dazzling competitive analysis of the industry. The colors, the graphics, the prose were superb. The Japanese were not mentioned even once. That's *1985*, yes.

Mirror, Mirror on the Wall, What Is the Worst Myth of All?

Perhaps the staunchest myth of all is not a business blindspot, but the one held by most Americans: Corporate leaders must know what they are doing. The deep need for heroes, the association of wealth with smarts and wisdom, and clever corporate public relations campaigns create the myth that senior executives are larger than life. In the automobile industry, many were much smaller. Sounds too harsh? I will let the reader judge after reading this segment. That the captains of the automobile industry were no geniuses is an understatement. Policies that at most were a "nice touch" and at least were common sense took the high-powered minds of the Big Three by surprise. Example: Toyota's policy of returning Lexuses, recalled for minor repair, washed and with a full tank of gas. This "creative breakthrough" was one of the major factors that transformed Toyota's image from reliable, but dull, to the standard in high class. It took the industry by storm. It really shouldn't take a genius to research this issue and determine that the customer who pays $35,000 per car would appreciate a little extra attention. But we can't expect that creativity from *everyone*, can we?

> **"It shouldn't take a genius to determine that the customer who pays $35,000 per car would appreciate a little extra attention."**

Beyond this tiny anecdote, there is little doubt that the story of blind-spots at the Big Three is the story of their leaders' blindspots. Sometimes a blindspot was just a personal obsession, such as Iacocca's fondness for squared-off roofs and vinyl padding that held Chrysler's styling back *a whole decade*. Sometimes it was a business blindspot, such as Smith's persistent refusal to see the failure of his vision of the automated factory, for which he spent billions of GM's cash, despite consistent counterevidence. Sometimes it was just amazing.

Iacocca and ChryCo

In 1980, a government-guaranteed loan of $1.5 billion saved Chrysler from bankruptcy. By 1982, a tax-loss carry-forward gave Iacocca a net profit of $2.4 billion. With this badly needed, taxpayer-funded cash, one would expect Iacocca to put Chrysler's ailing car operations on a sound track. Given the "near-death" experience of the company, the first order of the day for you and me would have been a radical transformation of the old ways, right? Instead, Lee Iacocca spent the next five years selling and buying assets, starving its car operations of cash, and culminating in the reorganization of Chrysler as a holding company, nicknamed ChryCo. It sounded like PepsiCo but tasted like New Coke: a resounding flop. The rental car acquisitions (General, Snappy, Thrifty, and the other four dwarfs) proved to be money losers. The Electrospace acquisition has been on the block since 1987 with little chance of finding a buyer. The Gulfstream acquisition was sold for a $188 million profit (average 5 percent return per year of holding), but considering the price paid by the car business for this use of the cash, it was a disaster. The AMC acquisition alone almost brought Chrysler down when absorbing it proved much more difficult than buying it. The stock repurchase at a price of $22 resulted in issuing new stock at $10. By 1990, Chrysler was on the brink of bankruptcy again. While the diversification and transactions raged, the car business was neglected and deteriorating. Every model following the K-car line was a failure!

How could Iacocca neglect the car business—the same business he grew up in and was called to rescue? How did his top executives let it happen? The answer can be found in two beliefs that permeated Iacocca's Chrysler during his reign. One, which became a *corporate taboo* (an incorrect assumption that becomes foolproof), was that the most important performance measurement was the stock price; the second was an *unchallenged assumption* that the Japanese were basically unstoppable.

Senior executives at Chrysler claim that Iacocca was driven obsessively by the desire to see Chrysler achieve the same stock multiplier as, for example, Xerox. To get there, he was determined to please the financial community, which, in the early '80s, saw diversification as a panacea (despite the strong warning voiced by such strategy gurus as Michael Porter). *Since Iacocca did not believe that the Japanese were stoppable,* he turned his efforts toward a buying and selling spree, singlemindedly aimed at raising the stock price.

The fact that Iacocca listened more carefully to *financial* analysts than to his own analysts should not surprise anyone who knows the type of convoluted relationships that exist between American CEOs and Wall Street. The fact that for the next five years no one in his close circle tried to break the corporate taboo of the stock price, despite mounting evidence that the company was going down the drain, is a testimony to the power of corporate taboos. The taboo was broken only when Iacocca *himself* became disenchanted with diversification. In the 1992 *Fortune* article, he admits, "We wasted a lot of time, a lot of effort, setting up a holding company. I never was a conglomerate type." We? Taboos are typically the result of a strong autocratic leader and his or her personal biases. There is no "we" in taboos. Perhaps if Robert Lutz, the bright Ford executive who was recruited in 1986, had put his foot down on the waste issue, something would have happened earlier. But Lutz, who eventually became Chrysler's president, preferred to confront Iacocca on the styling issue, the *other* taboo. Thousands of workers then paid the price.

It is interesting to note that when Iacocca eventually turned his attention to the car business, in 1988, and Chrysler decided to produce a new line, it dispatched *12 of its brightest young managers to study Honda.* The result was a complete reorganization of the engineering department at Chrysler. Following Honda, Chrysler eliminated the grouping of engineers along functional lines (such as electronics, suspension, etc.) in favor of platform teams. The new LH models were completed on time for their 1993 introduction and received rave initial reviews. There are two lessons to learn from this turnaround. The first is captured in the Third Law:

● *Third Law: The best way to overcome business blindspots is to confront the blindness head on—i.e., learn directly from the competition.*

The Third Law suggests that Benchmarking, the comparison of one's performance and practices to competitors or "best in class" companies, if done properly, is indeed more than a fancy corporate fad; it is a survival technique (more on this later). The second lesson comes out of the fact that the team Chrysler dispatched to study Honda was young; no one was over 35. Their success was no accident, as young managers still "learning the trade" are less burdened by the blindspots and myths associated with "years of experience."

"The fact that Iacocca listened more carefully to *financial* analysts than to his own analysts should not surprise anyone who knows the type of convoluted relationships that exist between American CEOs and Wall Street."

Roger Smith

Roger Smith has become one of the most infamous personalities in American business. He has been blamed for singlehandedly destroying America's industrial might with his grandiose policies. The truth is, Mr. Smith was not alone. He was supported and comforted by his top executives, in a culture as fertile to competitive blindspots as Napa Valley's soil is to grapes.

GM had a risk-averse bureaucracy even before Smith took over in 1981. In such a culture, mistakes are not easily admitted. Smith found this quality appealing. He did his best to promote a culture in which "no one admitted problems publicly." It is revealing that after 1984's disastrous reorganization failed miserably, executives were willing to criticize its *implementation*, not the assumptions behind it. The only one who publicly attacked the *thinking* was Jack Smith, the European chief who was later named the new president.

Little wonder that Robert Stempel, who succeeded Roger Smith and was eventually replaced by Jack Smith (confusing, isn't it?), failed to change GM. He shared many of his boss' blinders![30] This case exemplifies a more frequent finding that the only way to fight *existing* blindspots may be to bring in a new leader who does not wear the *same* blinders!

Roger Smith made many wrong decisions while at GM. However, his two biggest failures were his convictions that (1) the way to beat the Japanese in the productivity and cost game was robotics, and (2) as long as GM stayed the industry's undisputed leader, it would be the trend setter, and the consumer would *follow*.

Both assumptions acquired the status of blindspots, reinforced by the culture that would not admit problems. Roger Smith spent $80 billion on automation, technology, and robotics[31] with indifferent results, and GM turned from the lowest-cost producer to the industry's cost *leader*. In 1981, soon after taking office, Smith declared, "Technology leadership is what will keep us ahead in world competition."[32] This belief was formed while Smith was the head of GM's nonautomotive operations, where he had to sell units making home appliances and earth-moving equipment because they could not compete with the technology of their rivals. This kind of a trauma can shape an executive's convictions for the rest of his or her life, and Smith was no exception.[33] Once he made this declaration, though, the technology assumption became immune to reality—in other words, a corporate taboo. The clearest indication that a taboo was being created was provided by GM executives' unique experience with their chief competitor, Toyota, with whom GM formed a joint venture.

In 1983, GM and Toyota formed a company called New United Motor Manufacturing, Inc. (NUMMI). NUMMI was aimed at producing small cars in an old GM plant in Fremont, California. The joint venture was placed under Toyota's management.

NUMMI turned out to be a success story. It was able to produce a car in 19 hours with few defects and with American workers. A comparable GM factory needed 31 hours, and its cars were full of defects. *Surprisingly enough, the NUMMI factory was not highly automated at all*. Instead, the main differences from other GM plants were teamwork rather than the typical 200 job classifications at GM, workers' authority to stop production to fix quality problems (the famous "assembly line button" that nullified the need for large repair areas), job training, and other soft "people-issues."

One would expect GM to take a careful look at NUMMI and infer what an MIT team inferred in 1986—that technology was not the answer, since technology was not the problem. Rather, "lean manufacturing" techniques that had to do with management, not machines, were the secret behind the

Japanese success.[34] Instead, the corporate taboo created by Smith was so effective, it caused GM executives *at all levels* to simply turn a blind eye to the facts. At the top, even as the deal with Toyota was signed, Smith continued with his investment in Hamtramck, a high-tech plant that opened in 1985 with 260 robots and 50 Automatic Guided Vehicles (AGV), laser-based measuring instruments, and lots of computers. A year after it opened, the plant was still unable to go fully on line. The AGVs refused to move, the robots occasionally dismembered each other, and production would halt for hours while the software was debugged. At a lower level, a group of GM managers who returned from visiting NUMMI claimed it was a fraud: It must be hiding a *secret* storage area for car repairs (a la GM plants)! This inability to use experience to move forward is typical of corporate taboos, as set forth in the Fourth Law, below.

● *Fourth Law: Reality is bent to fit corporate taboos, not vice versa.*

Eventually, the high-tech gadgets at Hamtramck had to be removed and workers given more authority over quality. Smith's taboo about technology cost GM a whole decade, thousands of jobs, and billions of dollars. Yet another big change born of the shakeup at Hamtramck was the plant employees' attitude toward customers. Workers at the plant began calling on customers to check on problems. As one manager commented about the change, "There used to be a 'them and us' mentality."[35]

This mentality can be traced to a second widely shared myth that Smith reinforced—the industry leadership myth. This myth accounted for Smith's refusal to cut capacity even as market share shrank, a problem some experts see as the most significant for GM in the 1990s. A statement made by Smith to *Fortune* magazine reveals his thinking on this issue:

> We knew we were at a percent of the market that was unsustainable over a long period. In the early 1980s you had Chrysler in semibankruptcy and Ford with product problems. So what do you do? Do you say to yourself, 'The best I can do is a 38 percent market share, so I am not going to build any more after that?' Hell, no. You go out there and build every car you can.[36]

The car line rushed to the market was the new front-wheel-drive line, which, at the time, was still full of bugs. Naturally, you do that only if you *blindly* believe that the consumer will buy these cars, because *as the industry leader you set the trends, and the consumer follows*. The consumer balked.

The leadership myth can explain numerous other blunders. As the baby boomers aged and demanded family sedans, GM introduced four new coupes in 1988 (Ford, foreseeing the decline of coupes, never developed a two-door Taurus). As new niches such as sport-utility vehicles and minivans exploded, GM's offering was the weakest in these growth areas. When the Japanese, the masters of listening to the customers, brought diversity of models to the market and were rewarded by consumers who wanted more individuality, GM's Chevrolet, Pontiac, Oldsmobile, and Buick divisions had been selling the *same* car with different nameplates. The astonishing part of this sad saga is not the blunders themselves, but the fact that from 1984 to 1992 GM's market share declined from 45 percent to 33 percent, a loss of almost $16 billion in a normal car-buying year, yet only in 1992 did its board of directors face up to the myth. A slide of a decade down a blind alley is an unbelievable feat. If anyone needed proof that competitive blindspots are immensely powerful, GM provided it.

A Lesson in Anatomy

GM provides an interesting look at the anatomy of blindspots. First comes the leader with a strong vision. The vision turns him blind to contrary evidence. He works the vision throughout the organization, making sure dissent is discouraged. Over time, the vision acquires the strength of myths or taboos—untouchable, un-disprovable. Then the daily routine takes care of the rest. GM was well known for its working by committees. The *Fortune* article states:

> As decisions were passed up through various committees for approval, they developed a momentum of their own. By the time they reached the top, they had an inevitability about them, even if they no longer made sense. GM's top committees were notorious for ratifying, not deliberating.

Well, what is there to deliberate? A myth? The lower-level committee members knew better than to burst the bubble. Technology is the cure. Customers would follow the leader. Make it clear through promotions and demotions that this is what you really believe in, and the organization will produce decisions that are enamored with technology and ignore the consumer. Bingo! A blindspot is born, and somebody down the road—stockholders, workers, middle managers—will pay the price.

Ford and Fear

Of the Big Three, Ford has came out of the '80s relatively unscathed. The success of Ford is explained by the enormous popularity of the Taurus and the clever concentration in the truck segment of the market, where the Japanese were the weakest, tariffs the highest, and profits the largest. The success of the Taurus, ironically, is a lesson in the strange working of a corporate myth. The lesson of the success in trucks (a segment that includes minivans and sport-utility vehicles, as well as pickups) is a perfect example of the power of one insightful *individual* to make a difference in the fight against blindspots.

The Taurus, introduced in 1986, was a breakthrough for an American car manufacturer. It had a unique, European-style design. It put Ford, for the first time, in the position of a leader in design, after years of following GM. This was an uncomfortable position for Ford. There was an unspoken myth (assumption about one's strengths and weaknesses) that GM leads in design and Ford is the industry's conservative player. Roger Smith, GM's chairman, called the Taurus a jellybean, and his comment was widely publicized. That was the catalyst that brought the myth full-blown to the surface. Ford's design committee met the next year and said (as one member recalls), "We bit off a lot. Now let's capitalize on what we've got." In corporate-speak, that was the death sentence to original thinking. The models following the Taurus reverted to the old design, the product development process to the old inefficiencies. Costs were starting to get out of hand, market share dropped, and Ford would lose $2.4 billion by 1990. However, in line with its ability to see reality more clearly than its American competitors, the Ford board's early action forced CEO Donald Peterson to retire in 1989 and brought in Red Poling. This amazing story has a strong moral:

● *Fifth Law: Myths are like a Phoenix—once broken, they rise again, unless the company has a process by which myths are continually shattered.*

Louis Ross' Unique Role in the Theory of Blindspots

The success of Ford in trucks is a ray of hope in the battle against corporate blindness. It also exemplifies the value of using competitive intelligence regarding executives' *personal* backgrounds to help predict corporate strategies.

In the car industry, trucks got a bad rap for years. They were not glamorous enough, and therefore were neglected. Then Phillip Caldwell and

Donald Peterson, two Ford executives who ran Ford's truck operations in the 1970s, were eventually made CEOs. That completely changed the way Ford looked at trucks.

Caldwell became CEO in 1979 and developed the Ranger pickup (1982), the Bronco utility vehicle (1983), and the Aerostar minivan (1985). All winners. Ford was outselling GM in trucks.

Then came the Japanese, who introduced their subcompacts at $2,000 less than the small American cars. Ford was forced to sell its small, best-selling Escort and Tempo at a loss. The only remaining profitable segment was trucks, where the Japanese did not have much to offer, and where a high tariff kept them at a competitive disadvantage. A Ford executive, Allan Gilmour, recalls a meeting of Ford's strategy committee in August of 1986 to discuss Ford's future strategy. His description of what went on at that meeting should strike a familiar cord in every manager or consultant who has experienced such meetings. Among those present at the meeting were CEO Peterson, President Poling, and several top executives, including Louis Ross, then the head of Ford's North American operations. As Gilmour describes it, "It was not a meeting for bashful people." *But then, strategy meetings should never be, should they?*

At the meeting, Louis Ross made a fateful proposal—more a bold idea than a careful argument. Ross's recollection, quoted below, makes it clear this was not a carefully researched proposal (note the numbers he threw in) but a gut feeling of an angry executive whose company was losing the competition to better manufacturers of small cars. In the meeting, Ross said:

> Look, what we've got to try to do is move our spending to trucks. We want to spend 70 percent more on truck programs in the next five years than we have in the last five. It's pragmatic. First, there's the 25 percent import tax on two-door trucks, which holds back the Japanese. Second, we have good market leadership. So why the hell don't we, as a company, redirect our resources substantially to our trucks?

Yes, why the hell not, Ross? I would bet my 10-year experience with managers and students that at least 100 lower-level managers throughout Ford reckoned that this was the logical competitive strategy. Yet corporations do not make decisions by listening to their junior managers. Comments Gilmour, "*It was not that nobody had ever thought of those things, but there was a consensus on strengths, opportunities, weaknesses—how we needed to realign and charge full tilt.*" The important point is not that there was a consensus—GM's committees were notable for creating consensus—but that this consensus was relatively free of competitive blindspots. And yet, without Ross's bold proposal, punctuated with at least one "hell" (signaling emotional commitment to the idea), Ford's strategy committee might have gone the way Roger Smith's committees had gone. It was Ross who saw reality for what it was—Ford's true strengths, the competitors' vulnerability—and put his foot down. There is an important lesson to learn from this episode, which repeats itself numerous times across corporate America. It is the same lesson that the Old Testament describes in the story of Sodom and Gomorrah. As Abraham begs God to spare Sodom, God is reported to reply, "If you can find one innocent person in this town, the town will be spared." By analogy, here is Business Blindspots' Sixth (and last) Law:

● *Sixth Law: All it takes to spare the corporation is one person on the top team who maintains a relatively objective view of reality.*

As Ford's story reveals, that person does not have to be the CEO himself. But it has to be a person trusted by top management, who can pound on the table and say, "Look—" and "Hell—" and get the executives to look reality in its face. No doubt, in Ford's case, it also helped that the CEO "cut his teeth" in the Truck division.

The Japanese

One cannot end a segment on the automobile industry without mentioning the Japanese. So much has been said about the Japanese that one does not need to dwell too much on their strengths. As *Fortune* put it, "They are the leaders in productivity, flexibility, design, and niche marketing. They are the masters at probing the customer base and quickly developing appealing products." Yet, consistent with the theme of this book, their biggest advantage may come from a different angle, one relatively ignored by the admiring world. *When they make mistakes, they discover them quickly and change direction.* In other words, they suffer less from business blindspots' destructive effect. How they do it will be discussed in a later chapter. Can we do it as well? The answer in this book is a resounding YES!

The next chapter presents some possible explanations as to why companies develop blindspots, and why some have them much worse than others.

Summary Table: Blindspots' Laws and Most Frequent Characteristics

- *First Law: Unchallenged assumptions underlie every corporate activity, from strategies to tactics to operating procedures.*

- *Second Law: Unless managers have the ability (cognitive, emotional, and organizational) to perceive and question their implicit competitive assumptions, they are not going to perceive the value of learning from experience.*

- *Third Law: The best way to overcome competitive blindspots is to confront the blindness head on—i.e., learn **directly** from the competition.*

- *Fourth Law: Reality is bent to fit corporate taboos, not vice versa.*

- *Fifth Law: Myths are like a Phoenix—once broken, they rise again, unless the company has a process by which myths are continually shattered.*

- *Sixth Law: All it takes to spare the corporation is one person on the **top** team who maintains a relatively objective view of reality.*

Frequently Found Characteristics

- Large companies learn from large companies.
- With blinders on, *recessions* become a scapegoat and fundamental market changes go unnoticed.
- Taboos can often be traced to the executive's personal background.
- Breaking taboos can be a profitable enterprise.
- Having a strong corporate "style" often implies a whole bag of business blindspots.
- Young managers still "learning the trade" are less burdened by the blindspots and myths associated with "years of experience."
- The only way to fight existing blindspots may be to bring in a new leader who does not wear the *same* blinders!
- Corporate myths are powerful enough to wreak havoc. They must be subject to continuous testing. On occasion, breaking them just to test their validity may save a manager from losing his job.
- Restructuring that leaves people *thinking* the same way leaves them as blind as before.
- If you want to shatter a truly sacred myth, shatter a few related ones as well. There is power in numbers and you may never get another chance!
- No strategy is too radical to fight competitive sclerosis.

Chapter Four

A Theory of Blindness

What causes smart executives and successful firms to develop blindspots? This is the $64,000 question, or, if we add in GM and IBM and Chrysler, the $64 billion question.

The answer is far from simple. In this chapter I, will synthesize some of the research that has been carried out on decision making that might shed some light on the conditions under which blindspots may gain powerful momentum. Yet no research to date can explain why some top executives heed the signs of change and some stubbornly rest on their outdated laurels. To date, there is no theory of blindness—just strong confirmation that blinders indeed exist.

This chapter borrows heavily from a research program carried out at Rutgers University in the mid-'80s.[37] Our team of three researchers identified various research strands that were useful to our understanding of the phenomenon of blindspots. One clear conclusion from this research: Economics can add nothing to our understanding of strategy and strategic blunders, but psychology and management research can be a little more relevant.

Human Error at the Top

Business blindspots fall under the category of error in judgment. That executives, like other people, form wrong judgments is an accepted fact of life, except perhaps in economics. Neoclassical economic theory, the dominant theory among academic economists since the 1930s, does not recognize bad, or nonoptimal, decisions. Only in 1979 did two psychologists out of Stanford and British Columbia, working within a strand of economic research known as behavioral economics, demonstrate a systematic bias in the way people make (economic) judgments.[38] Their research, which confirmed what most people have known for ages, caused a huge stir among economists, giving the final blow to economists' notion of optimal decision making in the business firm. So we can't really expect to find much help from within traditional economics—but then, economic theory has little to add to our understanding of the (business) world, anyway. Our best hope for relevant research is in the fields of management and psychology—subfield: decision making.

Decisions are based on information. Information is a big term; it includes external facts, internal beliefs, intuitive feelings, etc. There are three ways in which decisions can go wrong: (1) not all the relevant information is available; (2) the available data are ambiguous and wrongly interpreted; and (3) available information is *filtered*.

The first factor is a fact of life in most business situations. Information is hardly ever complete. "If we only knew then what we know now" is a typical comment when projects go sour. The second factor is also very common: Information is often equivocal. Is the market really changing or is it just a cyclical event? *"Facts" are, in fact, often far from being facts.* Interpretation of ambiguous data is what separates the executive with foresight from the executive without. Neither of these factors has anything to do with blindspots. Therefore, I want to make it clear that not every bad decision is due to executives wearing blinders!

Was Iacocca's *initial* decision to embark on acquisitions instead of shoring up car manufacturing a bad decision? Probably. Was it due to lack of complete information? Most likely, like 99 percent of all decisions. Was it due to misinterpreting ambiguous facts? Perhaps. But was his *10-year* odyssey into conglomerate strategy based on lack of information or ambiguous facts? Not a chance. This type of behavior falls under the third factor: Available information is considered only after it is filtered through very *biased* sunglasses. It is what a very wise observer of human behavior once termed *the ability to stare at the facts and not see them at all!*[39]

Behavioral Research

Research in psychology and management to date has uncovered several behavioral processes that operate to filter the information we use to make our decisions. For example, experiments with human subjects in laboratory settings exposed a Prior Hypothesis bias—a situation in which a prior belief led to ignoring disconfirming information. Other experiments, typically with students, revealed the phenomenon of Anchoring: Initial assumptions or forecasts served as an anchor around one's neck, causing subsequent necessary revisions to be too small. Laboratory studies also confirmed the existence of the Escalating Commitment syndrome—a process by which an initial commitment caused discounting of negative information regarding the action taken, and a resultant continuation or even *escalation* of the commitment. This line of research brought the researchers to coin the term the "trapped administrator" for the decision maker in their experiments.[40] All this research would have been doomed as typical, contrived, laboratory-based, irrelevant research (like the vast majority of contemporary social science research) if not for the real-life affliction of powerful, sustained, pervasive business blindspots. What had been glimpsed in students pushing buttons in the lab seems to exist on a much larger scale in corporate America. The roots of all of this research into the filtering of information can be traced back to a 1957 research program undertaken by a psychologist named Leon Festinger.

Filtering Information Since 1957[41]

Back in 1957, Leon Festinger uncovered a psychological condition he termed cognitive dissonance. By 1982, more than 900 studies were published about this condition. Even allowing for the 90 percent of wasted research projects carried out for the sake of tenure and promotion in the exclusive monopolistic club called academia, cognitive dissonance still has been shown to operate in numerous walks of life. What is cognitive dissonance?

It is basically a very simple phenomenon. If I hold the assumption that smoking is not harmful, and a news item on TV shows rows of graves marked "Smoker, dead due to lung cancer," I might, under certain conditions, suffer a state of "cognitive dissonance." The dissonance created between the inconsistent cognitions is rather unpleasant, and therefore invokes behaviors aimed at reducing it.

Cognitive dissonance does not occur every time we encounter a state of affairs that is inconsistent with our mindset. Two additional conditions are necessary:

1. *The existence of a prior commitment.* Commitments create ego-involvement—i.e., once committed, the decision maker has a stake in subsequent events; his or her ego is on the line. Commitments also create anchors: The commitment becomes the cognition that is *resistant to change.*

2. *The perception of responsibility.* The theory of cognitive dissonance states that to feel a dissonance, the decision maker must feel responsible for the choice he or she made. Forced choices do not give rise to later dissonances. And then, too, the decision maker must have foreseen a possibility of adverse consequences to the

decision. Unforeseen, sheer bad luck apparently does not give rise to cognitive dissonance.

In short, an executive making a free commitment to a project, a vision, a strategy, with the understanding of possible adverse performance results, is setting the stage for a potential cognitive dissonance. If later information points to adverse competitive developments, low performance levels, changing market circumstances, etc., the executive may resort to *dissonance reduction.*

Dissonance reduction takes the route of changing dissonant cognitions, starting with those that are least resistant. One can see why strongly held beliefs, myths, and taboos will be the last to change. Instead, incoming dissonant information will be changed first. There are several ways in which the mind works on the problem of dissonance: It can add consonant cognitions ("everybody on my executive team has bought into this vision"), increase the importance of consonant cognitions ("if Bob says we are OK, I trust him; he KNOWS the industry, he has been our consultant for 20 years"), subtract dissonant cognitions ("I did not have time to read the latest analysts' report"), or decrease their importance ("Ben is known to be a doomsday prophet"). Underlying these mind tricks is the phenomenon of *selective exposure:* filtering out negative information and seeking out confirming data.

Selective exposure is not a monotonically increasing function of dissonance. In other words, when the discrepancy between established assumptions and reality grows too large, eventually even the most resistant assumptions will be changed—the pricing policy reversed, the mainframe influence eliminated. The problem lies with the low-level dissonance: Until the firm is suffering large losses, dissonance reduction in the form of ignoring or misinterpreting incoming market information can continue unchallenged for years.

Crisis Management: Does It Bring Out the Worst?

OK, so executives under ego-threatening conditions engage in selective exposure to information. Business blindspots resist change the most, and therefore, following the cognitive dissonance theory, a deterioration in performance is almost inevitable. But when the full crisis hits—sharp decline in earning, operating losses, loss of market share—one would expect the top executives to react swiftly and decidedly, adjusting their assumptions, changing course, staring reality straight in the face. Most executives are not known to be of weak heart or usually indecisive. Why, then, does it seem that when a crisis hits, some executives wear their blinders more tenaciously than ever? Why is it that in case after case, from IBM to American Express, from Tenneco to Goodyear, the only way out of a crisis seemed to be pushing out the CEO and often his top lieutenants with him?

The answer may lie in the way crises seem to affect information processing. While popular folklore holds that a crisis brings out the best in a person, in real life it brings out blindspots rather more often. Experiments conducted in the late '60s revealed a strange phenomenon: During crises, the decision maker tends to establish a dominant percept through which information is interpreted, and this percept is maintained tenaciously in the face of contrary information. Experiments carried out in the late '70s confirmed further that overload leads to screening of information according to personal preferences and expectations, and to disregarding of unsupportive data.

The similarity of this phenomenon to cognitive dissonance is apparent, but the two are not the same. The selective exposure to information exercised during crises is due to a different cause: information overload. The large increase in information typical of a state of crisis apparently leads to narrowing of attention span. It is not surprising, therefore, that during crises, executives who are facing the adverse consequences of their earlier strategies may narrow their attention span even further, adhering forcefully to old and "proven" assumptions and myths. One example of this mechanism can be glimpsed from the sad story of Atari, once the formidable leader in video games.

Packing Away the PacMan

In 1982, Atari was the generic name for video games. The company had pioneered the arcade and home versions of the game and was the main reason that its parent company's (Warner Communication) stock reached $54 by 1982. Then the market began to mature. There were growing signals that home video games were peaking and competition was coming on strong. Atari's top management, however, was committed to a growth vision. It therefore continued to predict accelerated growth. In 1983, as competition from Coleco, Bally Midway Manufacturing, Texas Instruments, and Commodore brought about a price war, Raymond Kassar, Atari's charismatic leader, was still making rosy earning forecasts.[42]

Atari ended 1983 with a loss of $539 million. At this clearly crisis stage, Kassar was quoted as saying, "We have made some mistakes. But we've had some extraordinary success, which people suddenly seem to have forgotten."[43] Narrowing his attention to proven past successes cost Kassar his job. When his replacement, James Morgan, came in, Atari was in a full crisis. Morgan acted swiftly, coming out with a new product line and cost-cutting measures. Both failed. By mid-1984, the company had lost $100 million more than in 1983. Then Morgan started to hit the information-filtering trail. Observers testified that "he did not want to hear the bad news but wanted desperately to believe the good news." Some former executives remarked that the problems were worse than Morgan was ready to admit "even to himself." In mid-1984 Morgan announced, "We recognize we have a problem but we are on the right track in solving it." Two months later Warner Communication virtually gave Atari away.

A Simple Model of Filtering

If one looks at the various empirical investigations and the behavioral processes they uncovered, it is possible to bring them together into a simplified model of information filters—the lethal side effects of business blindspots. Information filters can be expected to operate once a decision maker, committed to a particular course of action, develops a desire to see the world behaving in sync with his commitment: a stock price of $50, a multiple of 15, continued unlimited growth, etc. The higher the extent of ego involvement in the course of action, the larger the potential for disaster. The clearer the responsibility for the decision, the more likely it is that a motivational state may evolve capable of creating filters through which unsupportive information will be screened. Yet even without much ego involvement, research suggests that the mere information overload experienced by the average executive may be enough to narrow attention span—i.e., make adherence to proven practices, past successes, industry norms, etc., a rather efficient (though not effective) way to manage! With corporate downsizing (rightsizing, in corporate speak), this overload is expected to increase several times over, and the problem of information filtering can be expected to increase with it. And while individual differences will undoubtedly mitigate these factors, once the filters are up, *a belief stops being just a belief and turns into a blindspot*. Only when the discrepancy between the blindspot and reality grows large may a threshold be reached that will allow the filter to turn clear again.

The above discussion suggests, rather temptingly, that one class of beliefs or assumptions will be more likely to suffer from information filters: the beliefs and assumptions underlying strategies or visions. Strategies require heavy commitment, both financial and personal. They involve relatively clear responsibility: Strategies are not routine programmed decisions. The possibility of adverse consequences is rather large, given the long-term nature of strategies and the investment involved. In short, assumptions and beliefs associated with strategic decisions fulfill all the conditions to become sacred cows (in academic jargon, resistant cognitions) and therefore serve as fertile ground for filtering information.

> **❝Admitting the acquisition was bad is a very unlikely event for the top executive who sponsored it, given the large stakes, both financial and political, involved in such deals.❞**

A classic example, which also received some empirical support in recent years, is the class of strategic decisions involving mergers and acquisitions. Michael Porter, in his seminal paper "From Competitive Advantage to Corporate Strategy" (Harvard Business Review, May–June 1987, pp. 43–59), as well as in later interviews in the press, claimed that many acquisitions are based not on careful strategic thinking but on ego or fear. Several studies suggested—and I seriously doubt that this is breakthrough news to managers—that *divestiture* did not take place until the champion of the acquisition left the company or his position, regardless of the venture's performance.[44] Admitting the acquisition was bad is a very unlikely event for the top executive who sponsored it, given the large stakes, both financial and political, involved in such deals.

Why Some Companies Have It Worse Than Others

What conditions will prolong the effect of information filtering—i.e., raise the threshold to adjusting one's beliefs in accordance with reality? These conditions are the key to predicting how powerful blindspots will grow in a given organization. The following hypotheses are based on the psychological research cited above.

Optimal Growth Factors for Blinders

1. *How decisions are made in the organization can be crucial.* A famous study once suggested that when decisions are made in a decentralized way, the natural tendency toward bias in interpretation of information is balanced by the diversity of views and, if we follow the dissonance explanation for filtering, by the sharing of responsibility for decisions.[45] This suggestion makes intuitive sense. The only caveat is that the "empowerment," or decision sharing, should be real. In several corporations where culture was especially strong, task forces and committees did nothing to pre-

vent the blinders—cultivated by the top—from affecting all decisions at all levels. Convergence around blindspots can come from buying into a shared vision *or* from fear of antagonizing top management. Thus, decentralizing decision making is just one step toward reducing filtering of information. A culture that is open and encouraging to internal dissent or diverse views is another. Such a culture is not necessarily related to how much decentralization or power sharing or empowerment exists in the organization. It may be very related to the personality of the top decision makers.

Furthermore, before one jumps to the conclusion that decentralization of decisions is a panacea, one should remember the tradeoff: too much decision sharing, through endless committees and task forces, can quickly turn into slow decisions. The art of management is to find the balance—lower filtering, but keep the speed. If it was simple, executives would have been paid civil servant salaries.

2. *Do you celebrate failure?* One small California-based firm introduced the following organizational invention in the '80s: They celebrated flops. The explanation was that without recognizing and admitting a flop, the company would have been much worse off. It is reasonable that in companies where mistakes are swiftly and severely punished, vigorous filtering of negative data may be the norm.

3. *How uncertain is your industry?* Environmental uncertainty is like white noise: It masks the indisputable facts, allowing blinders to be kept on for longer periods. Causes of environmental uncertainty are numerous, but the most important ones are government policies (active fiscal or monetary intervention, regulatory changes) and industry-specific factors (such as the length of payoff periods for investments). Uncertainty not only makes it hard to interpret economic signals, but also allows decision makers to justify adherence to existing blindspots ("it's a cyclical trend"; "inventories are high because of interest rates"; "deregulation created chaos in the market"; etc.).

Uncertainty is also related to the rate of technological change in a given industry. It is not surprising that the computer industry has been a birthplace for so many examples of blindspots. It is not that computer companies are worse than other companies when it comes to management's openness to change. Rather, it is that rapid change exposes blindspots much more quickly than slow change, through deteriorating performance.

4. *How fat is the cat?* We have seen that the emergence of powerful blindspots is almost always associated with long periods of success. Success creates "organizational slack"—a term organization scientists use to describe hidden resources that allow an organization to maintain aspirations and expectations even during a relative performance decline. Slack comes in several forms, from cash reserves to management perks to excess staff. It is what managers call the "fat." While there is nothing wrong with accumulating fat as a reserve, this cushion against adversity enables management to ignore warning signals longer than if bad times immediately and severely affected the bottom line. As the behavioral economist Stan Kaish suggests, if one's rivals are lean, mean fighting machines, this means the awakening may come only when the sheriff padlocks the doors.

Some of those lean, mean fighting organizations are mentioned in the next chapter in connection with the battle against blindspots.

CHAPTER FIVE

Managing the Competition

Most audiences to whom I lectured about business blindspots during the past two years—senior management, middle management, information professionals, and competitive analysts—took almost instantly to the notion and found immediate examples inside their own firms. Once the enthusiastic nodding was over, though, the audience demanded satisfaction: Tell us how to solve the problem!

Well, let's make it clear—there is no three-step, modular, organic, flexible, hip, jargon-laden, faddish management recipe. I am not even sure the fight is always winnable. If I learned one thing over the years working with corporations, it is that the fight is continuous, tough, politically risky, and sometimes, when it is undertaken too late, doomed. Let's face it: GM would never have been able to examine some of its worst myths and taboos had Smith or his yes-men stayed on. Akers had to leave IBM for it to have a chance to fight years of unchallenged assumptions and taboos. The best thing that happened to Goodyear was the fresh view of its CEO brought in from a different industry. This does not mean that Gault of Rubbermaid had no blindspots of his own. They were not related to the rules of the game in the tire industry, though, and that was his biggest advantage.

When all is said and done, sometimes the only solution to blindspots may be to replace top management and bring in an outsider.

This is the extreme case, however, and for that solution you don't need to read this book. But you do need to understand the reasoning behind this solution. The need to oust the CEO and his or her top lieutenants is not based solely on bad performance—the yardstick used by the board of directors. Bad performance can be reversed, new strategies tried, etc. The real issue is blinders. After years of working in a given industry, and years of success leading to the rise to the top, it is almost inevitable that the top decision maker may simply be too blind to see a whole new reality. Think of the following analogy: It is well known that after a long period of traveling on snow, one can become partially or completely blind. The glare and shine of past success is easily as strong.

Keeping the ultimate solution in mind, no company should regard it as desirable. Instead, it makes sense for executives to devote whatever time and effort is required to fight against sclerosis. I haven't met an executive who, after listening to my explanation of how GM, Compaq, Goodyear, or Sears brought the fall on themselves, did not agree that the search for blindspots is of utmost priority. However, most managers do not realize how difficult the task is and how *devoted* the search should be. Indeed, as this chapter describes, some companies have used radical strategies to fight sclerosis. Executives who are not willing to commit whatever it takes to the fight should not even start. Halfhearted efforts do not eradicate entrenched paradigms.

Two Combat Strategies

In attempting to fight business blindspots, I distinguish between two very different strategies: (1) preventive and (2) interventionist medicine. How do experienced skiers protect their eyesight? They wear dark glasses. This is preventive medicine. It is also a very fit analogy to the preventive strategy advocated in Part III of this book. However, in the short run, companies have employed some ingenious strategies as interventionist medicine against competitive sclerosis. Some of these strategies were deliberate attempts to stay one step ahead of blindness. In other cases, the avoidance of blindspots was the very fortunate *by-product* of clever competitive strategies. I label these strategies "managing the competition." These were not specific strategies, such as Porter's cost leadership, or differentiation or focus. Instead, these were managerial approaches that seemed to have provided their initiators some short-term relief from the dig-in power of obsolete assumptions about the market.

What Is "To Manage"?

Webster's World Dictionary, 2nd Edition, defines *to manage* as follows:

> to train a horse in his pace; to have charge of, to direct; to get a person to do what one wishes, to manipulate; to control the movement or behavior of

The essence of the word *manage* is control. There are basically two ways one can keep a measure of control over the competition in one's industry: Reshape it or keep moving with it. Under the label "reshaping competition," I include Wal-Mart's contrarian strategy, United's and American's information control strategy, and Tiphook's change-the-rules game plan. Under the "moving with it" label, I include such diverse strategies as Merrill Lynch's and Tenneco's attitude campaign and Unysis' and ICL's "continuous restructuring" paradigm. And then there are those change strategies, also in the realm of "moving with the competition," that exemplify the old adage "the sky is the limit." In this case, it is top management's creativity that sets the limit so high.

Reshaping Competition

The Contrarian Strategy

The genius of Sam Walton, who built a company from one store in Bentonville, Arkansas, to a $40 billion leader of the retailing industry in 1991, is the genius of active management of the competitive battle against competitors whose blindspots could fill the Giants' stadium in New Jersey. Walton was the master of using a contrarian strategy: *Understand your rivals' management thinking, and do the opposite!*

First he attacked his competitors' unchallenged assumptions.

Example: Sears and Kmart were concentrating their stores in big shopping centers and urban areas under the accepted assumption that you need movement of large crowds to make a profit. Walton's strategy? Build attractive stores in small country towns, and people will come to you. The average size of a community served by Wal-Mart is 15,000 people.[46] The big, modern Wal-Mart stores chased out the small *local* rivals, and Wal-Mart was able to grow quickly without incurring the wrath of the giants.

Second, he found out their taboos and exploited them.

Example: In the '60s, Kmart was known for its unusually spacious stores and low prices. In the '80s, Kmart managers changed their mindset: from concentrating on the discount business, they came to regard diversification as the panacea strategy. They then diverted Kmart cash reserves into a buying spree: Waldenbooks, PayLess Drug Stores, Builder's Square, and PACE Membership Warehouse. Its once modern stores became old and obsolete. Wal-Mart's strategy? Invest heavily in Wal-Mart. It concentrated on building modern, well-lit, well-designed stores that offered shorter lines and lower prices than Kmart.[47]

Third, Walton uncovered his competitors' corporate myths and concentrated his strengths exactly in those weak spots.

Example: One of Sears' weakest points was its distribution system, which resulted in out-of-stock and frequent delays. Sears, of course, did not see its distribution capability as weak. Walton's strategy? If his rivals see distribution as less than critical, he will make it a competitive weapon. Wal-Mart built huge distribution centers and assembled one of the largest over-the-road truck fleets in America![48]

Then, of course, there is the human resource myth Walton managed to exploit just brilliantly. One of the most universal myths I encountered among my corporate clients was the belief that "our work force is our true strength" (said with pride, moist eyes, and a flag waving in the wind). How many times did I hear the statement "we are like a family here" just to find out later it was a family on the brink of divorce? Top managers are loathe to admit they have weakness in their managerial ranks, workers' attitudes, or general morale and loyalty. Sam Walton knew that in his industry this myth was very pervasive. So he did something about it.

Example: It was a known fact that workers throughout the retail trade were low-paid, unmotivated, and insufficiently trained. Walton's strategy? To call his employees "associates"; to give them a stake in the business through profit sharing, stock purchase plans, and bonuses; to train them constantly to be "merchants," not just workers; and to motivate them relentlessly through visits by the legendary Sam himself.

Finally, Sam Walton went contrarian on one of the most sacred cows in corporate America in general and the retail trade in particular. He made his workers partners in the competitive fight.

Example: Walton obsessively managed the competitive battle himself to the lowest tactical level. When Wal-Mart started to build supermarkets within its stores and Kroger responded with a price war, Walton would go into Kroger's supermarkets anonymously to check on its milk prices to make sure his were lower, and encouraged his managers to do the same. In paying a surprise visit to his store in north Memphis, what does he talk about? ". . . You know, that confounded Kmart is getting better, and so is Target . . . ." To make his employees partners in the fight against competitors, he shared a lot of performance information with them, including cost, markup, overhead, and profit. In secretive corporate America, sharing performance information with the lowliest of workers is equivalent to selling nuclear secrets to the Iraqis. No wonder one expert stated recently, "I don't think Kmart can ever match the management training and enthusiasm you see in the ranks at Wal-Mart."[49] This is a classic contrarian strategy: Find out how they think, what they believe in, what they take for granted as the "rules of the game" in the industry; then go full steam ahead in the opposite direction!

Change-the-Rules Strategy

Take a look for a minute at the container-leasing industry.[50] This industry supplies containers for shipping. Not a sexy industry, but quite essential. Why do companies get into the container business? The tax laws in America and in the United Kingdom made it attractive for corporations to convert profit into depreciable assets such as containers. Big conglomerates rushed to form subsidiaries to take advantage of the laws. Thus, the industry became dominated by big-pocket companies. The leader, for example, is a subsidiary of General Electric.

Playing against the giants is hopeless: The capital required to supply containers on a competitive basis is a big entry barrier, since companies must keep a large stock of containers in every port. Against this background, Tiphook, which was built from scratch by a British entrepreneur in 1978—a time of relatively easy money—has attained the rank of second in the world. How? By refusing to play the game according to the prevailing rules.

Containers are leased in two ways: long term contracts and master leases. The long-term contract is for a minimum of a year. The master lease supplies shippers with containers only when they are needed at the specific port. The large companies concentrate on long-term leases because, as Tiphook's CEO Robert Montague explains, their parent companies see them primarily as a convenient way to park profit, not as a profitable business on their own.

Knowing how his rivals *think* was a big advantage. Montague's strategy was then to turn the business on its head. Instead of depreciation charges as the primary focus, he looked at his business as a service business and concentrated on master leases. Providing superior service to the shippers (they don't have to log back empty containers, for instance), Montague was able to charge higher prices. The fatter profit margins allowed him to get the financing needed to build a large fleet and to disperse it all over the globe. Of course, master leases require quick transmitting of information on opportunities in the various ports. To that end, Tiphook developed a proprietary computer software that enabled it to spot a change in containers' movements within days. It is only natural to conclude that when you redefine the rule of the game in your own industry, one lucky by-product is a temporary insurance against blindspots. The other players, entrenched in their beliefs of what works and does not work in their industry, have to catch up to the change. Often they cannot do that very easily, as the success of Packard Bell proved.[51]

Computers are sold through computer dealers. Everyone knows that is the way to sell in this industry. Then, in 1985, along came Benny Alagem, the founder of Packard Bell. Alagem declared, "We knew that PCs were going to become a commodity purchase. Consumers wanted something like a television—just turn it on and it works." So he approached retailers who sold TVs, VCRs, and other electronics. By 1992 he had 25 percent of the business at department stores and 37 percent in consumer electronic stores. IBM tried it too, in 1990, with its PS/1 computer. However, IBM was used to marketing through its own network, not through consumer outfits. It flopped. Maybe IBM should have listened to one of its own, William McCracken, the new European chief for IBM PCs, who said, "Hanging on to the things we used to do for no good reason is foolish."[52] When Packard Bell was using end-of-aisle displays and paying retailers for shelf space, its competitors were still "scratching their heads about the meaning of these strange practices," as one analyst put it. Blindspots are tough to eradicate.

Information Control Strategies

One meaning of "to manage" is to cause or manipulate others to play by your rules. One of the most blatant examples of this interpretation of managing the competition is the case of the airline industry and the success of United and American airlines.[53] While the industry as a whole logged $1.4 billion in losses since its creation, these two airlines grew larger and stronger over the years. Two ingenious tools were used by the management of these airlines to gain control of the competition: a hub system and a computerized reservation system (CRS). On the surface, these tools look like any other marketing/management techniques, yet they are different.

The hub system funnels travelers to one central airport (the hub) dominated by one or, at most, two airlines. From the hub, passengers can continue on to other destinations. Naturally, the airline that concentrates on the hub market and achieves dominance there can offer more flights, as well as better promotions and more loyal local travel agents, than other airlines. Anyone stuck at a hub airport with a cancelled flight can attest to the hub system's power in forcing one to fly with the dominant airline. Using the hub system, instead of flying directly from one destination to another (which disperses the competitive strength among many small markets), United and American (and also Delta) actually squeezed weaker competitors out of the market. As a method for dictating competitors' behavior, the hub proved superb. When Eastern vacated its 32 gates in Atlanta's airport, no one jumped to fill in the vacancy. Though Northwest needed a strong southeast hub, it figured it couldn't compete with Delta's 82 percent market share in Atlanta!

The CRS is even more ingenious. American owns Sabre and United half-owns Apollo reservation system. Other airlines have to pay a fee to use them. And when they do, they have to hook up through a modem, while

United's and American's flight planners are connected directly. The travel agents using these systems find the vendors' information on seat availability more reliable than that of their rivals. The bottom line is that American and United receive 15 percent more revenue from an agent using their systems than the other airlines. This tool is so magnificently competitive that interventionists such as Michael Levine (the dean who was blamed by his own alumni for the decline of Yale University's Management School) asked the government to force the airlines to give it up!

Like redefining the rules of the game in one's industry, as long as you can *dictate* the rules of the game to your competitors, one fortunate consequence is that you don't have to worry about competitive blindspots. However, United's and American's control will last only as long as technological or regulatory changes do not bring about a change in the economics of hub systems or the control of information through a reservation system. In other words, these two firms should be very alert to the possibility that their winner strategies could become blinders.

Moving with It

What's Your Attitude?

Fighting blindspots depends to a large extent on attitudes, both managerial and staff. At times, it is simply a spirit of doing things. Just take a look at Merrill Lynch. With its 7 million retail customers and $400 billion in assets, it is the largest retail brokerage firm in the United States. Merrill Lynch enjoyed tremendous growth in one decade. Its 1991 assets were four times larger than they were a mere 10 years ago.

> **"**Compaq's manufacturing vice president quotes Pfeiffer as saying to his managers, '. . . Go out and *break paradigms.*'**"**

Anyone analyzing Merrill Lynch's phenomenal growth would realize the pivotal role of its network of 11,000 salespeople. In 1990, for example, they delivered 6 percent operating profit while the capital markets side delivered 2 percent. Since 1977, they sold $200 billion in Cash Management Accounts, the company's own invention, which met with a lot of skepticism upon its introduction in 1977. How did they do it? With a spirit of competition imbued from above. In 1982, John Steffens, the sales executive, told his people, "Find ways to *induce* our best customers to *disrupt* their relationships with their bankers, insurance agents, and other financial representatives."[54] (emphasis added)

This quote may look trivial to the reader who is used to corporate hype. However, its essence is the *lack* of set rules, of "this is how things work in this industry." Instead, notice the use of the words *induce* and *disrupt*, implying that established relationships in the industry (in this case, between customers and their traditional providers) should not be regarded as sacred. To *disrupt* the relationships between a client and his or her other suppliers is an act of wresting control over the competitive arena. With that dictum, Lynch's salespeople then found their own creative ways to poach customers from rivals. Management just made sure to clear the landscape of the wrecks of traditions.

The Masters of Change

Some of the strategies discussed above had the fortunate *side effect* of fighting competitive sclerosis. However, they were not in themselves created to fight blindspots. The following sample strategies are different: They were created by CEOs with the explicit objective of maintaining or realigning the company with reality.

At Compaq, new CEO Eckhard Pfeiffer needed to act in a hurry. Within a year he transformed Compaq's product, marketing, and manufacturing philosophy from high-tech to low-cost—a huge change for Compaq. In order to do that, he needed to eradicate some very entrenched blindspots. So, instead of an incremental move toward low-cost PCs, he decreed a complete line of low-cost desktops and portables. As he put it, "Sometime it's more difficult to achieve a 10 percent cost reduction than it is to tell people they have to achieve 50 percent. *Small incremental steps block your view of doing something fundamentally different.*"[55] (emphasis added).

To fight old habits and accepted practices, Pfeiffer initially held weekly meetings with all of Compaq's worldwide top managers, something previously unheard of at the company. Compaq's manufacturing vice president quotes Pfeiffer as saying to his managers, ". . . Go out and *break paradigms.*"[56] For all of you readers who were told by your boss, "this won't work in this industry," this one's is for you.

Mike Walsh was brought in to save Union Pacific in 1986 and did an amazing job. Then in 1991 he was called on to save Tenneco. Walsh has been one of the most inspiring leaders in corporate America, far ahead of his colleagues with the fat checks and bags full of blindspots. His philosophy is relatively simple: "I believe that the biggest enemy of progress is happy talk. You need to tell your people that if we do not change, and change fundamentally, we are going out of business."[57]

This may sound self-evident to many people. If the company is in trouble, in a crisis, of course you go out there and tell them to shape up! Yet Mike Walsh was not talking about a crisis stage. He was talking about his experience at Union Pacific, a company that in 1986 was celebrating a record $322 million in profit! No one at Union Pacific recognized there was a problem except for the Board and Walsh, who realized that at a rate of return on assets of about 4 percent, capital was not going to be reinvested in the company. Walsh had to *persuade* a cadre of happy managers and unions that the party was *over*.

> **66 . . . women are better suited than men to the new reality facing corporate America, *where recognizing change is a must.* Women are trained to listen, and men are trained to win. 99**

He employed a very old and amazingly rare technique—tell your people the truth, the whole truth, and nothing but the truth. "My experience," says Walsh, "is that people in companies can deal with reality and facts much better than their management gives them credit for."[58] Alas, many corporate executives don't give their people any credit. They starve their people of information. They use all kinds of excuses, from the danger of leaks to competitors (right, Sears and IBM disintegrated because of leaks), to morale and motivation. But as Walsh puts it so clearly, "If you don't deal with that reality and you paper it over in the name of undue apprehension about creating insecurity, I do not believe you can cause a revolution or major change or any of those 50-cent words we're talking about."[59]

I couldn't say it better even if I tried. Information secrecy is the biggest phony philosophy I ever encountered. It robs people of involvement in their own company's future; it makes them robots reacting to corporate cheers and annual report propaganda. It is a sham and it is stupid. My advice to corporate executives who snub information sharing on the grounds of "they don't need to know" is to recall (if they still can) the days when they were lowly juniors in the company, complaining about not knowing what the company was up to. Child abusers were typically abused themselves.

Information flows both ways. Chances of fighting blindspots are nil in corporations where the big boss believes his way is the only way. Walsh's taste for the truth seems to go both ways—a rare quality among the mighty. As one of his executives at Tenneco describes it, "He has always been open to criticism."[60]

This same executive, Rebecca McDonald, has a very intriguing perspective on fighting blindspots. She believes that age is not a factor in puncturing myths and obsolete assumptions. Many older employees at Tenneco seem to have welcomed Walsh's open challenge on accepted doctrines. McDonald speculates that they might have been doing the right things (in this case, focusing on customers) *despite* the pre-Walsh corporate culture, which was, in her words, "corporate arrogance." They were frustrated and then, when Walsh arrived, felt justified. These feelings must be shared by many readers and by millions of employees and managers across corporate America who have experienced a similar change in leadership in their organization. After the rituals of hailing the outgoing chief, his venerable strategy and his most accepted assumptions are slowly but surely declared nonsense or disastrous.

McDonald brings another intriguing observation to the table. She claims that women are better suited than men to the new reality facing corporate America, *where recognizing change is a must.* Women are trained to listen, and men are trained to win. With winning as the only worthwhile objective, she claims, comes rigidity. That brings to mind the discussion in Chapter 4 of the behavioral processes behind information filtering. Ego involvement was one big factor. With winning at any cost a basic drive for males, the ego is deeply invested, and denial of reality is not far away. Just ask yourself why Compaq didn't act before it started to lose money. According to Ross Cooley, Compaq's chief of North American operations, "We had so much success for so long, it got embedded in our DNA code." When performance started to decline, says Cooley, the reaction was denial—Compaq's managers (overwhelmingly male) blamed the economy.[61]

Acquisition as a Cure?

European companies are not known to be vigorous fighters of old traditions. Yet one company, British International Computers Ltd. (ICL), had the good fortune to be almost bankrupt in 1981 and then bought out by the Japanese giant Fujitsu.[62] The transformation allowed ICL's chairman since 1984, Peter Bonfield, to remain in his job while Siemens, Bull, Olivetti, and Nixdorf axed their top executives.

Apparently the contact with the Japanese did something to ICL, and not only in its technology. Management thinking has been exceptionally progressive. Bonfield shut down a whole line of mainframe manufacturing, closed five factories, targeted a few key customers, and by 1992 had 50 percent of ICL's sales from software. As one analyst described it, "Management has turned the company on its head." Turning a company on its head gets many blindspots to fall out of its pockets.

One example of the thinking that led to destroying blindspots is the way ICL handled a recent acquisition of a small Finnish PC maker, Nokia Data System. The traditional postacquisition philosophy of integrating a smaller company into the larger acquirer's culture was apparently unknown to Bonfield. Instead, says ICL's PC division director, "We bent over backwards to make sure Nokia changed ICL, not the other way around." First, control over PCs moved to Nokia, then the two PC lines merged into one. If this

> **"Turning a company on its head gets many blindspots to fall out of its pockets."**

was a one-shot deal, it would not have been that impressive. But this was a deliberate strategy. Bonfield has been seeking acquisitions not to increase market share or sales, but to revamp ICL! This extraordinary effort to shake sclerosis is a result of his belief that "if you've got the same structure you've got now in two years, you'll be out of business." ICL integrates itself with other companies—a PC distributor, software developers in which it bought stakes, and a joint venture with Bell Atlantic, which teaches it how to service IBM and Digital machines. "We are changing old mind sets" says Bonfield.

Restructuring Rx

In 1986, Michael Blumenthal merged Burroughs and Sperry and created Unisys. The merger required taking on enormous debt and put Unisys in a very vulnerable position. It had to get sales any way it could. So it sold computers made by other companies, shut down five factories, stopped making mainframes, and focused on four industries only: government, financial services, telecommunications, and airlines. The idea behind the focus was to truly understand the market—an unusual idea for most Western firms. Unisys' chairman, Unruh, was able to turn the company around after three years of losses and reduce debt to 59 percent of capital. His method? "Our phrase is 'a little restructuring every day.'"[63] Before you dismiss it as more corporate-speak, consider this: As a management philosophy, it beats most corporate credos I have read. How about you?

Other Remedies

And then there are the little things companies do to fight sclerosis. Vaughn Bryson, Eli Lilly's new CEO, is trying to fight a culture that sees success as a "birthright." So he sent several hundred *senior* managers to a week-long course that is supposed to make them more open to outside ideas.[64] Microsoft's Bill Gates does not have this problem. His people don't even know Microsoft is the dominant firm in its industry: "It's etched in our brain: Don't get complacent." An expert describes Microsoft as having a "siege mentality."[65] That is one way to counter the tendency to develop blindspots due to an "industry leadership" syndrome.

Microsoft's culture translates into practical acts: Its product chief goes on some two dozen off-site retreats a year with his *younger* managers and asks them to look at "Microsoft's culture, with its strengths and the weaknesses they could give rise to. We're smart—how not to be arrogant; we're aggressive—how to make sure we negotiate win-win contracts rather than going for all we can get."

And (couldn't you guess it?) in "Bill Meetings" with product development teams, the young managers, some just a few years out of college, stand up to the chairman "as if he were a classmate." Walsh, Gates—are we seeing a pattern here? Two very successful executives who are open to criticism. You are not convinced with a sample size of two? OK. But then consider this: If your junior employees cannot stand up to your CEO and call him an old hand who's blind to the new realities, how would he ever realize he has a blindspot? By watching the company turn a huge loss—and then, like Roger Anderson of the Continental Illinois Bank, claim that "the reputation of the bank and the confidence of the depositors has been hurt but not gravely wounded"?[66]

The examples in this chapter are evidence that there is no one way of fighting competitive blindness. They demonstrate that when it comes to attempting to free up a company from its long-held myths and taboos, unchallenged assumptions, and old and trusted habits, no strategy is too radical. The lucky companies will have winning strategies that hold their competitors by their collective throats, or reinvent an industry, thus not having to worry about old habits *for a while*. Others will acquire companies, hold week-long meetings, share information with the lowliest of their employees, develop a siege mentality, or restructure continually just to fight sclerosis. But for every success story such as Walsh's Union Pacific or Gates Microsoft, there are numerous anecdotes about executives who failed to move the behemoth. If you read this book like the typical successful executive reads books, skimming for a few *easy* ideas to implement, or brushing aside any radical concept, you may join Lego, Smith, or Canon sooner than you expected. Or worse—if you are a middle manager, you are not going to have the luxurious retirement of these fallen heroes. You will be looking for a job and worrying about the mortgage. *No strategy is too radical to fight a disease that brought IBM and Sears and Hoffman-La Roche and Goodyear to their knees.*

However, Walsh and Gates and Pfeiffer and Bonfield and their courage to wage an attack on every old myth notwithstanding, the situation should never reach the point where radical strategies are desperately needed to save a *once* very successful company. Moreover, some of these remedies can only be described as short-term penicillin shots in the arm of an immune-deficient patient. What can be done to *prevent* the onslaught of competitive sclerosis in the first place?

Those familiar with the discipline of homeopathic medicine will find it easy to relate to the following analogy. Those who are not may need more reading to become convinced. Homeopathic or holistic medicine does not believe in interventionist, classical medical treatment, such as antibiotics, which only suppress the symptoms. Instead, homeopathy believes that to foster long-term health, one needs to strengthen the immune system of the patient. A more vital person will contract fewer diseases, regardless of exposure. This book follows the homeopathic prescription. *The true challenge is to build up the immune system of the organization so that blindspots are systematically exposed and eradicated and sclerosis does not have a chance to develop. This is the purpose of the process of learning, which is described in the next two parts of the book.*

● CHAPTER SIX

Alexander the Great, Hannibal, Scipio, and Federal Express: Blindspots as a Competitive Weapon

The essence of competitive strategy, or any strategy, is to position one's company in such a way as to take advantage of its unique strengths (the so-called capabilities, competencies, or any other hot term) *against the competitors' weaknesses*. It must be obvious to the reader, as it is to me, that the identification of a company's unique *strengths* implies an assumption (correct, one hopes) that the competition is *relatively* weak in exactly those aspects of the business. However, positioning is an active term; therefore, it also implies the reverse: First, *discover* the weak points on the opponents' side, and then *develop* your competencies in exactly those areas!

Many managers have surely participated in discussions centering around competitors' soft points relative to customers' needs and/or the economics of the industry. Most of those discussions stay at the level of speculations, or worse, wishful thinking. When reverse engineering or the newest Quality Function Deployment[67] are practiced at a company, competitors' *product* weaknesses can be systematically identified. However, product weaknesses are not the same as strategic weaknesses. The competitor might be working on a better product right at this moment, *unless its management is certain its products are the best for the market!* In other words, one excellent way to evaluate competitors' strategic weaknesses is to identify *their* business blindspots.

Using blindspots as competitive weapons may sound like one more nice theoretical concept. It is not. The following examples made history demonstrating exactly this point. Alexander the Great, Hannibal of Carthage, and Scipio Africanus, the Roman commander, many centuries ago proved that the *principle of using the opponents' blinders against them is one of superior strategy.*

Finding the Angle[68]

Alexander the Great, who lived from 356 to 323 B.C., was one of the greatest military strategists of all time. His most famous battle was the battle of Gaugamela, October 1, 331 B.C. In that battle, Alexander's Macedonian-Greek army of 40,000 infantry and 7,000 horsemen faced the Persian King Darius' army of 100,000 infantry and 34,000 cavalry in what is now the northern part of Iraq. The Persian army was not only much bigger but also of high quality, equipped with new technology (a new armor, longer sword, and a spear instead of a javelin). Darius also chose a perfect battleground: a plain, which he ordered cleared and leveled to enable his war chariots to charge without obstruction.

On the morning of the decisive battle, the Persian army was deployed in a line running east to west and extending the entire width of the cleared plain. Alexander had no chance in a frontal confrontation with an opponent so much larger. Yet he won the battle, losing 500 men and killing 40,000 Persians, and opening the way to building one of the biggest empires in history. His strategy? He positioned his army in an angle.

Yes, in an angle. *Alexander knew that Darius would follow the classic maneuver for a larger force facing a smaller one: Outflank the smaller force.* The Macedonian line was naturally shorter than the Persian, having far fewer soldiers (see Figure 6-1). By placing his rear troops as far from the Persian line as possible, and moving units to his extreme right until they reached the end of the flattened area, Alexander prevented Darius from outflanking him *outright.* Yet he knew Darius would try the maneuver later. This is the beauty of identifying your opponent's blindspot: You *generally know* how he is going to act.

There were many reasons Alexander won that day, yet none was more decisive than the strategy described above. Darius had no choice but to attack Alexander's approaching right wing. While the attack was in full swing, and confident that Alexander was fully occupied on his right, Darius ordered his cavalry wings to try to envelope Alexander's line on both sides, *exactly as a believer in the outflanking paradigm would do.* This diverted

Figure 6-1: Alexander's and Darius' Formations

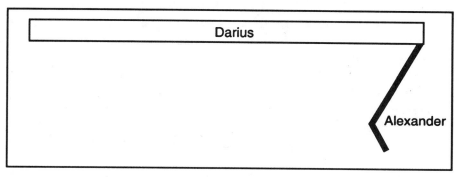

additional Persian soldiers to Alexander's right and opened a temporary gap in Darius' center. Alexander, waiting for just this opening, led his cavalry in a charge straight at Darius. Darius fled.

What was Alexander's secret for success? *He used the opponent's blindspot against him.*

So did Fujitsu Ltd. and Hitachi Ltd. in the Japanese mainframe market. For years IBM dominated that market in Japan. That domination led to a very weak service offering: IBM sold standard software with its machines. Then, in the 1970s, Fujitsu and Hitachi began their drive against IBM, concentrating on customizing software for customers and offering it initially at no charge. They knew IBM would not be able or willing to follow, given its huge market share and its philosophy (i.e., its blindspots). The strategy worked: By 1989, IBM was third in the market after Fujitsu and Hitachi. Only in 1992 did IBM-Japan declare a reorganization aimed at strengthening its service offering.[69]

The Power of Asymmetrical Thinking[70]

AUGUST 2, 216 B.C.—Forty-two thousand surviving Carthaginians, who, led by Hannibal, had just crossed the Alps, found themselves facing 72,000 Roman soldiers under Varro. Behind them was the Aufidus River. They could not avoid the battle.

Hannibal divided his forces into an advanced weak center and strong cavalry flanks. The flanks were positioned against a hilly terrain to hamper the Romans' advance.

Varro, a traditional Roman commander, noting Hannibal's deployment, massed 65,000 of his warriors at the *center* and ordered them to attack the weak Carthaginian front. He then divided the Roman cavalry, sending about equal forces to oppose Hannibal's flanks.

Varro lost the battle and the lives of 60,000 of his men because he was a traditional Roman soldier, and Hannibal studied Roman strategies carefully. *He knew that Varro would mass his strength for an attack on his apparently weak center.* That was the traditional way of fighting, and therefore Varro's blindspot. How did Hannibal win? His two cavalry flanks were of unequal strength. The left wing was larger and therefore outnumbered the Roman cavalry opposing it.

The rest was relatively predictable. As the Romans attacked the center, which was withdrawing orderly under the pressure, the Carthaginian left wing crushed its smaller Roman cavalry opposition. It then circled the Roman center to unite with the Carthaginian right wing and finish off the remaining Roman cavalry. Hannibal then ordered the center to halt its withdrawal and attack. Simultaneously, the cavalry attacked from behind. The Romans were so densely packed at the center that their weapons were of little use. Their large numbers turned out to be their weakness. They were slaughtered.

What was the principle behind Hannibal's success? *He used his opponent's blindspot against him.*

Pepsi used the same principle in its tremendously successful marketing strategy aimed at unseating the industry leader, Coca-Cola. Pepsi took risks it knew its rival Coke, a conservative and traditional company, would never consider. In the 1980s, it used advertising and celebrity promotions as a strategic tool to position itself as the drink of the "new generation," *knowing that Coke would not tamper with its traditional brand image.* Pepsi pioneered advertising that knocked Coke (e.g., showing Coke as a geriatric drink), the use of very hip celebrities for promotion (Michael Jackson, M.C. Hammer), and the use of jazzy ads with Ray Charles to create an image of a youthful, trendier company (the 1990 ads with Ray Charles scored highest in awareness among consumers of all consumer products). As expected, Coke continued for years to plow forward with its "stuffy" image and traditional promotions, and kept its ad agency, McCann-Erickson, for 30 years despite some disastrous campaigns (a corporate taboo). Only in 1991, with its image slipping and its supermarket share declining, did Coke start to react, signing with a "hot" celebrity agency (Michael Ovitz's CAA), and putting out its advertising account for review.[71] One can only speculate that Pepsi's chairman is a lover of history.

When They Bring Out the Big Guns[72]

The value of learning rivals' blindspots is never more rewarding than when they are using their really *big* guns. A Roman general, Scipio Africanus, an opponent of Hannibal, faced him and a larger Carthaginian army in the battle of Zama (today part of Tunisia). Hannibal, by then a very seasoned and successful strategist, deployed 80 *elephants* in front of his line. One elephant was able to disrupt an entire army!

Alas, Scipio had learned Hannibal's methods well. In the battle of Zama, the young and untraditional Roman, who was a *persona non grata* in Rome, was the one who used his opponent's blindspots against him. Hannibal opened the battle by ordering his elephants to charge the Roman center. *Scipio expected exactly this strategy, which was the traditional way of using elephants in battle.* He equipped his front line with trumpets. When the attack began, Scipio ordered a blare of the trumpets. The elephants were terrified by the unexpected noise, and many turned and crashed into their own troops. The others passed harmlessly through Scipio's deliberately designed open formations. Hannibal's wings were thrown into confusion, the Roman wings used the opportunity to attack them, and the road was paved for Hannibal's final defeat.

By now I guess my message is clear. The principle behind Scipio's success was the same as that behind Dell Computer's.[73] In the 1980s, all three giant computer companies—IBM, Apple and Compaq—fell victim to "margin creep" blindspot: They focused on the upscale market, where corporate customers pay higher prices for higher-margin, top-end products, and turned a blind eye to the lower-end market. Michael Dell then grabbed it from under their noses. Dell also knew that IBM could not react to his $1,000 machines without a serious shakeup of its most entrenched myths about the value of centralized management and the value of its product line. A simple calculation could show that as of 1992, with its 32 percent operating expenses (as a percentage of revenues), IBM would have lost $1.2 billion per year if it had tried to match Dell's prices (Dell's operating expenses were 16 percent of revenues). Without radically changing its cost structure and product line offering, IBM was just like Hannibal and his elephants.[74]

Let me reiterate the main lesson of this section about history and blindspots: *If you know your competitor is committed to a certain way of thinking about himself and his market, you have in your possession a lethally potent competitive weapon.* Toyota's Lexus and Nissan's Infinity cars exploited to the full extent possible Mercedes' advertising taboo: Its ads did not acknowledge competition even with a hint. Johnson & Johnson's Vistakon, the world leader in disposable contact lenses, took advantage of giants Bausch & Lomb's and Ciba-Geigy's unchallenged assumption that contact lenses were unsuitable for disposables, to snap up 25 percent of the U.S. market by 1992. Wal-Mart owes much of its success to exploiting Sears and Kmart's blindspot when it came to location: It opened big, modern stores in country towns, while they for decades concentrated on big malls and urban areas. Packard Bell used its big competitors' entrenched myths about how and where one sells computers (not in department stores or warehouse clubs, for sure!) to grow from nothing to $1 billion in sales in five years. *Yet no one proved the value of this principle more succinctly than Federal Express.*

The Battle of the Urgent Package[75]

In the early '70s, if you wanted to send an urgent package, you could go to domestic air forwarders such as Emery, Airborne, or UPS. The package would move through five to 10 different corporate hands and arrive at its destination between two and four days later, at the earliest.

> **❝A competitive intelligence study revealed the following state: Most air carriers considered the small-package business to be a money-losing operation or, at best, marginally profitable.❞**

The main problem with shipping an urgent package was that regulations prohibited air forwarders from operating their own aircraft. That left the airlines to move the packages—and they were a major headache. Over 60 percent of their movements were among the 25 largest markets in the United States, but over 80 percent of the urgent packages moved *outside* the largest markets. Only 10 percent of the flights were night flights, so if you played by the rules, getting a package *overnight* was "mission impossible"!

In 1972, a young entrepreneur, Frederick Smith, took on the huge airlines and the large air forwarders and won. First, he changed the rules of the game. His lobbying in Washington changed the regulation to enable his Falcon jet fleet air-taxi service to carry a load of packages. Thus he became the first forwarder operating his own planes, free from the cumbersome airlines. This move enabled him to put in place many technological and organizational innovations that were impossible with the old forwarder airline link, such as a hub system, automated central sorting, and "on call" pickup. Like Alexander, Hannibal, and Scipio before him, Smith's success rested on his ability to neutralize the size advantage of competing air forwarders and to attack their weakest points (time, reliability, convenience).

Yet to reach the necessary volume to reduce cost and expand the market by attracting new users, two conditions essential to the survival of FedEx, Smith needed some protection from competition. If any one of the big air forwarders decided to imitate his idea, tiny, cash-strapped Federal Express would have been wiped out overnight. The market was simply too small at that point to allow a small company to survive against the giants. Why, then, was Smith foolish enough to enter such a high-risk venture?

The answer is, Smith had uncovered a gold mine in the form of a blindspot. A competitive intelligence study (then called market research, for lack of a better term) for which Smith paid $150,000 from his precious start-up capital revealed the following state: Most air carriers considered the small-package business to be a money-losing operation or, at best, marginally profitable. *This unchallenged assumption held by his competitors bought Smith six years of near monopoly to build his volume.* Only in late 1978 did Emery finally start to offer a similar service. UPS responded only in late 1982!

If you think uncovering your competitors' blindspots is just another nice theoretical concept, you would probably not have been one of the very lucky and very wise investors who invested in FedEx—the most successful private venture in U.S. history. You might have been the Yale professor who gave Smith a "C" grade on his paper proposing a company that would ship packages and letters overnight.

But how do you discover competitors' blindspots? If I made it sound easy, I apologize. It took Hannibal years of studying Roman battle strategies. It took Scipio years of following Hannibal and learning the man's way of thinking. If one can rely on the stories and legends surrounding Fred Smith's founding of FedEx, he had spent close to 30 percent of his very scarce initial resources on studying the competitors. One thing is clear: You have to develop a deep understanding of your competitors to be able to pinpoint their blindspots. I mean understanding to the level that you can guess the way they think. The assumptions they make when thinking. The things they can't or won't see anymore because of who they are or how they think. This is *not* the stuff you get from reading the news about your competitors in the clippings summary reaching your desk!

OK, forget about finding your competitors' blindspots. How do you discover your *own* blindspots? This is the subject of Part II. But then, assuming you have discovered your company's more lethal blindspots, how do you challenge unchallenged assumptions, shatter myths, and open taboos to fresh air? Let me rephrase the question:

How do you keep your company in touch with reality?

The answer is, you need a *powerful, systematic, company-wide* process that is devoted to the identification and deciphering of weak, ambiguous market signals early enough to make a difference. It is *not* something that

CEOs or division heads or executive vice presidents can do *on their own in their spare time*. This is the subject of Part III. Read the following statement twice to let its significance sink in:

> *Due to the nature of the disease, decision makers will be blind to their blindspots!*

● PART TWO

Diagnosis

"*Facts do not cease to exist because they are ignored.*"

Aldous Huxley

CHAPTER SEVEN

The Tests

I hope that by now I have convinced you that blindspots in a changing world are very dangerous. After all, it does not really take a genius to realize that, does it? But it takes a special ability—call it humility, openness, greatness, whatever—to bring yourself to entertain the thought that maybe, just maybe, you and your company are suffering from some specific blindspots as well. Keep in mind: *One clear symptom of blindspots is that one is blind in regard to their sheer existence.*

If you are a top executive in the newspaper industry and believe that the future belongs to big cities and, therefore, big-city newspapers, you would invest heavily in newspapers. And if you happened to be the chairman of New York City's *Newsday* in 1986 and were deeply convinced that two of your three competitors, the *New York Post* and the *Daily News*, were about to expire, by the time you became the president of the parent company, Times-Mirror, in 1992, would you change your mind just because they were still around? No. You would complain that "people seem to want to keep papers alive no matter what the economics" and be somewhat blind to the fact that you are one of those people, with your paper accumulating operating losses estimated at $150 to $200 million.[76] And if you did not really believe in the future of electronic media, you might make only a small, lip-service investment in cable TV but then fail to follow through, instead spending heavily on your blindspot—big-city newspapers. It is unfortunate that the cash flow from the small cable operation now exceeds the cash flow from your entire empire of papers.[77]

We are blind to our blindspots, which is why they *are* blindspots. The first real challenge is to diagnose them. Naturally, beholders of the blindspots cannot do it. Assuming that they are open-minded enough to entertain

77

the possibility that they (and their companies) coexist peacefully with blind-spots, someone else must diagnose them—and then try to convince the executive that it is indeed a blindspot.

It may sound hopeless, and sometimes it is—when the executive's ego is just too large or his mind too closed—but not always. Some executives will give you the benefit of the doubt. And often doubt is all that is needed.

So now let's assume you were given a free hand to roam the corporation and "break paradigms," be one of the mavericks RJR Nabisco's CEO Lou Gerstner appoints to be "china breakers."[78] How do you find blindspots? It's easy. *Just ask around.* I haven't been to an organization that within five days of my entry interviews would not spit out a dozen blindspots. Middle and junior managers and staff are well aware of their companies' myths and taboos. The problem is to bring this stuff to the surface in a systematic way so the company has a chance to fight it before its future is ruined. This will be discussed in Part III. At this point, we need a road map to start. The following suggestions are exactly that: a way to start. They are not intended as exhaustive diagnostic tests, nor are they exact, nor do they give a nice quantitative index to present to top management.[79]

My methodology of diagnosing blindspots is indirect and is based on three tests of competitiveness. Some management thinkers believe that competitiveness is in capabilities. Others call it competencies. Many executives look at competitiveness as a cost-related issue. I believe that above all, competitiveness is in knowledge. I therefore designed three tests to give you an indication of how well your company is attuned to the world around it.

Ask yourself the following questions:

1. *The visceral test:* Does your company *viscerally* know its markets?

2. *The reaction test:* Can it predict *reactions* to its initiatives?

3. *The mute, blind and deaf (MBD) test:* Does it suffer from a learning disorder?

1. The Visceral Test

The visceral test is named after an October 7, 1991 article that appeared in *Fortune* magazine. Titled "Keys to Japanese Success in Asia," by Ford S. Worthy, it concluded with the following statement: ". . . Japan's edge in selling to its neighbors has come from understanding—*viscerally under-standing*—its customers, suppliers, partners, regulators, influence peddlers, and competitors." (emphasis added) I couldn't agree more, so I adopted the phrase for my test. (I could, of course, have called it a worthy test, but that might have been trivialized.) The test is deceivingly simple:

Do you understand—viscerally understand—your competitive arena?

Of course you do. Most managers I confront with this question regard it as an insult to their professional pride. "Of course I understand my competitors. Man, I have been in this industry for [fill in the blank] _____ years, what do you think I do for a living? I know them as well as I know my own firm!" (The higher the number in the blank, the more the indignation.)

Please don't take it as a personal insult. *Most Western managers do not have the luxury of the time, the patience, or the resources to piece together a good mental picture of the market.* Remember this: Just because your company's marketing vice president receives periodic sales reports containing competitive information, and just because your company's engineers meet with clients, and purchasing agents talk to vendors daily, and project teams go over some published material regarding competitors' capabilities as they relate to your company's new service idea, does not mean your company has developed a visceral understanding of its market.

A manager of an American chemical company once told me the following story after listening to my lecture about competitive intelligence. He was attending a conference in London, and the speaker was a Japanese executive lecturing about trade opportunities in China. After the talk, the American manager went over to congratulate the speaker and they chatted for a few minutes. The Japanese mentioned that he was familiar with the American's firm, which was engaged in three large projects in China. The American corrected him: two projects. The Japanese insisted the number was three. Back home, the American discovered that the Japanese was right: There was a third project of which he, the employee of the American company, was not informed. This tale's lesson is not about the Japanese but about the American manager: We don't always know our own organization as well as we think, *let alone the rivals'*.

The Visceral Test, Japanese-Style

The *Fortune* article described a very different style of learning about the competitive arena. Four anecdotes were illuminating.

How much would your company spend on information? Trading companies are known for the premium they place on good competitive intelligence. The fourth-largest trading company in Japan, Mitsui, has more than 50 joint ventures in Thailand alone with partners who belong to the Overseas Chinese network—ethnic Chinese families whose business networks extend throughout Southeast Asia. These joint ventures serve to plug into local information that no outsider can ever hope to obtain, from which bankers are easiest to work with to how to approach potential customers.

How much effort would your executives put into gathering information? Almost every Japanese manager plays golf. Some Western managers play golf, too. In Southeast Asia, Westerners play golf mostly with their Western friends, regarding their golf hours as "home away from home." The Japanese use golf as a tool to obtain intelligence and intelligence contacts, especially with local businessmen, politicians, and government personnel. Who is the handicapped, then?

How long would your company wait for good intelligence results? Vietnam is one of the poorest countries in Asia and still under an American embargo on trade. Yet several Japanese companies have posted people in Vietnam against the day the country's markets reopen. That might take years. These Japanese managers do little business but mostly lay the groundwork for future business by establishing human contacts—absolutely THE prime competitive intelligence source. Similarly, Japanese automotive companies, such as Honda, studied the American market for about 10 years before seriously attacking it. Can we say the same about American firms abroad?

How far would you go to get to know the people on the other side? The *Fortune* article tells the story of an executive from Sandoz Pharmaceuticals who visited a Sandoz supplier in Osaka. Upon arrival, he and his colleagues were whisked to a communal hot bath with their Japanese hosts in a hot spring resort, then to a sumptuous dinner plus geishas, then to a small bar where they sang and danced and drank until the wee hours of the morning. The next day when the negotiations began, the Sandoz managers felt "like we had been friends for ten years" with their Japanese hosts. To reach this point, the Japanese had carefully prepared a comprehensive personal intelligence profile of the Sandoz people.

Similar tales are told by some of my Israeli and American friends who travel to Japan for negotiations or even mere presentations. The Japanese hosts always have files on the guests and quote detailed and accurate information from them. Not surprisingly, the Western guests never know anything about the hosts. You think I got carried away a bit? Think again: In one of the largest and most successful American companies, the newly established competitive intelligence unit began its presentation to a top management group by posting enlarged photos of the top managers of the company's number one Japanese competitor on the walls and asking the group members to identify their counterparts in Japan. They couldn't name ONE. Advantage: Japan.

Benchmarking and Knowing Thyself

Xerox is one of the few American companies that were able to wrestle back some market share from Japanese competitors, and returned to previous competitiveness in quality and sales. This miracle happened after Xerox reached a dangerous point in its history. In 1979, it saw its world market share slipping and its earnings fall surprisingly fast as Canon and Ricoh entered the market with better-quality copiers at lower prices.

A new CEO, David Kearns, rescued Xerox. One of his most successful tools was a process called *Competitive Benchmarking:* Every department at Xerox was required to compare its performance against its counterpart at the best competitor. If the competitor was no match, then the comparison was to be done against the "best in class"! This intense study of competitors' practices, processes, and results required tremendous input of competitive intelligence.

Xerox's Competitive Benchmarking practice started in 1979 in a few units and became a companywide mandated practice by 1981. Xerox units benchmark themselves against competitors such as IBM and Kodak, against major account customers, and against known excellence leaders. The distribution organization, for example, has benchmarked some of its functions against L.L. Bean, the catalog sales company known worldwide for its warehousing and distribution excellence.

Benchmarking is more than just another method to improve performance and motivate workers. It is not a fad, a quick fix, or one more misapplied gimmick from the arsenal of Japanese management techniques. The principle behind benchmarking is 1,000 years old. It can be traced to the Chinese general Sun Tzu, who wrote in his "Art of War" treatise, *"Know your enemy and know yourself; in a hundred battles you will never be in peril."*

The beauty of benchmarking is not only that it forces you to look closely and understand competitors, customers, and other players. If it is done right, it is also a way to learn about yourself. There is no better way to burst a myth than to see how others accomplish better results with different methods. There is no better way to uncork a taboo than to wrap it up in information about competitors' practices. I have seen many instances, and I am sure that you have seen many more, illustrating that the quickest way to change some established routine in a company was not to point to the obvious merits of a new routine but to marshal evidence that a successful competitor has been using or is about to use the new practice. *My unequivocal experience is that companies that benchmark get rid of a few blindspots and myths about their own strengths.*

Benchmarking can be done not only after the fact (on cost, quality, or service performance) but before the fact, on product characteristics, customer/consumer demands, and customer/consumer satisfaction. The Quality Function Deployment method of Professor Yoji Akao from Tamagawa University in Japan, which is used by such heavyweights as NEC, Mitsubishi, and Bridgestone Tires, introduces benchmarking techniques into the product design phase, such as the design of the 32-bit chip by NEC. Using this technique enabled NEC to create a chip without a single misspecification![80] Benchmarking at the R&D stage enables a company to design a product specifically and deliberately to beat the competition. It does away with much of the random guessing as to how the product will meet consumers' expectations.

Poor Man's Benchmarking

Benchmarking is based on learning from your competitors and other excellent companies those aspects of their operations in which they *excel*. But how about learning from their *mistakes*? You will be surprised at the effect of doing reverse benchmarking. After listening to my seminar about competitive intelligence and its role in fighting blindspots, a marketing manager at a large Asian food company went back to his sales managers and asked them to do a quick exercise: to list the five areas in which they thought their number-one competitor was weakest, and to explain why. He told me that the mere question was a shock to the system. The sales managers, like sales managers everywhere, were always extremely busy comparing prices and reporting new promotional initiatives and new products so that the marketing staff could react quickly (in the food business, speed of reaction is everything). They never benchmarked the competitor in terms of its weaknesses. The exercise led to a flood of new ideas from the floor—strategic initiatives aimed at pushing against the competitor's *weakest links*.

In sum, if understood correctly, benchmarking can be used as one terrific way to diagnose blindspots. It is a SWOT analysis—strengths and weaknesses, opportunities and threats—with a twist: a reality twist.

The Visceral Test: Some That Failed [81]

It happens to everyone, even the best of us. Viscerally knowing the market requires meticulous attention to *details*. Strategic intelligence is a puzzle—a composite picture of the market made of bits and pieces of competitive information. Details, in themselves meaningless or of low priority, are required to complete some crucial holes in the puzzle. How crucial can be seen from the following examples.

Wal-Mart Who?

Family Dollar Stores is a retail chain that was based in the rural Southeast, in small, blue-collar communities where family incomes in 1987 averaged less than $25,000.[82] The year 1987 was "special" for the chain: After nine years of stellar growth, its earnings plunged and its image started to blur. The reason? Expansion. Every year, Family Dollar Stores added 20 percent to its existing store base, pushing into 23 states with 1,107 locations. Family Dollar Stores had the image of a discount chain, but in reality it was not: It relied more on its convenient locations, service, and limited merchandise to support higher margins. In short, a typical regional chain serving populations that do not have easy access to the large national discount chains.

> **"By the time the expansion was over, Family Dollar Stores was no longer tucked away in the Southeast. As a matter of fact, it had pushed itself straight into Wal-Mart's territory."**

Well, almost. By the time the expansion was over, Family Dollar Stores was no longer tucked away in the Southeast. As a matter of fact, it had pushed itself straight into Wal-Mart's territory. Unfortunately, Family Dollar Stores' management failed to notice this little fact. Prices on its most heavily advertised items were actually up to 10 percent higher than Wal-Mart's nonadvertised, everyday low prices. Little wonder its sales slipped from a 9 percent growth rate to zero.

Family Dollar Stores' failure to notice that its prices were no longer competitive was not a tactical failure, as it may seem. Companies do not typically neglect to check on competitors' prices, except for the government (see below). The vast majority of you readers are probably swamped with pricing data. Salespeople collect and fax price sheets regularly. Executives who are, or would like to appear, serious about competition sometimes venture into retail outlets to check on competitors' prices. In fact, I would bet that Family Dollar Stores' executives collected price information about what they perceived as their local competitors—small main street boutiques and assorted shopping mall stores. The moral of the story is not about tactical pricing information but about the fact that, more often than one would imagine, companies fail to notice the little detail of *who their competitors actually are*!

Where Did They Come From?

Sounds extreme? Consider the story of Mentor Graphics. The computer company was founded in 1981 by Thomas Bruggere and a group of his friends from Tektronix to produce a fast desktop to handle design work on integrated circuits. From the beginning, it was clear to Mentor's executives that they could expect stiff competition from two large competitors: Hewlett-Packard and their former employer, Tektronix. What they actually discovered, sometime during their first year, were two other companies, Daisy Systems and Valid Logic Systems, that were a year to 18 months ahead of them. As one of the founders put it, "We were behind from day one," and with a strategy that kept them behind.[83] Interestingly, as of 1988, neither H-P nor Tektronix had entered their market!

Chiquita Banana Slips Away

Before you conclude that I regard price information as an unimportant detail in the strategic intelligence puzzle, let me relay the following anecdote about the Port Authority of New York and New Jersey. In 1984, Port Newark was receiving 816,000 tons of bananas. By 1986 it was 688,000 tons. The decline might have aroused some suspicion in most companies, but the Authority is a state enterprise, and so perhaps more absentminded when it comes to knowing its market *viscerally*. So, in 1988, when Turbana Corporation and Chiquita Banana notified the Port that they were pulling out, both having found a *cheaper* alternative, and were going to truck the bananas into New Jersey, the news "came as a shock" to Authority officials and the 600 workers who lost their jobs.[84] Would you describe the Authority's top executives as alert?

The **Real** Pepsi Challenge

If you believe John Sculley's autobiography,[85] attention to details was not exactly the hallmark of the Coca-Cola Company. In reading it, one may conclude that it was the attention to details that allowed Pepsi to gain a strong second place (first place in the United States in 1993) in the cola market, despite the presence of an undisputed leader.

The story of Pepsi begins around the 1930s, when its "twice as much for the same nickel" campaign quickly brought in market share. The leader, Coke, whose dominance went back to the late nineteenth century, did not even know Pepsi existed. How was Pepsi able to gain on Coke without any reaction? As Sculley put it:

> . . . as we gained on Coca-Cola, we realized the Atlanta-based company was in reality a sleeping giant. Coca-Cola was still track-

ing market share on the basis of the number of bottles (units) sold, not ounces. A 48-ounce Pepsi bottle would count as much as a 6.5-ounce Coke bottle in the survey. Because so much of Coke's business was in its small 6.5-ounce bottle, their Nielsen data tended to disguise the real advances Pepsi was making. We converted our Nielsen numbers to 8-ounce-equivalent cases, because it more accurately showed the trend toward larger packages. This made sense, too, because Pepsi and Coca-Cola were in the business of selling beverage concentrate; the more cola ounces consumed, the more concentrate bottlers would buy from us.[86]

Made sense, yes—if (1) you knew which business you were in (in itself a somewhat significant piece of strategic intelligence), and (2) paid attention to the *details* of competitive information.

Then, as Pepsi grew in market share, its next strategic thrust was to change its image from lower price to quality taste. Thus was born the Pepsi Challenge. Put an average-looking consumer in front of a TV camera; place two wrapped glasses in front of her; ask her to drink, then choose—and Voila! she chose . . . Pepsi!

As Sculley describes it, Coke went berserk. It became obsessed with stopping the tests, claiming they were unethical and would destroy the industry. It tried to persuade the networks to stop carrying the commercials. It tried every legal maneuver possible. When these efforts failed, Coke invested millions in an advertising blitz. It produced counter-Challenge events in which a football player named Mean Joe Green would smash Pepsi vending machines; it ran taste tests with chimpanzees and ads in which people tasted a glass of tennis balls. Now read the punch line, from *Odyssey*:

> If Coke did its research, of course, it would have known that consumers overwhelmingly chose Coke over Pepsi when the brands were identified before the sip test . . . . It was the missing piece of research that could have unraveled our campaign. (p. 50)

In fact, Pepsi was growing by devouring weaker local brands, not Coke. A company that knows its market viscerally, knows these facts.

King Grocer [87]

Winn-Dixie is a supermarket chain based in Florida. By 1988 it had 1,252 stores in 13 southern states. Its margins ranked at the top of the industry throughout the 1970s and most of the 1980s. It paid monthly dividends, increasing them by more than 10 percent per year for 44 years. Then, in 1987-88, its margins fell to industry's average, its stock lost 30 percent of its value, its earning dropped 4 percent, and its dividends grew by only 3 percent. What happened?

Competition happened. As the South grew, it attracted supermarket chains such as Bruno's, Food Lion, Kroger, Pueblo International, and Albertson's. Winn-Dixie and its Florida market co-leader, Publix Super Markets, had to adapt and learn. Publix did it, preserving margins of 2 percent. Winn-Dixie flunked.

What was the difference? Publix took learning seriously. The national chains were moving in with 56,000-square-foot combination food/drug outlets with higher margin cosmetics and nonfood merchandise. Publix took note. It remodeled its stores, creating wider aisles, better lighting, meat counters, pharmacies, and restaurants, positioning itself as the supermarket with the best service. Winn-Dixie, which up until then sat quietly with its chain of outmoded 25,000-square-foot food-only stores, had to react. So in less than five years it opened 382 stores, closed 340, and remodeled 267. None was as well designed as the competitors'!

What does "not well designed" mean? Well, how about salad dressing sitting next to hair and bath products instead of next to the vegetables? How about high-margin vitamins buried next to cereals? In the 1980s, shelf-space management became an essential facet of managing supermarkets. Winn-Dixie ignored these little details and went from number one to a deposed king looking for new clothes.

The Devil Is in the Details

And to finish off the visceral test, here are some short anecdotes. In the late 1980s, Coca-Cola began its push into China. Fond of the English pronunciation of its soft drink name, for which it spent billions of dollars over the years, Coke had a translator come up with Chinese characters that would sound roughly like Coca-Cola. Only after bottling and distributing the product did Coke discover that the meaning of the Chinese words for Coca-Cola was actually "bite the wax tadpole."[88]

Anheuser-Busch launched its flagship brand beer, Budweiser, in Britain in 1984. After four years, three agencies and four campaigns, the brand had only 0.5 percent of the British market, the fourth largest beer market in the world. When Anheuser started to push into Britain, the trends seemed to have been on their side. The lager market was growing by 6 percent per year, British consumers were switching to the lighter lagers from dark ales, and there wasn't much competition. What more could someone ask?

Someone could ask for attention to details. Some 75 percent of beer in Britain is sold in 82,000 pubs, most of which are owned by other brewers. Anheuser followed a reasonable strategy: It licensed its brands to a local brewer with 6,000 pubs, hoping it would promote Budweiser in those 6,000 pubs and later sell to others. But the brewer had other plans. It saw Budweiser as just an addition to its already extensive international portfolio, so Budweiser was advertised as an exotic beer for yuppies. After four years it had been placed in only 3,000 pubs out of the 82,000.[89]

In Summary

All the preceding examples are of excellent companies. My intention is not to put these companies down or belittle their executives. These "slips" can—and do—happen to everyone. The point of these examples is that it is not so easy to gain a visceral knowledge of one's market, and it should never be taken for granted that a company already knows everything it needs to know. The quest for additional information about the market and its players should never cease. There is never *too much* understanding of market forces—be they competitors, consumers, suppliers, or substitutes.

2. The Reaction Test

The reaction test is a simple tool for diagnosing blindspots. In essence, it asks a simple question: When your company (or you) plans a strategic move, do you take into account the reaction of other players in your industry? Are you capable of predicting their response?

You may frown at the implication of the test. What executives don't take into account the way other major players around them are going to respond? You will be surprised, as was I. In company after company, I found either a perfunctory attention to other players' reaction *or no consideration at all!* When it came to competitors' responses, it was as if these very sharp executives were hoping rivals would just "sit this one out," or take their eroding share or lower profit as a sign from God that the good times were over. This was one of the most amazing phenomena I have ever encountered, and it was more ignorance than a deliberate lack of concern. When you don't really have strategic intelligence on your competitors, all you can do is hope they will not disrupt the success of your wonderful initiative.

Market Research Is Not Competitive Intelligence

If there is one thing no one can take away from corporate America, it is the fact that its consumer goods companies invented market research. Food companies elevated the discipline into an art. I suspect that an innocent bystander walking past some headquarters in Minneapolis or Cincinnati has a good chance of being kidnapped, brought to a secret chamber, and having his taste, color, and shape zones in his cortex mapped thoroughly before he even realizes he was taken hostage. Focus groups, the invention of the '60s, have mushroomed into a monster industry. What do they do there, anyway? On how many dimensions can a normal person rate frozen peas?

But I am probably just envious. With so much research power and those huge budgets, my intelligence processes could have saved the world, let alone IBM. But these same market researchers couldn't save Green Giant or General Mills from some very costly flops. The reason? Consumer products companies failed to understand that consumer research was not competitive intelligence.

William McGrath, Jr., a former vice president for business development at Green Giant and a reformed intelligence advocate, describes the following two incidents at Green Giant and General Mills in the '60s and '70s. While this (public) material may be old, I can vouch that the situation has not changed much.[90]

In the late 1970s, Green Giant introduced a line of single dish entrees. The market for singles in the United States was growing by leaps and bounds, and Stouffer was there first with a full product line. Like the good food company that it was, Green Giant invested a lot of money in market (i.e., consumer) research. The offering tasted good, looked good, and was priced right. Alas, markets include not only consumers, but competitors as well. The only thing Green Giant did not research was the expected reaction from Stouffer. In the war that erupted, Stouffer had the upper hand. It had superior cost structure and was dedicated to the market. Green Giant never made it as a dominant player. In the food industry, being a distant second is as good as being dead—you will never recoup the investment.

There are two lessons from this little anecdote (I am sure it was not that little to the poor executive at Green Giant who championed it). First, it is important to attempt a study of the economic (cost) structure of competitors (and suppliers; more on this later) in order to be able to estimate response *capabilities*. In most marketing departments, where corporations typically hide their meager attempts at competitor intelligence, the subject of cost is not among the favorites. Marketers are not accountants and surely not engineers. At best, one will consult the competitor's annual reports or analysts' reports and assume the costs "cannot be that much different than ours." This assumption, like most assumptions, tends to acquire over time the status of certainty. Time and many presentations make it easy to forget that the so-called "competitive cost estimates" are basically manipulations of one's own costs.

Second, it is important to study people, organizational politics, and power struggles at other major players to understand the response *intentions*.

Who's championing what? Where does he move to next? Stouffer's CEO might have come from the single-dish project—thus Stouffer's devotion to that segment. Ford's chairmen throughout the 1980s grew up in its Truck division. Their background would have made it easier to understand Ford's reliance on trucks as a center of its strategy. Lou Gerstner, the new chairman at IBM and former RJR Nabisco top man, grew up in American Express. He "cut his teeth" in premium brands, developing the platinum and Optima cards. One could have placed a very safe bet that at RJR he would push premium brands. Indeed, he spent millions on full-price Winston and Salem, ignoring for a long time evidence that competitors' generic cigarettes were winning out. At the end he joined the party, saying, "You have to be fast on your feet and adaptive, or else a strategy is useless."[91] I guess he read this book.

The second anecdote relayed by McGrath regards General Mills. In the 1960s, General Mills decided to enter the snack market. Again, the lights burned very late in the market research offices and poor consumers were forced to "sing" in the prison catacombs. The salty snacks had a very attractive offering to the consumer. General Mills just did not analyze Frito Lay, the major player in this market, too closely. It assumed that its distribution system was inefficient. Frito Lay had a store/door system that was indeed very costly but also allowed it to monopolize the particular shelf space in the grocery outlets where impulse buying took place. Salty snacks lived and died by impulsive purchases. General Mills' product bombed.

As an epilogue to this anecdote, it is ironic but not surprising that in 1993 General Mills formed a joint venture with PepsiCo, Frito Lay's parent, to distribute snacks in Europe. Not surprising because the General Mills of 1993, under Bruce Atwater, is not the General Mills of the 1960s. It is one of the most progressive companies around. Atwater himself is well-known for being a ruthless fighter against blindspots in his organization. The right person can make a heck of a difference, even if one airline cannot.

RJR Strikes Again

And since we mentioned RJR Nabisco, its pre-Gerstner chairman, F. Ross Johnson was also responsible for one classic example of how companies (in this case, his ad agency) do not understand the potential response of players in their field. The story occurred on April 4, 1988, when Johnson fired RJR's ad agency, Saatchi and Saatchi DFS. The move came as a complete shock to Peter McSpaden, Saatchi & Saatchi DFS's president and chief operating officer. The reason for the unexpected move? The agency produced an ad for Northwest Airlines promoting its ban on smoking on all its flights without notifying RJR of the campaign and its involvement. RJR's vice chairman and head of its tobacco business, Edward Horrigan, just noticed the commercial while watching TV.

A complete shock? An ad agency promotes antismoking and is completely surprised that a tobacco account gets mad? Did these people collect *any* intelligence about the people at RJR?

Double-Cross

At last, a story befitting a book on intelligence. A 175-year-old textile dynasty, J. P. Stevens, was about to be acquired by its rival, West Point Pepperell, Inc. In a desperate attempt to block the hostile takeover, Stevens looked for a white knight—a company that would leave management in place in a friendly takeover. Stevens' directors found Odyssey Partners, a New York investment group. As the bidding war erupted, Stevens' board embraced an offer from Odyssey. The deal would have prevented West Point from getting its hands on Stevens' prized lines of home furnishings, including Ralph Lauren and Laura Ashley sheets and towels. To further the deal, Stevens opened its books to Odyssey, invited its executives to plant tours, and, in short, accorded them treatment suitable for saviors from the mortal enemy. Imagine their surprise when they found out from the press that West Point and Odyssey had been discussing a plan to buy Stevens jointly.

The match was made by a former Citibank venture capitalist, who first agreed to buy some Stevens assets from West Point and then called an old friend at Odyssey to offer a "peaceful cooperation." According to the new report, Stevens' managers were "incensed."[92] Wouldn't you be?

But then, stop and think for a second. Is this type of event preventable? You bet. People's backgrounds give many clues to their future actions. If not in specifics, then in broad strokes of the brush. Did Stevens' directors run a check on these New York guys and their past deals? Was it at least *possible* that their integrity had been compromised before? Should Stevens' executives have at least tried to play likely scenarios regarding Odyssey's reaction to the request for help? After all, these were guys from New York!

Crafty Kraft [93]

In an industry, one can be a leader or one can be a follower. There is nothing magic in being the leader, and there is definitely nothing wrong with a *deliberate* strategy of following. Matsushita, for example, made an art of the strategy of being second (after Sony) and proved that sometimes coming in late is profitable.

The story is somewhat different if a company exhibits a follower strategy because it is simply *slow*. This was the case with Kraft. When the food industry was going through diversification, Kraft was among the last to join by merging with Dart. When the industry was going back to basics, Kraft was the last to spin off its nonfood business. The image hurt Kraft's stock, which spent the late '80s sitting out the rally on food processors in the stock market. To change the image, Kraft's chief executive, John M. Richman, hired Michael Miles away from Heublein, Inc. Miles, described as a hard-driving executive, was made Kraft's chief operating officer. That was 1983. In a 1987 article in *Business Week*, Kraft was described as having trouble growing through new products and new business development. The hard-driving Miles was quoted as saying that Kraft was preparing a push into fresh, refrigerated foods such as salads, pasta, and entrees. For a change, the proud Miles stated the move would be with Kraft's own products rather than with acquisitions. Hurray to the giant's new product development teams? Not so fast. The article does not fail to note that Campbell Soup Company and General Foods Corporation had apparently already entered the market with their own products. One can only wonder at Miles's ability to, for a change, *preempt* competitors' moves.

3. The Mute, Blind and Deaf (MBD) Test

Finally, the last test is the utterly preposterous test for companies suffering from a serious learning disorder. It is really a test for middle managers more than for top managers. Given the last decade's experience with corporations, it is the middle layer that almost automatically pays the price during corporate "restructuring." My advice to the reader who is a middle manager: Put your company through the test. If it seems to behave like the companies in the example, run for your life. Your top management is so arrogant and blind, and the culture so much against any learning, that I will bet the royalties from this book that you will be looking for new employment sometime in the next two years. The middle managers in the companies cited in the example have been doing it for the past few years.

The MBD Hall of Fame Presents:

There are many companies (including several pillars of the financial community), who have definitely *not* passed the MBD test. Let us all salute the puppets in Robert Campeau's circus.[94]

Robert Campeau was a real estate developer from Canada. He had a successful real estate company that in 1986, when our story begins, was earning a respectable profit of less than $10 million. In 1986, he decided it was time to take over the retail trade in the United States. He did not have any experience in this field. His first target, Allied—which owned Brooks Brothers, Ann Taylor, Jordan Marsh, and other stores—had 10 times his company's profit. Campeau was a real estate man. He thought that all one needs is to find the financing.

And he found plenty of it. In 1986 he took over Allied with a loan of $3.6 billion from First Boston, Citibank, and another successful developer. In 1988, he took over Federated Department Stores with an additional loan of $6.5 billion, again from First Boston and Citibank, but this time with additional financing from Olympia & York, Dillon Read, Paine Webber, a few Japanese banks, and even the Bank of Montreal. Between loans, he received interim financing from Prudential and Security Pacific Bank.

Alas, our fairytale is about to end. The old witch Reality steps in again. By 1990, just four years after he took these investment bankers by storm, the Allied-Federated-Campeau complex went bankrupt, leaving Citibank with a bad debt of $288 million; First Boston with $425 million; Olympia & York, $525 million; DeBartolo, $480 million; Paine Webber, *only* $96 million, and 300,000 suppliers, 100,000 workers, and 250 retired executives, whose severance checks "remained in the mail," in search of their money.

It seems that no one questioned these deals. No one. Not even the very senior executives who were too busy to notice the evidence, or Paine Webber's top brass, whose company had to sue him to get a $5.75 million fee for the Allied deal, and who later claimed that their bank needed the experience in bridge loans, so it lent Campeau another $500 million . . . . Couldn't they get the experience with a sound deal?

Let there be no doubt: Deals such as these were done by the top executives of these banks, with armies of young MBAs with red suspenders and black BMWs who were recruited to analyze financial statements to death. That also explains why a simple financial analysis, which showed that even in their best times (and these were not their best times) Allied-Federated's profits were $680 million and the interest on their debt $869 million, went unnoticed.

The story of Campeau is not only a story of a lack of any *strategic* analysis by banks; it is a story of organizations that did not want to learn anything from the environment—the classic MBDs. Let's look at the intelligence that was available to these brilliant financial minds.

Prior to the deal, Campeau had a direct record of psychiatric instability. In addition, a Morgan Stanley manager recalls that neither he nor his colleagues, who met with Campeau during his rounds of raising money to buy Allied, could understand what he was saying. This comment surfaces again: Executives present at a meeting between Campeau and a business associate reported that he did not seem stable. Guests invited to his celebration party after taking over Allied commented that he made a speech no one understood. In a meeting with a banker about selling a few divisions of Allied, he began to question his own purchase of Allied.

It didn't appear he was stable. The market, though, was in the midst of takeover mania. The deals themselves seemed good to the CEOs, regardless of the persona involved.

Well, if you believe that, you would believe anything. No deal has a strategic value when the leader's decisions are questionable. No strategic value, no financial value—but, as I pointed out, bank executives are typically hard pressed to come up with strategic understanding of the industries they lend to, or, for that matter, understanding of the meaning and value of strategic intelligence. Two years after purchasing Allied, Campeau replaced two CEOs. The third one objected to the additional debt that Allied would incur if Campeau brought Federated on but was forced to swallow it. Allied's performance in 1987, the year Campeau went after Federated, was far from stellar. Later on Campeau would sell its best performer, Ann Taylor, because he needed the money to pay a loan. But Olympia & York were *shocked* when he came to them for an emergency loan of $75 million for Allied. Only then did they send in their advisers to look over Allied, just to find out it could never survive its interest payments. Should we be surprised that Olympia & York's empire crumbled in 1992? Financial genius is not strategic genius.

If your company suffers from MBD—with brilliant financial wizards at the top and no one who understands the need for competitive learning—run for your life, and your mortgage. And try not to work for banks, which still don't understand that they, of all companies, need the best strategic learning process money can buy. Oops, sorry, did I catch you on your way to the local S&L?

In Summary: The Three Tests

The visceral knowledge, the reaction analysis, and the willingness to learn are three indicators of the company's *susceptibility* to blindspots. While not pointing out specific blinders, the tests indicate how well prepared the company is to identify competitive developments in its environment. The implementation of these tests involves the following steps:

1. The CEO (for corporate level) or the president (for strategic business unit [SBU] level) decides that the task of ridding the organization of its blindspots is of utmost importance; otherwise, it will be practically impossible to carry out his vision for the company.

2. The CEO (for corporate level) or president (for SBU level) appoints a "china breaker" (more on that in Chapter 14).

3. The china breaker is given a free hand to roam the organization, exploring and exposing (E&E) significant myths, taboos, and unchallenged assumptions.

4. To start the E&E, I recommend that the china breaker studies the following three issues:

- By which process does top management acquire its knowledge of the competitive arena?
The principles behind the visceral test above are the starting point. The china breaker must keep in mind the type of activities and examples I presented that provided a visceral knowledge of the market or exposed its absence.

- How much reaction analysis is carried out before and during strategy implementation?
The china breaker must identify, chart, and attend the various meetings where competitive moves are planned. He or she must read the various project and strategy documents floating around the company and look for reaction analysis. Although this study is somewhat different for each company, I believe that new product review meetings can be a reasonable starting point.

- How conducive is the organization to competitive learning?
This is the most ambiguous of the china breaker's tasks but not necessarily the most difficult. The successful completion of this task wholly depends on the china breaker's skill in coaxing answers to sensitive issues from the hierarchy. Some people will tell him or her nothing; some will break out of the corporate line. The china breaker's talent is indirectly tested by his or her ability to locate the latter in the organizational maze.

With the three tests completed, the CEO or president has a rational basis for answering a simple question: Is my company competitive? If the answer is "not quite," it is time to act.

In the next chapter, I will recount the amazing amount of information my colleagues and I were able to obtain by using a very simple methodology for exposing blindspots. We had the advantage of being outsiders, but a good china breaker, with support from the top, has the advantage of unlimited access. Perhaps a combination of outsiders and a designated insider is the best approach to flushing out the blindspots *without acquiring them in the process.*

CHAPTER EIGHT

A Case Approach to Flushing Out Blindspots

One method of identifying blindspots was designed by the Rutgers team during its research on quantitative indexes for competitive intelligence flows in an organization.[95] The method's most useful aspect was its relative ease and the quick look it provided at deeper problems. It was never meant as a substitute for the three "tests" discussed in Chapter 7, but rather as a jump-start for a qualitative, interview-based study of how knowledgeable a company is about its markets and its competitors' responses.

The method was based on the reasonable assumption that past decisions can yield a clue or two as to how much competitive information was collected and how well it was used in the company.

Following this rationale, our method involved the following steps:

1. Identify a decision to be studied. The decision was to be a specific project, such as entering a new market, acquiring a company, or introducing a new technology.

2. Identify categories of competitive intelligence that should have been germane to this type of decision. If we needed help, we consulted knowledgeable line and staff members (but avoided those too involved with the decision!).

3. Identify the people who were the key players in making and implementing the decision.

Step 4 in our original research involved a rather complex and unnecessarily sophisticated index that translated subjective responses from our decision players into one number. That is the name of the game in academe—a too simple (although just as effective) approach would never have been published. For the purposes of this book, when a china breaker is entrusted by top management to assess the company's competitive readiness, I propose a qualitative approach, as follows:

4. Ask these players two simple questions: (1) Did they have enough competitive information about the category at the time they finally made the decision? and (2) How important did they think it was to have this information in this particular category? The result is a matrix such as the one in Figure 8-1 at the end of this chapter.

Example: In 1990, GE acquired the Hungarian bulb maker Tungsram, which turned out to be a huge cash drain on GE. Apparently, in its haste to enter the Eastern European market, GE did not look too closely into the Hungarian company's financial, technological, and human aspects. This was not an exceptional state of affairs: Among the most blindsided decisions are acquisitions. As I discussed in Chapter 4, acquisition decisions are ripe for information filtering. However, if GE wanted to learn a lesson from the experience (identify blindspots and try to prevent them) as opposed to punishing the managers involved, the above methodology is especially well suited. I would have started by identifying competitive information categories to which attention should have been paid in the deal. One reasonable category is "profit." I would have broken it down to subcategories such as "accounting method," "cash flow," "state transfer policy," etc., then asked the executives who were involved how much information was actually *available* on Tungsram's true state of profitability before they agreed to pay $150 million for the acquisition and heralded it as one of the "most promising in Eastern Europe."[96] I would then have tried to get into their reasoning by asking them how important it was for them to have this particular information. Often executives know they lack information, but the information would not have made a difference in the final decision anyway! It makes little sense to work hard on readying a company to gather intelligence that will have no real impact.

Comparing the notes from a series of informal discussions with the decision/project players is an opportunity for identifying and fighting blindspots. Some managers might have had the information, but never thought it was important to pass it along. Some would have withheld it on purpose (but then they will not tell it to the china breaker either, will they?). Availability is a rather straightforward issue, and one can identify where the information *could have* been obtained, to ensure a better-informed crowd later. For example, the *Business Week* reporter on the GE case comments that the Hungarian workers at the original Tungsram were apparently better informed than the GE negotiators.[97] Had a competitive intelligence expert been on the team of GE's managers, he or she might have seen to it that some discreet conversations would have been held with knowledgeable employees. Finally, asking the managers what they thought was important to get and what they thought was not so important to get is very revealing of blindspots. Here hidden assumptions, myths, and taboos surface very rapidly.

There are several ways a china breaker can manage this hindsight analysis of a decision. One way is to informally interview the participants in their offices. Another is to gather the original team around a table for a half-day analysis and lessons. Naturally, the second choice is not feasible in many corporate cultures. It is good for those organizations with a chief who can look you in the eye and admit, "I screwed up" without feeling that his or her authority has been undermined. But then, these executives are the type who call me in to organize a continuous process to study their companies' blindspots anyway.

To illustrate what type of information can be obtained from this method, I have included three case studies.[98] Remember that we employed a rather sophisticated indexing method and were not at all familiar with the organization. A china breaker with blessings from the top can achieve 10 times the insights we obtained.

The first two cases were decisions studied after the fact: a new product development decision and a market extension project. The third applied the method to a consumer product company's current problem of procurement.

Case I

The first decision, involving a large firm, was whether or not to engage in a large-scale pilot production run of a new product. Because of reasons described below, however, the implementation of the decision was terminated approximately 12 months prior to our study. A panel consisting of our team and two people from the company compiled a list of 15 relevant competitive intelligence categories (Table 8-1). We then divided the key participants in the decision into three groups: general managers, marketing managers, or technical managers (including R&D and Production). Similarly, we identified each intelligence item as dealing with either marketing intelligence or technical intelligence.

Overall Results of the First Study

The competitive information categories judged most important (indicated by asterisks in Table 8-1) tended to deal with the future market size, competitor costs and capabilities, and availability of raw material, whereas the least important dealt primarily with existing competing products or substitutes. However, while information on potential future conditions was of most interest, there was little information available on the potential for competing products to be introduced into the market. Nevertheless, that did not prevent the managers from proceeding with the decision. We smelled a blindspot from miles, and indeed, as we kept talking to participants, it became obvious that a corporate myth underlined the nonchalant attitude toward competitors. There was a general feeling that the company stood far above its rivals in the relevant technological skills ("no one had the technology we did") although there was no hard evidence at all to back this feeling up. There was even an admission that the Japanese represented an informational black hole. As one manager observed, "No one does primary research on the Japanese"; and from another, "the Japanese always surprise." Yet despite this lack of information about activities in Japan, the research director chose not to meet with a group of Japanese researchers who visited the company.

As subsequent events unfolded, it became obvious that expectations of competitive developments were badly off the mark. For one, a European company came out with a competing product that seemed to use a cheaper processing technology. Ironically, the company we studied had excellent access to European data. But no one ever asked the European contacts for information about this particular competitor, nor was there a mechanism for routine exchange of competitively useful information.

The lack of information on competitors was not due solely to negligent collection efforts. When a North American firm came out with a competing product, several senior managers expressed surprise, but a technical manager claimed knowledge (if not in detail) of the competitor's efforts in the product category. Not surprisingly, there was also a lack of consensus concerning the interpretation of intelligence. A marketing manager indicated he would have made significant adjustments to his projections if he had known a certain competitor would enter the market, but several colleagues dismissed this competitor's activities as irrelevant to the company.

One classic unchallenged assumption uncovered by our method was related to cost. Our index showed zero availability of direct information on competitors' cost, yet every manager on the team subscribed to the *assumption* that costs were similar in the industry. This is a widely prevalent practice, used extensively in benchmarking studies, consulting firms' "market studies," and internal planning. The justification? It is better than nothing. I vehemently disagree. Wrong assumptions are worse than nothing—they can actually wreak havoc. One classic example was the refusal of GM's board to believe the cost figures coming out of Isuzu, in which GM owned a sizable minority share. The numbers showed that Japan was beating Detroit in the small-car manufacturing game by such a margin that it was impossible for GM to compete. The tendency to say "their cost couldn't be that much off ours" caused GM to lose huge amounts of money until several years later when it conceded the point and turned to Toyota for a joint venture in small-car manufacturing.

"Our" company was no different. A recent price drop on the Japanese version of the product left one expert puzzled. This manager then reacted to the drop by assuming again: "They must be dumping, no one can have that low a cost"—still without any hard information on the subject.

The final blow to the American market resulted from constraints ultimately imposed by a regulatory action. While some of those interviewed shrugged this off as unpredictable because of politics, others did not agree. The division head admitted, "I could have done a better job of anticipating their actions," and a technical manager reported that he was made aware by the lawyers that the attitude of the regulators was tightening and he should have contacted the agency's division head directly. The forecast of the future market having been so badly off the mark, the product had to be shelved after completion of the production run.

Hierarchy and Functional Effects

Our analysis indicated that the availability of important competitive information was lowest among general management. This is consistent with previous studies showing problems of information filtering in an organization hierarchy.[99]

All managers felt more comfortable with the marketing intelligence they received than they did with the technical intelligence (see Table 8-2 at the end of the chapter). The technology myth led to complacency with regard to the lack of direct intelligence on competitors' actual technical capabilities. An alternative possibility, that technical intelligence was harder to get, did not seem to be valid, as the technical people indicated that one could easily learn what is going on in a field by attending the right technical meetings and socializing with the right people. Prior to our study, however, no one thought this should be done in a *systematic* way.

Case II

The decision we studied for this well-known, diversified manufacturer involved penetrating an additional market segment with a lower-quality product. The company's entry into this market failed to produce results that met the initial expectations.

There were 11 decision and implementation team leaders. We investigated 27 competitive categories.

Results

As in the previous company, abundant intelligence was available on tactical items about current market conditions, all of which had low importance rankings. A paucity of information occurred in strategic marketing issues, such as those dealing with competitors' potential responses and capability for response, as well as in the company's ability to market the product successfully against the competition's strengths. Breaking down the results by management function and information type (including a new category, Competitor Strategy), revealed a profile of relatively little strategic intelligence *generally* available, but—more revealing—little *senior* management dissatisfaction with its unavailability (see Table 8-3 at the end of this chapter). This suggested an organization that was potentially more at risk from intelligence blindspots than was the first. And, indeed, a few years later the company suffered performance decline and went through a wrenching cost-cutting drive.

Case III

The methods described above were applied to a third company in a prospective rather than a retrospective manner. The company was a mid-size consumer products firm that had identified the procurement area as one that could possibly benefit from a (supplier) intelligence analysis.

Results

A matrix was compiled that listed intelligence issues and major players in procurement decisions. Interviews then revealed two major blindspots where corporate myths about company strengths led to false conclusions and flawed decisions. One was the belief that the purchasing function was able to extract the largest possible discount (relative to competitors in the industry) from the two suppliers of bulk raw material. The other was that the majority of the purchasing contracts represented "good deals" because suppliers would not wish to be caught "underhanding" this company due to its size and influence in the market. However, zero information existed to support either assumption, and counterinformation was either not collected or ignored. Subsequent collection of hard data ultimately proved both myths to be just that. The company then moved to change the entire procurement decision process by imposing a *mandatory intelligence review* step on contracts above a certain size and on renewals of contracts that had existed for longer than a specified period of time.

Conclusions

The three cases studied using our method revealed what was to me a rather shocking fact: an absence of any systematic planning for intelligence gathering, analysis, or distribution. Given the cost of failure, and the management hours devoted to information gathering, report writing, debates, and discussions in the process of making a strategic decision, one would expect some systematic attention to be paid *in advance* to questions such as:

1. What competitive intelligence is needed for the decision,
2. Who is going to get it, and
3. How and to what extent will it be shared?

The mere exercise of listing the important categories of competitive intelligence required for a well-reasoned decision proved to be an eye-opener to many managers involved in the studies.

This competitive behavior is the easy-to-generate result of a systematic competitive learning process, which is the subject of Part III.

Figure 8-1: An Outline of a Response Matrix

	Participant 1	Participant 2	Participant 3
Intelligence item 1	Importance; Availability	Importance; Availability	Importance; Availability
Intelligence item 2	Importance; Availability	Importance; Availability	Importance; Availability
Intelligence item 3	Importance; Availability	Importance; Availability	Importance; Availability

Table 8-1
Case I—Competitive Intelligence by Functional Area

Marketing Items
* Who the competitors are
* Current market size
* Future market size
* Competitors' prices
  Who might enter the market
  Supply/capacity conditions of close substitutes and competing products
  Competitors' experience with their existing products
  Relationship of competitors with our company's clients
  Consumers' perception of product and close substitutes

Technical Items
* The cost of production and distribution of close substitutes and competing products
* Raw material availability
* R&D efforts by competitors in this product category
* How costly would it be for competitors to add similar value?
* The state of technology

Unclassified
  Relationship of competitors with their parent companies (if applicable)

---

* An asterisk denotes an item rated important or critical by the majority of the participants in the first case.

Table 8-2
Percent of High-Importance Items
Rated Adequately Available
Case I

Information Type			
Team Member's Function	**Marketing**	**Technology**	**Total (N=14)**
General Management	71%	25%	54%
Marketing	75	42	60%
Technical	78	50	65%
Total (n=10)	75%	40%	

N: Number of items rated important or critical
n: Number of respondents classified by function

Table 8-3
Percent of High-Importance Items
Rated Adequately Available
Case II

Information Type				
Team Member's Function	**Marketing**	**Technology**	**Competitor Strategy**	**Total (N=20)**
General Management	63%	76%	91%	73%
Marketing	48	43	42	45%
Technical	47	54	45	49%
Total (n=11)	51%	57%	58%	

PART THREE

Treatment

"Learn as though you would never be able to master it. Hold it as though you would be in fear of losing it."

Confucius

"He who can see three days ahead will be rich for three thousand years."

Japanese proverb

CHAPTER NINE

Competitive Learning—The Deciphering of Weak Signals

By now you have walked with me from the banal declaration that "success is one's worst enemy" to the understanding that the culprit is the emergence of blindspots in successful (and unsuccessful) organizations. Since we are blind to our blindspots, no amount of stern warning—"success may lead to complacency!"—will have any *real* effect (although it can still make a good headline in *The Wall Street Journal*). Just like a virus that hides inside the body's own cells, so that the immune system does not recognize the disease exists until the virus bursts out in force, so are blindspots protected from discovery and eradication by the mere fact that no manager knows he or she actually suffers from them! Therefore, it is not success one should fear. The key to understanding is as follows: *A successful executive who keeps on learning will stay successful. The same is true of companies.*

Examples abound, but one example may be familiar to many. The executive's name? William Clinton, CEO, U.S.A.

Everyone knows that Bill Clinton was governor of Arkansas, although some people may not be sure where Arkansas is. How long was he a governor? Most will answer since 1982. The fact is, Clinton was Arkansas' governor two years earlier. He was then defeated by a Republican challenger, Frank White, in 1980. But he was back in office within two years.

By all means, Clinton is a successful executive. His story is like a small company's CEO who, after being fired, comes back, takes over, and then proceeds to acquire General Motors. What was Bill's secret? Did he not let success "go to his head" (whatever that means)?

No. Bill Clinton simply *learned* very well from his early defeat and applied the lesson consistently over time. As reporters relate it, he talks about his defeat in 1980 as if it is still very fresh in his mind.[100]

What he learned, apparently, was that pushing through an aggressive agenda ahead of public opinion might be dangerous. Compare his behavior his first time as governor with his later strategies.

In his first term, Clinton raised car license fees to finance highway repairs, campaigned for a new system of rural health clinics, and considered limits on logging in state forests. He was young, an activist, idealistic, and kept a chart of how legislators voted on his issues. He planned to revolutionize education, conservation, and all other politically correct ideas. Arkansas' voters were basically politically incorrect. They booted him out.

When he came back, Bill Clinton was a changed man. Instead of his brash style, he adopted a cautious, compromise-laden approach. He backed off from proposals that had offended Arkansas' powerful industries and began relying heavily on public polls. As one critic put it, "He does not like to make enemies." Clinton's love of consensus became legendary—a far cry from his first term, when he pushed his agenda almost belligerently.

Clinton learned his lesson well. The emphasis is on "learned." In an interview, he recalls spending the two years between elections studying, analyzing, reading, and discussing the reasons for his defeat. How many executives do you know who devote two months, let alone two years, to studying the causes of the decline of their companies? In his first term, he appointed outsiders to high-level positions in his administration. He found out it alienated his voters, who already regarded him as "an Easterner." In his second term, he made sure Arkansans filled those same positions. His analysis revealed that people regarded him as inaccessible; well, we all know the lesson he learned. The Township meetings could have been predicted by watching his past.

After alienating his voters once, Clinton became averse to alienating anyone. He would express agreement with all groups sparring over an issue, and once he even changed his voting on a bill to provide tax credit for contributions to colleges at literally the last moment (a state trooper fished out the bill from under a legislator's door) because its backers said he was reneging on his promise.

Elizabeth Kolbert's analysis of Bill Clinton's record is one seminal piece about competitive learning. It is also, coincidentally, a *perfect* example I often use in my classes in Competitive Intelligence and Analysis to demonstrate the power of *Personal Intelligence*—information on competitors' executives, suppliers' executives, clients' executives, or governmental executives that is used by a company to understand the strategy and future moves of these players.

If you are skeptical about this point, I can't blame you. Psychology is a very *soft* art, and psychologists have given it a bad name by touting it as a science. Scientifically predicting human behavior is mostly nonsense. Predicting companies' behavior based on executives' personalities is not a science. It is an art based on common sense, historical observations, and visceral knowledge. But then, competitive intelligence in general is an art, too.

Just reflect on Clinton's strategy in the first few months since his election. Issues he espoused enthusiastically during the campaign that proved controversial later on (homosexuals in the military, abortion funding, health reform) were watered down. Compromise on budget, environmental issues (logging, for one), etc., became the dominant strategy. He tried not to antagonize anyone in Congress. Even his election campaign was a replay of his tactics in 1982. While in his first campaign he avoided negative commercials despite his opponent accusing him of responsibility for riots by Cuban refugees in Arkansas, in his second he plunged right into it. By the third, and presidential, campaign, he could teach anyone on Madison Avenue what negative comparisons were. The only ones who *could* have been surprised by Bill Clinton's moves would have been those people who didn't read Kolbert's article.

Competitive Learning

Bill Clinton managed to return to office in two years and then go on to the White House because he learned from his experience and never again let his personal agenda blind him to the wishes of his constituents. Learning seems to be the only defense against the onset of blindspots.

What is learning? *Webster's New World Dictionary* defines learning as the acquisition of knowledge. *Competitive* learning is a company's acquisition of knowledge from its environment—from competitors, from customers, from suppliers, from strategic partners, from consultants—from anyone and anything that can impart knowledge about the company's *competitiveness*.

How does one learn? There are many ways to learn: by instruction, exploration, study, experimentation; or accidentally, serendipitously, subconsciously.

How does a *company* learn? By collecting, analyzing, spreading around, and incorporating into its daily routines the so-called *competitive intelligence*.

There are probably very few concepts or terms that have been more abused, misused, misinterpreted, and misunderstood than this one. If some readers feel a little uncomfortable with the term, I can't blame them. If it automatically conjures up cloak-and-dagger images, it's only natural, especially for senior managers who are 50 or older. Though the term has gained considerable respect since the mid-1980s, it has done so mostly with junior-to middle-level managers, the younger generation. If you haven't kept up with the times, you wouldn't know it had a renaissance. Even in a prestigious journal such as the *Harvard Business Review*, which claims to be at the forefront of executive thinking, competitive intelligence has typically been relegated to outdated issues of unethical espionage. The latest *HBR* survey in 1973 (that's how up-to-date *HBR* is) asked a bunch of busy managers to rank their approval of such esoteric activities as "subscribing to a trade journal" or such common practices as arranging to set up a competitor in "a compromising position with a woman."[101] Moreover, *HBR* immediately paired competitive intelligence issues with "security"-type issues, such as how many guard dogs a company employed.

The situation is a little better with the leading business presses, which seem to have kept more in touch with developments in the corporate world. While in 1988 *Fortune* carried an article titled "Corporate Spies Snoop to Conquer," in 1992, just four short years later and as a sign of the times, the same topic received the less sensational heading of "The New Race for Intelligence." *The New York Times*, an early and sophisticated reporter on the growing use of competitive intelligence in corporate strategy, used the title "Keeping Tabs on Competitors" in 1985, and in 1990 the heading "007 It's Not. But Intelligence Is In." *The Wall Street Journal* still needs to update its files a bit, although it is not as obsolete as the *Harvard Business Review* (oh well, it's a daily after all). In 1988, in reviewing a serious book on corporate intelligence that emphasized issues of competitiveness, the *WSJ* still felt the need to use the title: "*Spying* on the Competition: Costly Benefits." (italics added) In 1989 it relented, and dropped the "spying" nonsense, and replaced it with "Competitor Intelligence: A Grapevine to Rivals' Secrets." (italics added) Well, you have to get the reader's attention somehow. *Forbes*, the most conservative and traditional of the bunch, stuck to spying in a 1990 article about the Japanese and how they dare to send engineers to read our publicly published patents, and executives to take notes when speaking to American counterparts, and plant tourists to take pictures, and experts to translate articles about almost anything. *Spying*, indeed. By this criterion, your child reading the comics is a dangerous KGB agent!

No wonder that competitive intelligence is the most misunderstood term among American managers. Guard dogs? Blackmailing? Secrets? What do these have to do with competitive learning?

Nothing. Simply nothing.

*Competitive intelligence is deciphered signals from the market that tell the CEO (at the corporate level) and the president (at the business unit level) if his or her organization is still **competitive**, or how to make it **more** competitive.*

By this definition, competitive intelligence is any information that has a bearing on the company's *blindspots*.

Competitive Intelligence

Recall the story of Sears and its competitive sclerosis. Now compare that story with the following.[102]

In 1992, J.C. Penney earned $777 million on $18 billion in revenues. That same year, Sears lost $1.3 billion from operations alone (restructuring cost an additional $1.7 billion). Once, Penney and Sears were almost identical in the consumer mind. Today, Sears is a disaster, Penney is fashion. How did that happen?

Like everything else, because of executives who kept their eyes open. Donald Seibert and William Howell, the last two chairmen of Penney realized early on that what worked for them and Sears for generations would not work forever. The advance of the age of information meant that small-town folks were exposed to the same trends as big-city folks. So Howell, back in 1982, started a drive to change Penney's image. Penney began remodeling its stores, ridding itself of appliances and automotive parts. Then Howell tried to sign on the big brands, such as Liz Claiborne and Arrow shirts. They said thanks, but no thanks.

Some other big names said yes—Levis, Van Heusen, Vanity Fair, and Maidenform among them. The problem was that it wasn't enough to change Penney's image. So Howell made the riskiest jump.

Until then, private label brands were always considered a lower-quality, lower-price item for the downmarket. That was an industrywide blindspot. Howell, however, was about to break all the china he could, and make a lot of noise in the process. He created house brands such as Worthington and Stafford (there is nothing like good old English names to impart nobility). Then he hired designers, assigned brand managers, test-marketed new designs, made sure suppliers met specifications or took back the garment—in short, shattered every myth and taboo and accepted assumption about how one manages a private label. Penney's private labels were very different from "slapping a label on someone's else thought process."[103]

It worked. Yet the story does not end there. In 1990 the recession hit Penney hard. Its profit dropped 28 percent. In analyzing the situation, Penney's top managers realized that their pursuit of fashion distanced them from the price-conscious middle-income customer.

As Howell put it, in an interesting choice of words, his team did not "sit and defend itself." Instead, they put pressure on suppliers, buying fabrics directly from textile manufacturers and ensuring that the cut fabric was made into clothing in their most efficient plants. Penney then dropped prices on all items, competing with such chains as the Gap on brand quality and identity, but with such low-price chains as Dayton Hudson on price.

Most revealing of its executives' style, Penney then dropped its advertising agency and moved the account to another one. The reason? The first agency did an excellent job in creating the new image. It was now time to emphasize *value*.

Where is "spying" in this saga? Where are the dogs? How many compromising positions did Howell get his rivals into? None.

> **❝Sears, with its market research, continued to see its customers as polyester freaks.❞**

Where is competitive intelligence in this saga? Everywhere. Recall the definition of competitive intelligence: deciphered market signals and any information that has a bearing on the company's blindspots. Realizing your customers are changing requires very patient collection of bits and pieces of technological, competitor, social, and consumer data, and putting them all together so that the inference regarding a change in consumer preferences jumps out of the puzzle. Some may call it old-fashioned market research, but traditional market research never had any influence on corporate *strategy*. Nor did it take technology, competitor, and consumer information and put it all together. Sears, with its market research, continued to see its customers as polyester freaks. Recall also Schwinn's blindness to its changing market. It probably held as many focus groups as any of the big marketers. What it did not have was competitive intelligence—*strategic information with a view of the entire competitive arena that tells the CEO and president if their organization is still competitive.*

Looking at Sears and its general merchandising strategy, and realizing that it presented an opportunity to break away from the Penney's-is-like-Sears image in the eyes of the consumer, was the result of Howell's insight into a decade's worth of competitive information. Enforcing standards on suppliers, finding the best ones rather than enjoying years of cozy relations with traditional vendors (a classic blindspot) requires a whole lot of competitive intelligence. Analyzing the decrease in competitiveness in 1991 was a courageous exercise in competitive analysis. To realize that your prices are too high, you need to understand all competitive offerings and your position against them. Recall Apple Computer and RJR Nabisco: Pricing policy is frequently a *very* sticky blindspot. Breaking the taboo on private labels required accurate competitive information about how national brands such as Liz Claiborne, the Gap, and Hart Schaffner & Marx competed. Finally, dropping the ad agency required a clear conviction that its people were unable to change with the changing needs. Companies don't just drop their successful agencies (well, except for RJR). Many stick with their agencies well beyond the business requirements or the latter's usefulness. Breaking this taboo required an accumulation of clues or signals that indicated a need to switch. *Somehow* all these competitive signals were deciphered, reached Howell and his lieutenants, and *somehow* they paid attention to them.

In sum, this case reeks of competitive intelligence: information that told Howell and his top team that Penney was no longer competitive in 1982 and again in 1991. Information that told him how to gain competitiveness. Information that pointed out blindspots. None of the information was "secret," none required espionage or wiretapping. The basic data were all there, in the open, for everyone to see. Though they were in the form of market signals and needed patience and insight to decipher them, Sears could have read these signals. Montgomery Ward could have used the information. They didn't.

The example above demonstrates one important characteristic of competitive intelligence. It is never raw **data***. It is the recognition and deciphering of raw, often weak, never equivocal, signals. Intelligence is the outcome of putting together bits and pieces of data, evaluating them for reliability and* **strategic** *relevance, and analyzing their fit with the total strategic puzzle—a picture of the company's competitive arena and its position in it.*

It should be clear that competitive intelligence is not an incidental task for a busy CEO.

So while the data may be out there for everyone to see, first one must be able to *see* them (have an effective collection process), then one must be able to put them together (have an insightful deciphering process).

The confusion over the (true) meaning of competitive intelligence and the popular concept of industrial espionage can be easily resolved if we change terminology: Instead of using the term competitive intelligence, use competitive *deciphering* or *learning*. After all, it is the essence of this concept. Decipher the weak signals from your competitive arena; learn from them; avoid blindspots. The problem is, I *like* the term intelligence: it easily relates to IQ, and indeed *intelligent* corporations are masters of using intelligence correctly. Intelligence is what allows policymakers to navigate nations in a very complex world. Intelligence separates the leader who pursues an eccentric dream from one who astutely reads the market signs early on. In short, intelligence is not an insult to one's intelligence! Competitive intelligence does not connote information only; it can indeed be interpreted as an executive's competitive IQ—a measure of the ability of an executive to compete!

So I will use the terms interchangeably. But understanding that competitive intelligence is essentially deciphering and learning is important in dealing with the thorny issue of ethics.

The (Non)Issue of Ethics

Rarely have I encountered more hypocrisy than in discussions of the legality and ethics of competitive intelligence. Companies that don't mind sending defective or low-quality products to market, executives who will abandon you in a minute when political troubles appear on the horizon, and managers who will fix the blame on everyone around, will all rise to question the ethics of collecting competitive information.

Well, I am not naive, and some methods of collecting competitive data may be questionable. For example, misrepresentation (the most often quoted breach of ethics): "Hi, I am doing research for . . ." or "I am a student at . . ." and other dishonest ways to hide one's affiliation with the interviewee's rival. As if we don't use similar lies in our day-to-day life, boosting our resumes just a little bit, attempting to impress the impressionable with bogus heroic stories, pretending to agree with the boss, etc. Or the atrocious act of pretending to be a headhunter or a customer—almost as bad as ignoring or fighting evidence that the company has been consistently poisoning the environment or its customers for the last decade!

What has all of this to do with competitive deciphering of weak signals from the market? *Nothing.*

What has all of this to do with competitive learning? *Nothing.*

The type of competitive data one needs to fight blindspots does not require misrepresentation, unless one needs the excitement. The data are out there. They need to be collected and put together, which requires patience and insight. Wining and dining a competitor's secretary to find out what its expansion plans are will not change anything about a company's blinders. Even getting your hands on the competitor's secret five-year strategic plan—though definitely a nice thing to have—will not affect *your* competitiveness one iota. Strategic plans are one thing; actual strategies are another. Only those who fail the reaction test fail to understand this distinction. Understanding your competitor's executives' blinders will make a difference. Viscerally understanding your market and where you stand in it relative to competitors will make a difference. For that, one does not need to set up bogus employment interviews with competitors' managers.

Almost all the confusion about ethics comes from a basic mixing up of *tactical* versus strategic intelligence. Tactical details such as new prices, promotion spending, content of an upcoming ad campaign, a possible strike at a competitor's plant, a new product introduction, or a new product's market testing require a quick reaction in the marketplace. Getting information on these items sometimes may be possible *only* through some breaches of the corporate policy on ethics (as if firing a 50-year-old loyal manager whose only sin was following a CEO who was *blind* to changes is consistent with any ethics policy!). Those in need of tactical intelligence are typically product managers, marketing managers, and plant supervisors who do battle day-in, day-out. Top management hardly ever needs to know these details; *yet without exception, this is exactly what they like to know more than anything else!*

I am certainly not degrading tactical intelligence. The daily battles are a fact of life. Executing them perfectly is the hallmark of great companies. No strategy will be successful without the tactics that support and implement it. But by now you should have realized that this is not (strategic) deciphering and learning from early market signals.

One needs both tactical and strategic intelligence. Most companies have some informal or even formal systems or procedures to marshal tactical intelligence to the right places quickly. Many of these systems need improvement, but I know of no company that does not collect, deploy, and use tactical—usually *marketing*—intelligence. Moreover, companies I worked with had an explicit policy against unethical behaviors regarding the collection of (tactical) data. Yet because most executives don't pay too much attention to the difference between marketing intelligence and strategic learning, they feel uncomfortable with the ethics of competitive intelligence.

Competitive intelligence should prevent the inevitable decline. It should go to the root of myths, taboos, and unchallenged assumptions. It should change, in the total scheme of things, the way a company competes.

This type of information does not have to be there *yesterday*. Typically, no overnight action is needed. What is needed is

- *patient* collection,
- *insightful* analysis, and
- a clear-cut organizational process that ensures a direct *influence* on the thinking of the CEO (on the corporate level) and the president (on the business unit level).

This is competitive learning, and this is where most Western companies fall short.

The Competitive/Competitor Distinction

Another reason competitive intelligence arouses such mixed feeling among top executives is that they confuse the term with one of its submeanings: competit*or* intelligence. But competit*ive* intelligence is not competit*or* intelligence, and those who confuse the two will never become truly competitive.

A firm does not become competitive solely by following and imitating competitors. I doubt that many senior executives dispute this notion. A firm that is always reacting will never have the edge (although a firm that is always *late* in reacting will never survive). Understanding your competitors and your position among them in the eyes of customers is the essence of competitive strategy, and competit*ive* intelligence addresses exactly this issue. Therefore, in addition to information on competitors, competitive intelligence sweeps in data about all other competitive forces in one's industry, from suppliers, to buyers, to regulatory bodies, to end users, and to partners.

Allied Intelligence

In recent years the topic of relationships with partners, as opposed to rivals, has gained tremendous importance and exposure. It started with the Japanese model of supplier partnership, gained momentum with the wave of acquisitions in the early 1980s, and peaked with the hot new fad of "strategic alliances." It brought the issue of *allied* intelligence to the fore. Since most companies are less than skillful in the art of competit*or* intelligence, no one should be surprised that they do an even poorer job with their allies. Yet at least in this, activity executives should not be able to hide behind the argument of ethics. Competitive intelligence on allies should be relatively easy to get, and if the allies have skeletons in their closets, *it is unethical to hide them, not to expose them!*

Take supplier relationships, for example. Presumably, the Western model of managing suppliers is based mainly on price. Yet anyone who works in corporate America knows that even that is often just another myth. The lowest bid might have been the guiding principle, but many companies have been locked into long-lasting relationships that defied scrutiny for many years. Marriages of convenience and comfort: two *separate* bedrooms.

In the same way that assumptions about consumers might go stale, so might assumptions about who is the best supplier, who has the best technology, what a vendor can or cannot, will or will not do for you, etc. And I am not even touching upon the issue of corruption.

That supplier relationships have been moved to the center of competitiveness is clear. Lawrence Bossidy, the new CEO brought in to ailing giant Allied-Signal, made it a central piece in turning the conglomerate around.[104] He brought Raymond Stark from Xerox to head material management. The goal: to drastically reduce the base of vendors in order to increase productivity, which Allied-Signal measures as net sales divided by all costs.

Stark summoned 1,500 suppliers to a mass meeting to inform them of new relationships: Allied-Signal expected them to come up with plans to reduce prices by 10-15 percent and decrease lead time by 30 percent, while keeping the high-quality standards Bossidy had mandated earlier on. To help alleviate the new demands, Allied-Signal offered to help suppliers reduce their costs by letting them join in on its purchasing orders and get volume discounts. That is especially important to small companies. On the more fundamental level, Allied-Signal formed cross-functional teams of engineers, designers, and finance and purchasing managers to pick the best suppliers in such areas as castings, electronics, machine parts, and raw material. The chosen few were to get a long-term contract which would allow Allied-Signal's people into the supplier's bedroom to help out with TQM programs, but also get the supplier's people into Allied-Signal's bedroom to see designs early on and connect electronically with purchasing agents. In short, Allied-Signal and the supplier will no longer sleep in separate bedrooms.

This type of relationship is not new. Motorola, Xerox, Ford, AT&T, AMP, and other firms have been using it for a while. They learned it from the Japanese, of course. But think of the essence of these new partnerships. The real difference between the old and new style of managing the suppliers is access to (competitive) information. If you and your suppliers are locked into one bedroom, you will know much more about their performance than you ever knew during your decade-long arm's-length relationship with them.

The disturbing question about this move: If Allied-Signal's suppliers and General Motors' suppliers and Compaq's suppliers (Compaq recently renegotiated its contract for disk drives and terminated a relationship with Conner Peripherals, which its departed CEO helped found)[105] were all capable of reducing their prices and delivery times, why didn't they do it before? Why was the company satisfied with suppliers that delivered higher costs and slower turnaround time?

The answer is, of course, blindspots. Relationships with suppliers are often subject to sclerosis—no one questioning, no one breaking china. If the supplier is large and might even place an executive on the client's board, the blindspot is stuck in cement. Cross-functional teams collecting competitive intelligence, doing competitive deciphering on suppliers? Not here, baby. Our accounting vendor is fine. The vice president of finance, who used to be a partner there, told us so himself.

Supplier relationships are one example of competitiveness issues that typically do not receive the competitive intelligence attention they deserve. Other examples include mergers, acquisitions, joint ventures, and strategic alliances. I lump these diverse forms of business relationships together since they all require the application of "allies' competitive intelligence." And, boy, do companies botch up these relatively easy operations!

The Corporate Binge/Purge Era

Coming down hard on *American* companies for the careless, sloppy way they acquire other companies is no longer fun. Michael Porter has done such a superior job showing how 33 large and prestigious American companies botched up their acquisitions, with divestment ratios ranging from 60 percent in new fields to 74 percent (!) in unrelated acquisitions, that not much is left for others to criticize.[106] Among the companies he named were such legends as Johnson & Johnson, GE, Exxon, CBS, United Technologies, ITT, and Procter & Gamble. While many of the top executives who were responsible for the binge have since left these companies, one wonders how much more prudent is the new leadership.

The reasons why so many acquisitions fail are numerous. Not all of the failures are due to poor competitive intelligence. Acquisitions can fail with the entire industry, or they may not meet financial expectations, or unforeseen changes in the market may render them less than star performers. However, acquisitions can fail also because the acquirer did not read signals from the acquiree too carefully. *This is simply unacceptable.*

The example of GE's acquisition of Tungsram in Hungary is only the tip of an iceberg. Every time one reads about mergers or acquisitions where the "corporate cultures did not mesh," one is in essence reading about another sloppy operation. Collecting and deciphering competitive data about the acquisition's internal culture, morale, attitudes, beliefs, and blindspots and turning them into competitive intelligence is so basic that companies that are not good at it should not be playing the acquisition game at all! The masters of acquisitions, such as Henry Kravis, are also masters of information. When Kohlberg, Kravis, Roberts and Co. worked on a deal, their associates crawled all over the target company until KKR knew everything possible about every dollar invested in it.[107]

The new game in town in the 1990s is no longer acquisitions but strategic alliances. According to a recent study by two McKinsey consultants, about one-third of the 49 alliances they tracked were flops.[108] What is the number one problem? Lack of trust. The way the McKinsey guys explained it: "We Americans are used to acquisition and control."[109] The prosecution rests its case, your Honor—the poor intelligence work underlying so many acquisitions has simply been transferred to alliances. I wonder why only one-third of them failed . . . .

Interestingly enough, one of the corporations that seems to do a good job at alliances is Corning, the glass and ceramic maker. One of the corporations with the most advanced competitive intelligence systems in North America is—Corning, the glass and ceramic maker. Surprise, surprise. How many times did you tell your kid, "Do your homework"? You do your homework and you reduce the chance of a flop. This is competitive intelligence. It has nothing to do with sexy and shadowy "espionage." It rarely, if ever, gets entangled in legal or ethical problems. *It is homework.*

Ears to the Ground

In many respects, competitive intelligence is listening: listening to competitors when they send signals—had Kodak done so, i.e., listened to Polaroid's signals for "detente," it would have saved a lot of money when it entered the instant photography market back in 1976;[110] listening to partners—Ford's engineers videotaped Mazda's engineers walking around and criticizing a prototype Navajo, Ford's Japanese version of the Explorer, so that they could take it to their managers and get some changes on the *Explorer*, which until then had been denied;[111] listening to acquirees—Prudential bought Bache Halsey Stuart Shields, a stockbroker, turned it into Pru-Bache securities, and then tried to turn it into an investment bank and failed miserably (a $243 million loss in 1990). The mistake? Instead of helping its acquiree with its extensive contacts, Prudential declared off-limits to Bache anything that might have jeopardized Prudential's dealings with its big clients, such as pension funds, or Prudential's own investment opportunities—in essence, shutting Bache out of the enormously profitable hostile-bid game.[112]

And finally, it helps when you listen to your customers. Each year Whirlpool mails a Standard Appliance Measurement Satisfaction survey to 180,000 houses, asking consumers to rate their appliances on various attributes.[113] When a competitor's product ranks higher than Whirlpool, its engineers will take the product apart and study it. That type of patient collection of competitive intelligence paid off. Consumers always claimed they wanted easy-to-clean cooking ranges. Previously, it was translated into pushbuttons that were easy to clean but not to operate. The consumer didn't buy. Then the issue became an industry blindspot—"no one will touch the twister knobs anymore"—until Whirlpool engineers came up with electronic touch pads that were easy to clean *and* easy to operate. It has become one of Whirlpool's hottest products. Whirlpool listened to its customers.

Kmart, on the other hand, though a dominant force in retailing in the Northeast for years, has seen many of its customers flock to Wal-Mart. The reason? "We haven't listened to our customers enough," says Joseph Antonini, Kmart CEO.[114] What did the consumer want? Quick checkout, wider aisles. As one ex-Kmart customer put it, "We used to shop at Kmart, and we'd wait for hours in line. Sometimes we'd get so disgusted we'd leave the stuff and go."[115] Have you been to your local discount retailer recently? Perhaps you should photocopy this page and mail it to the retailer's CEO. As one who used to stand in lines at Caldor stores in New Jersey (and leave stuff and go, disgusted), I can vouch to the fact that Wal-Mart still seems to be years ahead in listening to consumer signals.

In Summary

Fighting blindspots is best done through strengthening the company's *immune system*—its ability to learn.

Competitive learning takes place anytime executives apply knowledge acquired from the competitive arena, rather than follow long-held traditions and assumptions.

Competitive learning requires systematic identification and deciphering of ambiguous signals from the competitive arena.

Competitive intelligence is any deciphered signals from the competitive arena that tell the CEO (at the corporate level) and the president (at the business unit level) whether or not the company is competitive.

Competi*tive* intelligence, by definition, addresses internal myths and taboos as well as external unchallenged assumptions—all business blindspots related to your competitiveness.

Competitive intelligence depends on a continuous flow of competitive data—the bits and pieces of daily interaction with the outside world—into a place where a decoder puts together the puzzle, and breaks the market code.

Without such an effective process of competitive intelligence/competitive learning, a company is setting itself up for eventual and inevitable sclerosis and decline.

You can always ignore this advice and resort to CPR: restructuring, reengineering, or anything else that starts with "re-," costs millions, and attempts to revive a corpse. Or you can beef up the immune system.

Make your choice.

CHAPTER TEN

Organizing Intelligence Activities—The American, Japanese, Korean, Israeli, and Yes, Russian (!) Experience

Articles on American corporations' intelligence activities started to appear in the popular business press around 1985, with *The New York Times* reporting that "intelligence efforts grow."[116] The rate of reporting on the new activity accelerated significantly in the next few years, and then, just like a consumer product life cycle, fell off.

This flurry of reportage and the leveling off of interest paralleled to a large extent the ups and down of corporate interest in the topic. In 1985, a dean of one business school remarked that business intelligence was one of the hottest topics on the seminar market. By 1990, one veteran president of a research company complained that "every corner you turn around, there's a new service."[117] And indeed, the number of seminars, consultants, data collection services, and similar supporting casts grew exponentially from 1985 to 1990.

What did not grow was the number of American firms that possessed a *true* intelligence capability. Recall what competitive intelligence is all about: *Deciphering of early and ambiguous market signals that tell the CEO at the corporate level, and the president at the business unit level, if their organi-*

*zation is still competitive. Competitive intelligence is any market information that has a bearing on the company's **blindspots**.* Given this definition, the overwhelming majority of American companies in the 1990s still don't really understand the meaning of competitive intelligence, nor do they know how to learn competitively.

You will not realize it by reading the articles in the popular press. There, experts and consultants and academics and corporate competitive analysts extol the virtues of their system and the benefits it bestows on the corporation. But talk to the practitioners when they meet among themselves, and their need to do public relations for their role is less obvious. The overwhelming feeling is of frustration. The most common attitude is that in the next cost-cutting drive they may lose their job. And indeed, several have.

Corporate America has played with the idea of organizing its competitive intelligence activities in a variety of ways, and many of them came out short of initial expectations. The higher the expectations, the greater was the disappointment at the eventual outcome. In many companies, once the idea champion left the company or his or her position, the competitive intelligence function, if it was an independent function, slowly dissolved—or worse, deteriorated into one more line item in the overhead budget. If you are small enough, and your company is large enough, you can survive for years without anyone questioning your value, merely on the strength of inertia.

How come the swell of initial interest laid such a small egg? It wasn't for lack of effort on the part of the analysts. It wasn't for lack of data or seminars on *where* to find competitive data. It wasn't even for lack of success of these fledgling efforts, as the following section demonstrates. Some intelligence programs yielded substantial benefits.

Ever since the first article appeared in 1985, they've all seemed to carry the same "war stories" about the same companies: Marriott, Coors, Motorola, Corning, Kodak, and several others. Either reporters recycled old names, or no one else would talk to them about successes, or *there weren't too many good, clear-cut intelligence victories to tell about.* It is also not surprising that the anecdotes relayed by the press were about Marriott, Motorola, Xerox, and Corning. These companies are perhaps the closest to the "real thing."

Success Stories as Reported in the Press

Marriott

For six months during 1986, a team of Marriott's marketing, finance, human resources, and operations people visited nearly 400 hotels in the economy hotel category. At each hotel, they played the same routine: One team member would call for a spare shoelace, one would note the toiletries in the bathroom, and one would produce as much noise as could be expected from a couple having sex while colleagues registered the level of soundproofing in the adjoining room. Later they would identify themselves as Marriott employees (of course—remember corporate ethics policy!) and ask the local manager for operations, price, and other details.

To augment the efforts of the intelligence team, Marriott then hired a headhunter to set up interviews with 15 regional managers from each of five economy hotel chains around the United States. Marriott informed these managers that no openings were currently available, but there might be some in the future. It then learned about pay levels, career paths, morale, training, values, and beliefs (blindspots?). It eventually hired five of the interviewees.

Why all these efforts? Marriott wanted to enter the economy hotel business. After the six-month intelligence study, Marriott spent $500 million on a new hotel chain, Fairfield Inn, which it launched in 1987. The chain had an occupancy rate 10 percent higher than the average in the industry.[118]

McDonnell-Douglas

In 1987, McDonnell-Douglas was looking into the possibility of launching a new generation of aircraft powered by a rear prop-fan. Early on, Boeing had stated that it was considering a similar move. There was little room for both in this market, so McDonnell-Douglas needed to know how serious Boeing was. It assembled an intelligence team that, for the next few months, studied Boeing's capabilities and intentions in this area through annual reports, factory capacity data, R&D spending, etc. Their conclusion was that Boeing could not produce the aircraft at a competitive price or within a competitive deadline.

McDonnell-Douglas then proceeded with the prop-fan jet named MD 91. Boeing announced it was delaying its development plans.[119]

Coors

Coors, the beer maker, desired a position in the wine cooler segment of the market. In 1985 it came out with a product that failed. So it assembled an intelligence team (after the fact) to study the cost structure of competitor Gallo. The team bought Gallo's wine coolers, determined their ingredients, priced those ingredients, and concluded that Gallo was the low-cost producer, and that against Gallo's vertical integration—it grows its own grapes and produces its own labels—Coors could not compete. In 1986, Coors decided to abandon the market for good.[120]

Motorola

During a meeting in 1985 between Motorola's top management and its European managers, top executives queried the European people about the Japanese in Europe. The Motorola-Europe guys were not impressed. They reported that the Japanese were not really that aggressive in Europe.

That did not fit with the character of Motorola's Japanese rivals. Motorola then sent a Japanese-speaking intelligence analyst to Japan to dig out information on the Japanese competitors' capital budgets. After researching for a while, the manager turned out the numbers. They showed that the Japanese planned to double their total capital investment in 1987, but not in their TV and VCR factories, as everyone expected. Instead, they were going after the *semiconductor* market in Europe. Based on that information, Motorola changed its strategy: It aligned several European partners and worked closely with customers. Despite the Japanese attack, Motorola either retained or increased its market share (depending on which article one reads).[121]

Corning

Back in 1990, a buyer from Corning noticed crates of a glass-making material on a dock. The crates were addressed to a competitor's plant. The buyer passed this information to an engineer, who used it to determine the kind of glass the competitor was planning to produce. As a result, Corning incorporated this information into its marketing plan.[122]

Coors Again

I told you there are a few favorite stories that seem to get cited every time the subject comes up. Coors monitored the court proceedings of a trial involving one of its rivals. Using the information, which was often quite revealing—courts don't care too much about "corporate secrets"—Coors' analysts were able to develop an econometric model that predicted how many barrels of beer the competitor produced and shipped each quarter. The prediction was accurate to about 1 percent. Coors should have sold its model to the competition.

McDonnell-Douglas Again

In case you weren't impressed enough with the intelligence ability of M-D, here is another story from Robert Margulies, who was an intelligence manager with the company. According to Margulies, McDonnell kept tabs on competitors' executives so that when and if one of them died, McDonnell-Douglas could predict the changes that might occur.[123]

AT&T

In mid-1985, AT&T launched an on-line service for its employees called AAA—Access to AT&T Analysts. The service was an information broker-age service—an internal "yellow pages" listing employees at AT&T by their areas of expertise. Workers were invited to list their qualifications and experience and register with the data base. They could then use it by logging in key words that retrieved the appropriate list of experts along with their titles and phone numbers. Thus, if a strategist was looking for information on Northern Telecom's PBX technology, he could get a list of AT&T people who had experience with the technology and the competitor. That saved the company a lot of time and money, since it was no longer necessary to reinvent the wheel every time its engineers started working on new projects. The system worked both ways: On the same electronic network employees broadcast competitive information to the network's subscribers.[124] Upon launching the system, the intelligence unit in charge of the network put on "road shows" and demonstrations near the cafeteria at lunchtime in order to entice employees to join the network. The network was still operative in 1993, with several hundred subscribers.

Xerox

In the late '70s, an article in *Fortune* reports, Canon came out with a copier that retailed for less than Xerox's manufacturing cost on a comparable ma-chine. Xerox's market share in copiers declined from 49 percent to 22 per-cent in a few years. Xerox then assigned a team of engineers to take Canon's product apart. The benchmarking produced results. Xerox's slide stopped.[125]

An earlier article in *The New York Times* seemed to suggest that Xerox made the practice a routine at its technology complex near Rochester. It discovered a change in the composition of the materials in Canon's copiers, with an increase in the use of plastics that made the copier cheaper to produce and more durable. Xerox copied the trend.[126] The *Fortune* article also reported that Xerox trained 200 managers to collect competitive data on pricing, technology, and new entrants to its markets.

Success on a Smaller Scale

And of course, there are always the heartwarming stories of the small guys whose eye for intelligence saved the day for their companies.[127] Nathan Katz, CEO of Dana Imports, a six-year-old importer of lamps and office furniture, learned in 1989 from one of his retailers that a competitor had raised prices on a line of lamps in the South. He immediately faxed the information to his salespeople, who were able to pick up some extra sales.

Maria Iriti of Serpintina Glass, a small glass maker in Massachusetts, submitted a bid to repair a window at a local church without checking out the competition. She won the bid with a price tag of $18,000, while the second lowest bid was $76,000. Since then she has started keeping competitor files and has asked her *friends* to write and ask competitors for price lists and brochures (you know those horrible small companies: no corporate ethics policy!).

So where has corporate America gone wrong in organizing its intelligence activities? Why has initial enthusiasm turned into discontent? Is it that these sophisticated companies do not understand the importance of information?

To judge by investment alone, the answer is a resounding "No." Some companies have devoted substantial resources to gaining better access to competitive information—and I am not talking about the expenditure on the competitive analysis function with its three to four analysts, one-half of a secretary, and $500,000 annual budget. I am talking *substantial* investments. Judge for yourself.

Taking on Japan

Eastman Kodak

In 1987, Eastman Kodak opened a $70 million research center in Yokohama, Japan. Texas Instruments, IBM, Du Pont, W.R. Grace, Dow-Corning, Pfizer, Digital Equipment, Upjohn, and Dow Chemical are operating similar basic or applied research centers in Japan. The purpose? To do research, of course—but also to *"hear of new technologies long before they surface in the United States."*[128] Dow Chemical has a nine-person team whose sole job is to collect ideas and develop relationships with Japanese universities—deciphering market signals *early on.*

Kodak's line of reasoning is illuminating. Its research director in Japan in the early 1980s mapped out the locations of leading electronics research labs. He found they were concentrated in a cluster of Tokyo's suburbs. *To be able to tap into Japan's face-to-face information network*, the director recommended this location to Kodak.

Kodak then built its research center and began a whole series of investments in information networks: It financed researchers at universities, provided scholarships to students, and hired star scientists away from Hitachi and Toshiba. In short, as its current research director put it, Kodak's people were becoming "full members of the Japanese community, with access to the *kind of information our competitors have.*" (emphasis added) Kodak's staffers at the Japanese center pick up competitive bits and pieces when they are out drinking, socializing, or playing tennis with customers, competitors, university friends, etc. "Compared with the relative isolation of Rochester . . . [i]n this environment, information flows like electric current."

Sound familiar? This was my first test of competitiveness: Does your company have a visceral knowledge of the market? Japanese companies such as Honda and Toyota and Sony and Hitachi and Fujitsu passed the test with flying colors, because they did what Kodak has been doing—only 20 years earlier.

Applied Materials[129]

Long before it was fashionable to set up operations in Japan, Applied Materials, a small company that in 1980 showed $69 million in sales, established an office in Japan and staffed it with seven people. The expense was not trivial for a company that size, and its CEO, Jim Morgan, admits he spent a few sleepless night wondering how he was going to pay for the Tokyo venture. But, as he says, "I've always had a long-term philosophy, and my board has supported that." One can easily see that this philosophy is about competitive learning.

Morgan's company produces the ultrasophisticated machines that make semiconductors. By 1980 he realized the gravity center was shifting toward Japan. He wasn't the only one who understood the need to penetrate the notoriously difficult Japanese market. His competitors, however, "continued to do things the lazy way, using Japanese partners," only to find the partners dumped them the minute a local company came out with a similar product. Morgan decided to enter the Japanese market as Applied Materials Japan. To do that, he first studied the way Japanese do business. He learned about supplier partnerships long before it became another slogan in the States. Eventually he built his plants in Japan to let NEC and Fujitsu's engineers join in new product development. In 1990, one-third of Applied Materials' sales were to Japanese semiconductor manufacturers.[130] In 1991 the company broke ground for a new technology center near Tokyo's international airport.[131] Jim Morgan and his Applied Materials exhibited exactly the type of competitive learning I referred to earlier on.

So at least some American firms, such as Kodak and Applied Materials, invest heavily in competitive intelligence. They reveal a surprisingly deep level of appreciation for the role of visceral technological knowledge and technological competitive learning in their survival. So why has this investment yielded so few apparent results for most of the companies mentioned above? Because enormous investment and effort in gathering *technical* intelligence have no parallel in how companies regard *strategic* intelligence. Some progressive American firms may at last mount a serious effort to develop R&D intelligence capability, with the appropriate organizational and financial commitments; but at home, inside their headquarters, in their executive suites, they still exhibit all the symptoms of Western companies that look upon strategic intelligence like most men look at table manners: *It's a nice thing to have, but it's not necessary for life.* Kodak, IBM, Upjohn, and the other American firms' top executives have a long way to go before *they* are plugged into strategic intelligence the way their own research directors are to the Japanese information network.

The Koreans, the Iraqis, and Intelligence as a Culture

The Koreans do not share the Americans' casual attitude toward strategic intelligence. We know this fact only because of an obscure doctoral dissertation about the intelligence activities of Samsung, the Korean Trading giant, written by S. Ghoshal at Massachusetts Institute of Technology back in the mid-'80s.[132] While the thesis itself with its curious statistical tests is not very interesting, there are pearls of information hidden among the jargon, especially in terms of revealing the importance Samsung's executives place on intelligence. Most of the managers interviewed for the dissertation expressed the opinion that information was Samsung's number-one asset, and they meant it. They also regarded its future success as dependent on the company's ability to collect and react to competitive intelligence.

Trading companies, of which Samsung is a respectable member, depend on market intelligence for their transactions. Though their intelligence needs may look tactical on the outside, they are not. Their *targets* are constantly moving. What may be a disastrously shortsighted strategy for a manufacturer is the essence of their strategy—a deliberately opportunistic game plan, moving fast from one opportunity to another. However, long-term trends create opportunities. Therefore, trading companies must be masters of strategic intelligence as well as able to move fast in reaction to more tactical "windows of opportunities."

At Samsung, they *devour* information. As one executive put it, they need to know when a government in the Middle East starts *thinking* about importing, because when the official bid is out, it is too late to win it. Another executive explains the importance of predicting fiscal and monetary policies of various governments, because the cost of financing is a large component in a trading firm's total cost. "Six months ago, the three-year interest swap was 11 percent. We should have made our deal but we did not. Now the rate is 12.5 percent. To me, that is an intelligence failure."[132]

A company that feeds on intelligence like Samsung must devote a significant chunk of its resources and attention to intelligence activities. A planning department with 100 full-time employees includes two—not one—intelligence functions, and is headed by an executive vice president. The two intelligence units are Overseas Planning (OP) and Research and Information. The two are distinguished mainly by the types of sources they use. Research and Information focuses on published information. It scans government studies, private reports, trade and special publications. This type of information is never too current. It suits the department's focus on monitoring macro issues (economic, political, product and market, supplier and buyer long-term trends). Overseas Planning collects intelligence mostly from field sources. The department is composed of four groups, organized geographically. There is a group monitoring ASEAN, one for the Middle East, and one for North and South America. The fourth group coordinates the three regional functions.

Each regional group is responsible for the collection and analysis of reports from its area. The coordinating group synthesizes the three regions' reports and delivers a comprehensive document to senior managers at headquarters, product divisions, and overseas offices. The four groups are staffed by five managers and 12 support personnel.

The managers of the OP department are all experienced line managers. The department's head rotated through all four groups before his current assignment.

Despite this awesome staffing, Samsung's competitiveness does not rely on these headquarters analysts. It relies on a culture. *One painful lesson learned by American firms was that no headquarters unit can be truly effective without a total organization commitment to competitive intelligence.* Money spent on headquarters intelligence analysts has never been shown to directly correlate with performance, although "performance" for an intelligence unit has never exactly been defined or measured. Given American executives' basic misunderstanding of the role of intelligence, this is not surprising.

Every overseas office of Samsung is obliged to send in intelligence reports, the bits and pieces of which are compiled into a puzzle. Depending on the size of the office, the reports may be daily or less frequent, but never less than three times per week. Faxing the report is often the last activity the branch manager performs at the end of the day. If he does not, that may be the last activity he performs (or does not) as a Samsung employee.

The obsession with intelligence collection goes beyond what we Westerners can comprehend. At the height of the Iranian revolution, when the CIA and the Savak were on the run, Samsung's office kept sending in reports. Since the office could not use its own telex machine, it used its banker's. When Beirut was under siege by the Moslems, the Christians, and the Syrians, the Samsung office kept on going. If this starts to sound like a commercial for a Duracell battery, it is, because the flow never stops. On average, 40 reports were received *each day* in 1984-85, when Ghoshal was conducting his interviews.

To get the information, branch managers exert pressure on their officers to include at least one item of intelligence per day in *their* reports. This hierarchy of pressure creates a very forceful routine of data gathering.

The headquarters office of Overseas Planning communicates this flow of daily intelligence from the branches in the form of a mid-day summary report in Korean, and each manager who receives it is expected to read the report and share it with his department that same day.

A separate analysis interpreting (deciphering) the daily data flow is sent in a sealed and numbered envelope to senior managers only, who are expected to destroy the report after reading it. Though this type of behavior may sound a trifle spooky to Westerners, and most American managers will consider it too close to "Mission Impossible" for comfort, if you ignore the drama, the analysis is superb. Take, for example, the following inference reported by Ghoshal:

> If Iraq is ordering such large quantities of army uniform materials suddenly, fresh army recruitment must be anticipated. This may mean that an escalation of the war is imminent. That, in turn, implies that Iraq may face a further strain on its resources, particularly with regard to availability of foreign exchange for payment of non-defense materials. They may therefore be likely to defer payment on such materials.[132]

The analysis then points out the extent of Samsung's involvement with Iraq in nondefense areas and the resulting financial implications.

Any way you look at it, this is a brilliant piece of intelligence work, putting together unrelated pieces (uniforms, escalation of war, payments) with implications for Samsung's financial position. When was the last time you read something like that in your company? Just yesterday, you say? Then you are *very* lucky! Most of your peers across the executive suites in corporate America have neither people nor an organizational process that can deliver such an intelligence analysis. Most of them would not read it even if they were lucky enough to have an intelligence function somewhere in the organization that could put together such a marvel (Room 238A, down from the Office Supply room; be careful with the renovations going on out there!). They would probably hope it would find its way to the credit department, where its tactical value would (one hopes!) be explored. And thus the intelligence flow circles the corporation, away from the busy life of the top brass, like an undercurrent of low-voltage electricity, waiting to be amplified to strategic intelligence, and instead being dumped into the black hole of the internal paper shuffle (no, not 238F, 238A! Oh, for God's sake, it was there last month!).

The Japanese

So much has been written about the Japanese's inspiring power of competitive intelligence that I doubt I can or *should* add much to it here.[133] Evidence of its raw power, such as the fact that Mitsubishi Trading Company has hundreds of intelligence staffers occupying two whole floors in an office building in Manhattan, substantiates this perception. Interestingly enough, most descriptions of corporate Japan's intelligence activities come from a few *American* consultants whose names seem to be recycled again and again in newspaper articles. The Japanese themselves are quite open on the topic of government activities in the area of commercial intelligence. (The Japanese government provides competitive intelligence to Japanese firms through such agencies as MITI, JETRO, and other government bodies.) But they are surprisingly silent on how specific corporations organize their activities. When they do address the issue of organized corporate intelligence, they claim to be behind the West in this area! So who is right? Both sides. The way Japanese handle competitive intelligence is rather different from the way we do it in the West. But that may be changing fast.

One of the most familiar and *least* understood Japanese institutions is the trading company and the role it plays in providing other companies with the awesome power of competitive intelligence. We don't have anything like it in the West; therefore, we cannot truly comprehend its meaning. But think of it this way: Let us imagine that several industrial giants, such as GM, IBM, GE, Exxon, and Du Pont, to pick a few arbitrarily, decided one day to combine their entire overseas trade in the hands of *one company,* in essence making this company their marketing department. How powerful would that marketing organization grow to be? This, roughly, is the concept of a trading company. And as a premier marketing apparatus for Japanese manufacturers, the trading companies specialize in one thing, and one thing only: competitive intelligence. The large Japanese trading companies, the *Sogo Shosha* (did you notice how I became an instant expert on Japan when I was able to plug in some original Japanese terminology?), are not much different from Samsung but for their huge scale of operations—each with annual sales between $30 billion and $120 billion. Together, the nine trading companies account for more than 30 percent of Japan's GNP, 50 percent of its export, and 70 percent of its import.

The typical trading company employs networks similar to Samsung's. The culture is similar. The people's devotion is similar. The statistics are staggering: According to one U.S. expert, executives at Mitsui, a large trading company, exchange 80,000 messages each day on a satellite network connecting Mitsui's 200 overseas offices. That may be because Japanese executives just like to talk, or have to repeat everything twice; but according to the experts, the vast majority of these messages are related to competitive intelligence.[134] The networks are so effective that the Japanese government used Mitsui's during World War II.[135]

The Japanese do instill a competitive intelligence culture, just like the Koreans. The nine largest Sogo Shosha, among them Mitsubishi, Mitsui, Sumitomo, and Nissho-Iwai, have around 60,000 employees in 2,200 foreign and domestic offices, and each one of these workers and managers stationed abroad is required to submit a written report on a regular basis. Urgent information is faxed or called in to a special relay person in Japan. According to Ryuchi Hattori, an assistant director of the American division in the overseas research department at JETRO's Tokyo headquarters, "It is altogether possible . . . that based on a piece of information gathered overseas, a Japanese CEO might receive a call in the middle of the night, at home."[136]

Well, maybe or maybe not. But there is little doubt that every Japanese employee, whether in a trading company or an industrial corporation, is expected to carry out the collection of competitive data as part of his or her job. The corporations, in turn, collect these data in central research departments. These have between 10 and 20 people, and sometimes more. As one American executive reported, at the Tokyo headquarters of Marubeni Corporation, a trading company serving the business group (keiretsu) Fuyo (which includes such household names as Fuji Bank, Canon, and Nissan), he noticed "row upon row of clerical workers [who] were diligently filing away slips of paper, photographs, charts, and reports sent from far-flung employees on competing businesses and businessmen."[137] Well, as the average American manager would comment, these might actually have been photos of their grandchildren, who knows?

Some of the larger corporations, such as Nomura, Mitsubishi, and Daiwa, have their own "think tanks"—research institutions employing hundreds of people. But then, as another expert notes, the significant fact is that "there's no such thing as a Japanese entity that does not have intelligence gathering built in . . . . Pulling in information is part and parcel of what the Japanese are paid to do."[138]

The infrastructure is so impressive because it delivers exactly the type of input a company needs for *competitive deciphering of early signals*. The mundane nature of the sources used and the bits and pieces sent in are as far from industrial espionage as possible. It is not that Japanese companies are models of purity. The cases of Hitachi in the United States and Mitsubishi in Japan, in which the companies allegedly paid large sums to industrial spies, are "showcases" to any American executive who is nervous about the Japanese's incredibly effective knowledge of the market. Yet the industrial espionage cases have very little to do with the awesome power of the Japanese to understand markets and competitors. It is the work of the rows upon rows of clerks filing away reports and charts (I hope they have learned to use computers since that article came out . . .) that constitutes the infrastructure that yields the power. The reports and photographs and charts come from the most open, public, boring, unmysterious sources. Japanese managers are rewarded for hard work by getting to go on a tour of plants in America. Large American firms are inundated with calls for tours. The Japanese take pictures. One Japanese employee of Nissan took pictures of his neighbors in a small California town as part of his research into the lifestyle and tastes of the American driver.[139] The American family sued (of course), but Nissan cars are now better suited for the "human race," and Altima is a hit.

The Japanese read and translate everything: patent information, technical journals, newspapers. They are the masters of cultivating legitimate, open, human contacts. In an amazing paper by one of Japan's foremost experts on competitive intelligence, Juro Nakagawa—then a vice president for the New Ventures Development division at Nichimen Corporation, one of the large trading companies, and today a business professor at Aichi Gakuin University—he lists 19 cases of successful transactions carried out by Nichimen, ranging from exporting synthetic fabrics from Japan to Italy to importing American billiard tables to Japan. In seven cases, the initial information came from such mundane sources as a local daily newspaper, an economic bulletin put out by an embassy, or a trade newsletter.[140] The rest came from people. In another paper, Prof. Nakagawa reveals:

> I had worked for a Japanese trading company for 33 years, with 20 years overseas assignment traveling on business in over 60 countries . . . . I have cultivated and established contacts within government circles, international agencies, trade circles, and research institutes. I have attended innumerable conferences, exhibitions, and social gatherings. I have gathered the important and sometimes vital information from trade magazines, newspapers, and business associates all in order to establish, create, and develop new business. In my case, an overwhelming amount of information has been obtained from person-to-person contact, which we call HUMINT—human intelligence.[141]

An American expert comments, "The Japanese hire five people to ask the same questions."[142] They endowed six chairs at Stanford's engineering and business departments alone at an average cost of $1.2 million. They have 34 affiliation programs at Stanford through which they establish informal links to individual faculty members and place some of their people in joint projects.[143] When Motorola decided to give some serious thought to its intelligence-gathering activities, back in the mid-'80s, it approached experts at various American universities just to find out that "in three out of five instances" they had already been contacted by the Japanese.[144]

The Japanese go to trade shows. Well, the Americans go there too, don't they? Yes, if they are in the United States. The Japanese sent 300 people to an office furniture convention in Chicago. The crowd was actually well organized into teams of marketing, engineering, and research people. The teams picked up literature and took pictures and asked a lot of questions.[145]

The strength of the Japanese is in this massive human "infrastructure" that sends in bits and pieces of competitive data in a continuous flow, like a giant net that makes sure very little can be or will be missed. As one expert remarks, "The Japanese are information barracudas."[146] The philosophy behind it is: Who knows what might be important?

This is the infrastructure that almost guarantees competitive learning. We don't have it in the West and probably never will.

If we had Keiretsu, the big business groups that combine hundreds of industrial and service companies, and trading companies serving the member organizations, we could compete with the Japanese raw power of competitive intelligence. As it is, each American firm is left to its own competitive learning, without any help from the vast collection networks of trading firms or the deciphering power of government agencies.

That is not a reason to despair. One can approximate the benefits of a massive human net with a *process* and a *structure* that give the company a chance to read early market signals and fight the onset of blindspots. Interestingly enough, with the growth of the Japanese companies, they themselves are looking into importing the structure and process from the West.[147] If they do not lose their obsession with intelligence collection, they may become even more formidable competitors than they are today.

The Israelis

Small and simpatico, Israeli companies have for years been lagging behind developments in world markets for several reasons: the relative political and geographical isolation, the local mentality of self-confidence and reluctance to learn from "outsiders," the energy dedicated to the Arab-Israeli conflict, the protectionist government policies, etc. No more. In recent years, with the influx of very well-educated, highly professional Russian-Jewish scientists and engineers, the Israeli economy has taken off at a rate similar to the little dragons out East. In particular fields such as biotech, high tech, defense systems, and avionics, Israeli firms have acquired a reputation for innovation, agility, problem solving, and resourcefulness. And now Israeli firms are adopting competitive intelligence practices faster than one can say "chutzpa."

What distinguishes Israeli firms from a typical American firm are two factors: size and mentality. On the size side, most Israeli firms are tiny compared to corporate America. The Israel Aircraft Industry, the largest employer in Israel, employs around 15,000 people. Most high-tech companies do not exceed $100 million in sales. Yet they survive side by side with GE and Intel and Texas Instruments and Merck, and moreover, some of these giants have started to build research centers in Israel to tap the local ingenuity. However, when it comes to resources, a typical Israeli firm cannot devote even 10 percent of what American firms can to the collection and analysis of competitive data.

Nevertheless, on the mentality side, Israelis absorb intelligence with their mother's milk. The mandatory military service for both men and women, the rich heritage of wars and heroes, the revered Mossad—the equivalent of the CIA—and the sheer understanding that the fate of the country's 4 million citizens depends on its intelligence capability creates a very fertile ground for the spread of competitive intelligence techniques in the business community.

The result has been an explosion of seminars and courses on the subject similar to the trend in the United States in the late '80s. What has been different is the way Israeli firms adopted the intelligence model.

Most Israeli CEOs have been officers in the Israeli military. Many ex-generals turn to managerial careers upon retirement (at the relatively young age of 45–50). These people bring to their companies a deep appreciation for the value of competitive data—so deep that indeed they want to know every bit of competitive data *first*, and employees who gain access to such data would benefit from rushing to tell the boss.

If my complaint about the American executive was that he basically preferred not to have anything to do with intelligence activities, and typically hardly knew where in the organization his intelligence analysts were located, the problem with the Israeli executive is that he cannot be pried away from every tidbit of intelligence!

Both approaches to intelligence are wrong. To understand that, let me take you back to the three requirements of competitive intelligence: *patient* collection, *insightful* analysis, and above all, a clear-cut organizational process that ensures a direct *influence* on the thinking of the CEO (on the corporate level) and the president (on the business-unit level)—i.e., competitive learning.

With the CEO as the intelligence analyst, the last requirement seems to be fulfilled. The problem is that CEOs have no patience, and only a limited insight. The reason for the first problem is clear. The reason for the second has to do with the way top executives handle competitive data. Whether in Israel or in the United States, competitive tidbits are processed *on the spot*. They travel among the top people during meetings or, more rarely, by phone messages, and what goes in at that moment is what counts! Insights, the deciphering of early signals, require very long, very detailed memory: the type that a data base may support. Insights require many little pieces coming together *over time*. The tidbit that someone whispered in the CEO's ear, and that he later shared with his top lieutenants, does not count as strategic analysis. This is not patient deciphering; this is "hot flashes."

The Israeli firms are internationally renowned for quick response time. Sometimes too quick. When the CEO is the analyst, there is really very little patient analysis and only transitory insights, good for that moment when the information was registered. This is an excellent basis for an opportunistic strategy, but not for any other long-term vision. What is worse is that it does not guarantee a continuous fight against blindspots. For example, the Israeli Aircraft Industry registered a huge success with its development of the first sea-to-sea, sea-hugging type missile, Gabriel. Gabriel I and Gabriel II soon dominated the category. Then consumer tastes changed. Many navies came to prefer longer-range missiles that reduced the risk to their own vessels. The Israeli company ignored the intelligence, probably because its executives were already committed to Gabriel III—a *short*-range, very sophisticated version of the missile. The project proceeded, the technology was superb, and the missile was a marketing flop.[148] Still, if I had to choose between the CEO as the company's chief intelligence decoder and the CEO without *any* strategic intelligence support, I would choose the first any time, any place, any day!

The Russians

I could not end this chapter without at least a word about the Russians. *The Economist*, a respected business publication, reported back in 1990 that the KGB had set up a business-information service.[149]

In a television interview, one Major Andrei Oligov announced that the KGB, with the blessing of its head, General Vladimir Kryuchkov, would sell information services to Soviet firms, cooperatives, and joint ventures dealing with foreign firms. The KGB would provide credit checks, market information, and other information of "economic character." Given the flocking of Western entrepreneurs to do business with the former Soviet bloc, such a service may be very valuable. Especially the credit check.

The KGB can provide the service with distinction. For years, it had the number-one industrial espionage operation in the world, with its own directorate devoted to the duty. Its agents infiltrated and stole every possible technology from the beleaguered West. *If there is one lesson to learn from this story, it is that anyone who still confuses competitive learning with industrial espionage just hasn't learned anything from the phenomenal economic "success" of the Soviet Union, Inc.* Stealing the golden egg is not equivalent to raising the goose. For those who aren't smart enough to grasp the difference by now, here is an important piece of information: Call Moscow, 921 0762 and ask for Andrei. Or write: The KGB, 2 Dzerzhinsky St., Moscow, What's left of the U.S.S.R. No ZIP code is necessary.

The Americans

At last, we are back home. American firms have been very active in the field of competitive intelligence, to judge by the articles cited earlier in this chapter. To judge by reality, they are a little less organized than it may seem. There are two basic models by which corporate America has organized its intelligence activities, and these will be presented in the next chapter. Suffice it to say that at this point few American companies are using intelligence the right way. With time, and growing competitive pressures, I believe this situation will change dramatically.

CHAPTER ELEVEN

Strategy, Decisions, and Intelligence

This chapter presents the intelligence systems of a few well-known American firms, and then infers design principles guiding Western firms in organizing for intelligence. The choice of systems to present was based on two criteria:

1. Availability of *public* information about the intelligence organization in these firms

2. Some worthwhile features of the system

The reader should keep in mind that as far as I am concerned, none of these systems provide adequate answers to the most basic role of competitive intelligence: deciphering early signals from the market to fight the onset of business blindspots. The reader will also note that certain famous firms are conspicuously absent from the short list. For example, some experts consider IBM to be very skillful in using business intelligence. Indeed, the marketing representatives (i.e., salespeople) of IBM have traditionally been very well equipped with data about competing products, product announcements, technical literature about competitors, etc. Only this is not competitive intelligence; at best, it is tactical marketing intelligence. IBM's fortune was never related to how much its salespeople knew about NCR's machines. No company's fortune depends on how much tactical intelligence its employees possess, though doubtless a company's *day-to-day* operations are greatly enhanced by tactical knowledge possessed by its employees.

The four people on IBM's management committee never really understood the lesson of this book: If you have blindspots at the top and no process to break some china, in the long run, the company is doomed. As the following chapters demonstrate, only a radical change in the approach, attitude, and priority of Western firms to the role of competitive intelligence and how to organize to accomplish this role can save them from the possibility of suffering through the misfortunes of IBM, Sears, Hoffman-La Roche, and other fallen giants.

Since the "best practices" benchmarking I am about to present falls short of fulfilling the role of intelligence in competitive learning, why present it at all? There are three basic reasons:

1. Because one can learn from mistakes as well as successes;
2. If you identify your own company's approach to intelligence in this chapter, at least you would know where to go from there; and
3. Each system, though in need of some improvements, offers some excellent features that are worth adopting in an overhauled intelligence process. I highlighted with italics those features I judged worthy of your attention.

Overview

Let me start with a broad overview of intelligence programs across America.

Affiliation: The largest percentage of intelligence functions are housed in a marketing-type department, including Market Research, Marketing Services, etc. Next comes the Planning function, a dying breed, then Business Development, a reporting relationship on the rise. Some very curious corporations placed their fledgling competitive intelligence activities in an information system department, thereby killing any chance that the activity will bear any benefit *ever*. Computer types have no idea what intelligence is. I doubt that they know exactly what information is.

Budget: Average: $550,000
Median: $200,000
Range: $15,000–$6,500,000

This information is rather old. I admit I never tried to keep in touch with it, because the next cost cutting is just around the corner and the second budget to get cut is the competitive intelligence budget (the first is the Christmas party's). *In my experience, there is no correlation between the amount of money thrown at intelligence and its effectiveness.* On the other hand, there is never a free lunch. Just like our education system.

Budget lines: Salaries (around 50–60 percent of total), contract research, information sources and on-line data bases, equipment (PCs, fax).

Staffing: Corporate unit—director + 2–3 analysts, one administrative person

SBUs—vary greatly. Most cases are lucky to get one hapless "coordinator."

Oversight: Management Advisory Committee (examples: Nutrasweet, McDonnell-Douglas)

Policy Committee (Motorola)

Nobody (Typical Inc.)

AT&T[150](Note: Please read the important qualifying endnote.)

The intelligence unit within AT&T is a corporate unit, part of the Strategic Planning department. It provides AT&T with three basic services: a central competitive analysis group, a centralized expert directory (introduced earlier as the AAA), and a centralized data base.

The AT&T data base is an impressive monster. It has three heads: a market data base, a financial data base, and a competitive digest. The market data base, with 1,400 products, 580 companies, 180 industries, and 65 countries, is updated at least annually. The data, which are gathered and input by AT&T business units, pertain to products, customers, and applications.

The financial data base is a masterpiece of reconciliation of accounting standards and conventions across the globe. A specialist is devoted full time to the task of cleaning and analyzing the data. A user can retrieve the data by years, companies, accounts, or ratios.

The third head of this chimera is the competition digest. It is based on published news from all over the world that touches upon subjects of interest to AT&T. A special unit translates the clippings into daily reports, which include—and this is an incredibly important and innovative procedure—*strategic impact statements*. These are comments made by AT&T experts on the news items. The digest with the strategic impact statements is sent to senior managers. In addition, the unit maintains an archive that allows access to news reports and cross-referencing.

The competitive analysis group responds to information requests from management, initiates distribution of internal reports from the business units, and coordinates tracking of competitors by several business units. Given the sheer size of the mammoth that is AT&T, it is not surprising that such tasks are actually needed.

The AT&T intelligence service has some exceedingly nice features befitting a communications giant. The system has an Alerting service that can alert employees to developments of interest to them. It has a hotline and an on-line customer feedback capability, and it responds to information requests. It is based on an electronic mail system, it can broadcast mail, and, of course, it gives access to AT&T Analysts for everyone who needs to "let their fingers do the walking."

Pfizer

The competitive intelligence unit at Pfizer was housed in the Corporate Planning department, but each operating unit had its own intelligence "elements." This is a rather typical situation in a parent corporation. Often, business units differ greatly as to their intelligence capabilities, and the corporate unit has no power to impose intelligence "discipline" on them. It is not uncommon for business units to have no intelligence capabilities at all, while the corporate parent proclaims a great deal of interest in the role of intelligence in its bottom-line success. The legacy of portfolio management with autonomous business units has yet to be eradicated from corporate America's halls, even a decade after it was shown to be the most disastrous management model around.[151]

The central unit was geared to corporate studies, industry-level analysis, etc. It had informal relationships with the divisional staff and served as an in-house consultant on information issues.

The unit used mainly published information sources, from trade publications to analysts' reports to data base searches. One of its main roles was to support business development efforts by providing competitors' and companies' profiles in targeted industries.

Finally, intelligence at Pfizer was made part of the strategic planning process. *At the managers' annual reviews, the business units had to include a section on competitive analysis or top management would embarrass them publicly.* This interesting feature was the personal victory of the unit's head, a smart ex-military intelligence officer who understood that without it, most of the business units' managers would not do anything about collecting data, not to mention *learning* from their market.

Kraft

The Central Business Research Services Group was housed in the Marketing Research department. The unit utilized the principle of distributed intelligence: A network of 30–40 key experts (middle managers) from every function scanned journals, newspapers, magazines. They then sent the clippings to the unit. The unit prepared a quick browse list, one- or two-sentence summaries of each clip, and mailed them to 150 senior and middle managers.

The unit also served occasional information requests from management. It farmed literature searches out to an outside vendor and a network of consultants. It had one interesting principle: Its director *discouraged the walk-in-type service* in which people would drop by with weird questions. He also tried to push the unit toward more strategic and softer-type information, such as personnel changes at competitors, plant openings, competitive advantage, key success factors, etc.

General Mills

While General Mills did not seem to have a central intelligence function per se, or at least did not advertise one, it has always been one of the more progressive companies in this area. According to an article from 1987, it *trained all members of the organization* in recognizing and tapping competitive intelligence.[152] To augment the massive collection effort, it then set up distributed analysis: In-house focus groups would periodically discuss such issues as the way competitors competed, what made the competitors effective, how the industry climate was changing, etc. The focus groups were deliberately mixed, with participants coming from various functions in General Mills.

Motorola[153]

Bob Galvin, Motorola's former chairman, was once invited to serve on the Presidential Foreign Intelligence Advisory Board. He came back convinced that one cannot run a multinational giant such as Motorola without the full support of an intelligence unit. He brought in an expert, and there began the saga of what might be the best unit in the United States today.

Galvin established an interesting office, called Office of Strategy. Within it is the intelligence operation. It has gone through several changes, the most significant of which was the downgrading of the computerized data base, which started big (with big investment) and then ended up as PC-based local files. Because of its location, it has, at least in theory, direct access to the CEO and the heads of the various business units.

The central unit is divided into collectors and analysts, though over time the distinction has eroded somewhat. Collection is distributed based on a selective internal and external network of sources. In addition, each business unit is responsible for collection of competitive data. The central unit coordinates this collection effort. *The emphasis is definitely on human sources,* though every project is backed by thorough and competent literature background searches.

The people in the unit are highly trained, probably the best professionals in the field, some with *both* intelligence and business experience (a rather rare combination in this field). They provide analysis, present alternative courses of action, and do not shy away from making recommendations to top management. Whether management listens or not is a different issue. At Motorola, at least, indications are that it does. The projects they carry out are strategic: industry success factors, competitors' internal drivers, business development projects, etc. Serious emphasis is placed on foreign intelligence; i.e., trips to Japan are not considered a luxury. The way the system was set up, a *Policy Committee, made up of all group vice presidents and heads of headquarters functions, assigns the intelligence priorities to the unit.*

The unit's charter is to study corporate topics, to support the collection and analysis of the business units, and to maintain strategic files. Its most unique feature is its place in the pecking order at Motorola. *From its birth, the unit was dedicated to supporting top management only, both corporate and operational.* It remains to be seen, with Galvin out of active management, how the role of the unit will be defined and redefined in future years. One can only hope his son inherited his smarts.

The Guiding Principles Behind Corporate America's Intelligence Programs

The previous section summarized the main features of five corporate intelligence systems. I could have delved into many more examples, but the overall picture would have remained about the same. Corporations tend to imitate "best practices."

The "gospel" of competitive intelligence spread fast among American corporations. I am ashamed to admit that I probably share some of the responsibility for the way the corporate model has evolved. My 1988 coauthored book, *The Business Intelligence System,* was the first dealing specifically with how to *organize* an intelligence function. For the next five years, I worked with practitioners who read my work and were either building intelligence functions in their companies from scratch or attempting to attach the new role to existing units. During these five years, I realized that a typical corporate response to the need to strengthen its intelligence activities was to adopt the easiest portions of the model presented in my book and to ignore the more difficult and risky but meaningful portions—those that required cultural and organizational commitments, political guts, and openness to change.

In general, corporations approached the activity and role of competitive intelligence from two incompatible directions. One was based on the assumption that intelligence was relevant for decisions. This is what I will term a *Decision-Based* model of intelligence. The second held that intelligence was information like any other information. This approach I will call the *Information Center* approach.

Which Type Is Your Company's Intelligence Organization?

The easiest way to understand the two competing approaches to the role of intelligence is to classify a company's approach along two dimensions: strategic thrust of the intelligence activity and decision relevance (see Figure 11-1).

Figure 11-1
Classifying Functions

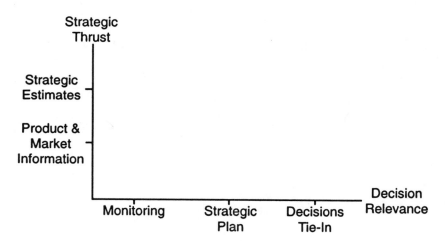

Source: Reprinted by permission from "A Self Examining Test for the Corporate Intelligence Professional: Where are YOU on the chart?," *Competitive Intelligence Review*, Volume 3, No. 1, Spring 1992, p. 4.

Strategic thrust refers to the products of the intelligence function. On the lower portion of the vertical axis in Figure 11-1 I put marketing-type reports, financial analysis, and any other output with a strong tactical tilt. The "competitor reports" that come out quarterly in your firm with market share, product mix, and maybe quick financial performance bullets are all tactical products. The news summary that goes on an executive's desk first thing in the morning in many companies is tactical information (or even data, if one cares to make the distinction).[154] The higher one goes on the vertical axis, the more strategic is the orientation of the functions' activities and products. A study of the threat of biotechnology to traditional pharmaceutical firms and the alternative courses of action (acquisition, internalization of some of the production methods, niche focusing) is strategic. A project dealing with how to compete with generics, based on studying the experience of the tobacco and food industries and the vulnerabilities of generic manufacturers is strategic. A 250-year strategic plan a la Konosuke Matsushita's 250-year corporate strategy requires strategic intelligence or a good sense of humor, or both. And so on.

Academics in the field of strategic management, perhaps because relevance of their work to corporations is *not* one of the criteria for their promotion, fill whole books with definitions and distinctions between what is tactical and what is strategic. The popular wisdom uses time as a yardstick: long-term (3–5 years? 2–7 years?) is strategic, short-term (under a year? 1–2 years?) is tactical. Other distinctions include the size of the investment required. I prefer to think of "strategic" simply as the effect on the company's future.

Think of the following two examples. Let us assume that you are a very senior executive working for RJR Nabisco. Let me further suggest that your company has an intelligence function. The function delivers a flash report about an upcoming price change on Marlboro cigarettes. Is this tactical or strategic information?

Don't rush. A price change is often a tactical move, a short-term change. However, in this case the Marlboro price cut was 40 cents per pack. It signalled a marked change in Philip Morris' philosophy.[155]

So this is a strategic piece, right? Maybe. But the real strategic intelligence would have been an analysis of how Philip Morris reached its decision.

The decision to mark Marlboro down by 20 percent was based on a month-long market test in Portland, Oregon, where Marlboro gained four share points. The critical point is that a month-long test is not enough for competitors to respond to. Recall my Reaction Test in Chapter 7: *Can a company predict reactions to its initiatives?* Philip Morris, like many other companies I know of, did not consider competitors' reactions at all. You don't believe it's possible? Listen to the evidence: A distributor to whom Philip Morris pitched the new move recalled asking the managers, "What have your marketing people given you to work with in the event of a competitive response?" Philip Morris's people responded: "Nothing."[156] The distributor further recalled that they looked pretty embarrassed. I would, too.

Furthermore, competitive response is not merely compet*itor* response. Thus, John Nelson, a senior vice president of planning for Philip Morris, admitted that the possible *government* response was never discussed during the development of the plan. And this was during the time Hillary Clinton's task force on health care was debating how large an increase in the federal excise tax on cigarettes was required to help finance health care costs.

Knowing the way Philip Morris, William Campbell (its U.S.A. president), its Board, and Michael Miles (its CEO) make decisions under pressure is the most strategic intelligence of all. It gives the rival a weapon—a blindspot—that enables it to understand many Philip Morris moves, not just a single one. Thus, strategic information comes in shades or hierarchy of strategic value. The higher in the hierarchy, the broader the effect on the company's future. In this case, knowing how Philip Morris makes decisions without regard to competitive response is of higher strategic value than knowing it is discounting Marlboro by 20 percent.

Many managers don't understand this point. The American inclination toward action makes managers inclined to see content as more important than process. Here is a quote from an article on why IBM, GM, and Sears ran into trouble. A former senior Sears executive remarks, "I've talked to a friend who worked at IBM, and we agree that when a company gets to the top, the *processes* of how decisions are made become all-consuming. You start focusing on how decisions are made rather than on what you decide."[157]

Unfortunately, that Sears former executive is wrong. Processes have a more profound effect on companies than a decision here or there. Companies with good decision processes will make better decisions overall than companies with decision processes that ignore competitive intelligence. A good decision without an intelligence process to back it is, at best, a *lucky* decision. If Sears had a process guaranteeing a reality check, it might still be a powerhouse, even if it fumbled in a decision or two. Thus, an intelligence function that focuses on understanding a competitor's *processes* is more strategic in its orientation than a function attempting to predict a particular decision.

The second dimension in Figure 11-1, *decision relevance*, refers to the actual organizational standing of the intelligence functions, *regardless of their aspirations or claims*. The question here is rather simple: How well is the function plugged into the routine decision processes in the organization? To how many meetings where decisions are reached, or at least debated, has the intelligence staff been invited? Don't be ashamed to count. It is an extremely important question.

Decision relevance goes to the core of the distinction between monitoring-type operations and decision-based operations. Think of AT&T's system: Its daily news summary with strategic impact statements is an exercise in continually monitoring what is happening in AT&T's environment. To an organization like AT&T, with so many environmental events that might have an impact on so many of its different businesses, continuous monitoring of the flow of events and information might be a necessity.

Most monitoring functions typically acquire such names as Business Information or Business Research centers. Their products, whether strategic or tactical, are mainly in the form of newsletters, reports, alerting flashes, competitor file updates, clipping services, etc. They release their products into the corporate stream with the purpose (and hope) of sensitizing employees, supporting proposals, and raising executive awareness. One never knows when the information might be useful to someone at some stage of making decisions, formulating strategies, dealing with customers, etc.

Next on the horizontal axis are those intelligence functions that are housed in Planning departments and support planning documents. Their relationship to decisions depends on the relevance of their bosses, the planners, and the relevance of their output's hosts, the planning documents. It is therefore hard to make an a priori judgment. The more powerful is the vice president of Planning; the closer he is to the center of decision making, the more decision-oriented the intelligence analysis becomes. However, when the vice president of Planning goes, so goes the intelligence functionaries' influence on actual decisions.

The farther to the right on the horizontal scale one progresses, the stronger is the tie-in with the *routine decision processes* at the company. Each company has its own rituals regarding decisions. The Wednesday's New Products Committee in company X is well known for making decisions, but the Monday's Senior Managers Half-Day Head Bashing in company Y never reaches any concrete action, or if it does, in company Z these are never implemented, and so on. Actual routine decision processes are not the same as the decisions themselves. Tying into a process does not *guarantee* that intelligence will have an impact on decisions. But it is definitely the case that when intelligence functions do not tie in with the decision process, their chance of affecting the content of decisions is close to nil.

To *which* decision processes can the function be tied? In IBM, MCI, Southern New England Telephone, and many other companies, the intelligence activity was specifically geared to support salespeople and marketing reps. The competitive data were fed directly into the rep's laptop or presented during special gatherings or promoted during annual Florida balls, or all of the above. Sales decisions regarding pricing and negotiations, which competitors' products to harass, how to react to new product introductions, what rivals' promotion campaigns to counter at the retailer, etc., were directly based on competitive data fed from these functions *in real time*. And in regard to time, the following is a typical corporate meandering.

A division of a large pharmaceutical company decided to establish a competitive intelligence system. After a few years, the system failed. The reason? It became clear that compiling reports every three weeks (the average time it took from collection to distribution) was too long a wait to make them *relevant*. The company switched to a computerized system that channeled data almost instantaneously. Any pretense as to analysis was dropped in favor of speed. Another division replaced a monitoring system that processed huge amounts of data and then distributed reports to everyone with an e-mail system serving marketing planners *only*. The focus of the system then became the operational data required for marketing planning decisions.

In short, decision-based intelligence functions can be designed with an eye toward supporting tactical decisions or, like the system at Motorola, supporting major decisions and actions. In this last case, *the decision process to which the function must tie in is quite different*. Thus, at Motorola, "future strategic decisions and anticipated actions by [corporate and operational] senior managers were the basis upon which the intelligence collection and analysis effort would be developed."[158] The unit was founded on the assumption that it will *not* serve everybody. The tie-in to particular senior managers, and them alone, was a very important, and very successful, decision early on in the life of the function.

Based on Figure 11-1, it is possible to create a classification scheme into which you can place your intelligence program—assuming your company has one, assuming you know where it is, and assuming you know what it actually does—*in line with its predominant role in the corporation*. The major classes are presented in Figure 11-2.

Information Inquiry Desks

Placed in the west-south corner of the chart are the units whose main role is to serve as data providers to callers. The typical caller or customer is a middle or line manager who needs a technical detail, a market share figure, a 1983 growth rate, etc., for a document he or she is preparing for management. Some managers call only after they themselves provided the function with some information. Others make "cold" calls unabashedly. "Hi, this is Joe from logistics over at____. I hear you might have the floor plan for [company x's] plant in . . . ."

No intelligence function starts by deliberately aiming to become an information inquiry desk. Many functions find themselves constantly fighting the slow slide into activities of this nature.

Figure 11-2
Decision Relevance

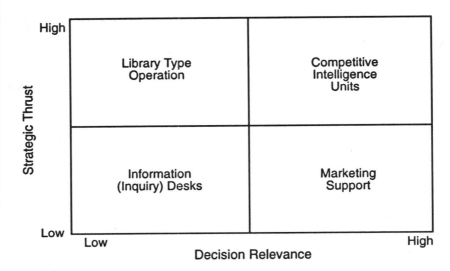

Source: Adopted from "A Self Examining Test for the Corporate Intelligence Professional: Where are YOU on the chart?," *Competitive Intelligence Review,* Volume 3, No. 1, Spring 1992, p. 2.

The Information Inquiry Desks do not typically know the purpose of the information requested. Often, when they try to understand the nature of the request, they find out the manager did not need the data requested, needed different data, did not know other data could be found at all, etc. The greatest value an Information Inquiry Desk type program can offer to the corporation is in educating the managers as to (1) what information they need, (2) what information can be found, and (3) why information should not be pursued only to support an already-reached conclusion.

Glorified Libraries

Libraries are the backbone of any corporate attempt at research, be it R&D, marketing, or strategic. It is not rare to find librarians who are smarter and more strategic-oriented than their managerial customers. However, libraries are not competitive intelligence functions.

Some competitive intelligence functions, however, are nothing more than glorified libraries—glorified because the status of libraries and librarians in the corporate hierarchy is rather low, while the title "analyst" sounds so much better. Yet if the intelligence function spends most of its effort and time on producing volumes of research, mostly based on *data base searches,* and then distributing it to senior managers in the hope that someone will read it and comment, the function is nothing more than a library-type activity.

Intelligence functions that maintain competitor files, send alerting bulletins around, and publish quarterly updates and newsletters are basing their information on published data and their role on the distribution of information, hoping to find readers and educate young minds. This is very similar to the traditional library's function. Don't misunderstand me: These activities may be extremely valuable. But this has little to do with affecting the future of the company or its survival probabilities.

Marketing Intelligence Systems

The east-south corner of Figure 11-2 is occupied by Marketing Intelligence Systems. These are the oldest and probably the most popular form of intelligence systems. They existed way before the current craze of "competitive" intelligence programs.

The Marketing Intelligence Systems rely mainly on published data from trade magazines and reports from the sales force to provide marketing and sales personnel with vital tactical information needed for the day-to-day battle. Often they are housed in or supervised by marketing support departments. No one doubts their relevance and usefulness, since the common wisdom is that to do their job, salespeople need to be armed "with all the competitive intelligence they can have." The irony is that no one thinks *top* management needs to be armed with the best strategic intelligence money can buy.

In better companies, the Marketing Intelligence Systems use very sophisticated electronic transmission and storage facilities, the latest gadgets in interfacing and retrieval, and very little analysis. What is transmitted are data. What is used are data. Everyone is happy. Articles on productivity in service functions extol the improvement in performance of service and salespeople based on better and quicker information that is made available to them. And top management stays blind.

Competitive Intelligence Units

Finally, at the upper-right corner of the map I placed the functions that tie directly into the corporation's *strategic* decision process. The functions' main role is analysis—i.e., deciphering. They integrate data from published and human sources into a strategic puzzle, which they feed to decision makers involved in strategy formation. They typically work on projects requested by top management. They are involved with new business development activities, benchmarking exercises, new market assessment, new product directions, etc.

There are few American corporations with this type of unit. Motorola is one. Some other companies would prefer I did not name them. *However, the vast majority of American corporations responded to the need to significantly improve their competitive learning capabilities by creating one of the three other types of operations.*

The Typical Corporate Experience: Does It Sound Familiar?

The typical corporation became aware of the new management trend of "business intelligence" through a public seminar or an executive briefing, which proliferated in the late '80s. Its managers either listened to a speaker or read an article which described how companies saved a few hundred thousand dollars by finding out a competitive detail in advance, or lost millions of dollars by *not* finding it out.[159] They then read the model my coauthor and I presented in our 1988 book, which pioneered the call for a *formal* intelligence function. A corporate champion—usually a planning or market research executive—would then take the concept upstairs, and after an initial suspicious response (ethics, remember?), upstairs would decide to form a competitive intelligence *unit*. Of course, they would give it a "respectable" title, such as Business Information Center. They would start by placing Mary or Bob from market research or marketing (with an MBA, preferably) in the role of "competitive analyst." The function would report to a marketing or planning director, who reported to a vice president somewhere in marketing or planning.

Soon it becomes clear that *one* Mary or Bob cannot collect and analyze the tons of competitive data floating around. John, Tracy, and a secretary will be added. An intelligence director will be named (maybe even Mary or Bob will be promoted to this role). A unit with three or four analysts is now in operation. Its director still reports to a vice president, who reports to an executive vice president, who reports to the president.

The unit will get the best help in performing data base searches either from outside or inside the company ("you will not believe how much information can be found from these data bases"). Attempts to gather information from the sales force will fail ("they really don't have time or give a damn"). The unit will produce several reports, which will get to the vice president and disappear. A central, company-specific data base will be created with outside help and a lot of money. Soon the unit will begin promoting its services and capabilities around the company and during lunchtime. Managers, the few and the brave, will call with questions like "how many people live in Mexico City?" The unit will be able to pull this datum quickly and efficiently, especially with the new software, which is the director's pet project. Within a year, the calls will become much more frequent. The next strategic studies will go the route of the first two, into the black hole "upstairs."

Then the company will go through its cyclical cost-cutting drive. Bad times, pressures from stockholders, a new chief financial officer, or simply a feeling that it is time to raise productivity—Western managers' obsession since Japan bloomed into a world power—will bring about a call for a 15 percent cut in overhead. The competitive intelligence unit is overhead. The director will fight like a madman; the vice president of Planning, whose department was already shrunk twice last year, will pitch in. The vice president of Marketing Services will fight less, because he was never sure about the difference between this new creature and the old market research department, and the competitor profiles that the unit produced were nice but not really of operational use. No one upstairs will defend the unit. There will be a few who will be *surprised to hear it exists.* The president and the executive vice presidents will remark dryly that the organization lived without the unit for many years, and what exactly are the benefits from it? The director, furious now, will bring his boss memos from middle and line managers who testify that they used the unit's output and gained *valuable* insight into the competition. The cost-cutting round will leave the unit with a director and one "senior" analyst. One analyst (John? *His* MBA was not from Harvard, you know) will be let go. Bob will be transferred to market planning (we need all our good men in the trenches for the upcoming line fight). Mary will stay (she will probably stay there forever if the unit survives. This is a nice, middle-level appointment, *perfect* for "a woman"). The unit will become a permanent fixture (once created, bluntly eliminating an organizational function is all but impossible). The director has by then learned the real game. Every year the unit will do less and less, but produce more and more reports. Productivity at its best. The director will wait for the lateral or upward move.

If you believe this is an overly cynical description and that I probably exaggerated a little, and that in reality corporations and their executives are more rational than that, you probably also believed Nixon.

If, on the other hand, you believe in GE's Jack Welch's definition of management as "looking reality straight in the eye and then acting upon it with as much speed as you can,"[160] you realize that none of the intelligence operations described in this chapter except the strategically-oriented competitive intelligence units can do what Welch's definition *commands* them to do: *Make sure management looks reality straight in the eye.* And even the strategic units can do it *only* if they follow certain rules, which are outlined in the next three chapters.

A radical change in approach is needed for the age of the global competitive pressure-cooker.

CHAPTER TWELVE

The New *Old* Paradigm of Competitive Intelligence

Ever since the trite statement "Nothing fails like success" succeeded in becoming a corporate critics' slogan, treatments for the "maladies of success" have abounded. The maladies are typically diagnosed as complacency and size,[161] and, naturally, medicine is offered for both symptoms. Among the more recent cures for complacency are restructuring and reengineering, two enormously successful (at least for the consultants) management fads. Restructuring typically takes care of the size problem as well: Corporations are urged to break into smaller, more entrepreneurial units. Let me examine these two management ideas more closely. I don't mean no disrespect, fellas; I just want to explore how these two concepts relate to blindspots, OK?

Restructuring

Restructuring is one of my most favored corporate concepts. It started as an *externally* oriented corporate strategy: A parent company buys failing companies, restructures them, and sells them for huge profits. One of the most successful examples of a corporate restructurer is Lord Hansen and his company, the British conglomerate Hansen.

The concept then emigrated inside, into an internal corporate management technique. Within this paradigm, companies restructure *themselves* in an attempt to revive their flagging business, acquire intrapreneurial spirit, get closer to the market, and a host of other rationales. The restructuring typically involves hiring one of the famous consulting firms, leaving a substantial chunk of one's resources in their very capable hands, shedding excess "fat," and facing the world like a new person.

The restructuring approach makes intuitive sense. No one can deny the logic of reorganizing a company so as to make its operations more suitable to the demands of the market. However, there are a few problems with the approach. The first and minor one is the fact that those advising on the restructuring are the same consulting firms that brought corporate America to its pre-restructuring sorry state. I never understood the logic of bringing in the same guys whose advice executives have been following since the 1950s, and who are therefore *as* responsible, if not *more*, for the decline of corporate America. But I guess golf course ties are stronger than logic.

The second and much more disturbing problem is that restructuring does not remove blinders. It is similar to *moving a terminal patient into a new room in the hospital.* The corporate patient remains as sick as ever, regardless of whether the reporting relationships appear on the right-hand side of the organizational chart or at the lower left!

Moving a terminal patient to another room does not make him recover. It does not change the course of the disease. A company can restructure, then restructure the restructured restructure, and its top managers will still hold the same blinded view of reality. IBM and Kodak are living proof.

Restructuring that leaves people thinking along the same lines as before is like painting over a rusty boat.

The New Paradigm of Reengineering

The ink hasn't dried over the term restructuring and corporate America is up to a new craze: reengineering. The truth is, it is not as bad as restructuring. It does not hold that the panacea is laying off people and cutting cost—as if having fewer secretaries, fewer managers, and lower expense accounts will wake up top executives to see fundamental changes in their markets more clearly.

Reengineering is built along very similar lines to the argument advanced in this book: Traditions and old assumptions underlying the old ways of doing business can become a burden on corporations. What is exciting about reengineering is that it suggests that managers should ask the most basic questions: "Why do we do what we do? And why do we do it the way we do?"[162] The advocates of the new paradigm call for reinventing the corporation. Sounds great, and I couldn't agree more.

But then the consultants pushing the new idea provide an example. It is taken from IBM Credit, the company that finances all those purchases of IBM services and products. Once you look closely at the example, reengineering appears not to provide the answer to a company's worst enemy: executives' blindspots.

IBM Credit had a problem. It took about six days to process a customer's request for credit. These six days allowed too much time for the customer to look for alternatives. "One day" write Hammer and Champy, the two leading advocates of the new paradigm who wrote the book, *Reengineering the Corporation,* "two senior managers at IBM Credit had a brainstorm." They took a financing request and followed it through, and discovered unnecessary steps, redundant paperwork, irrational procedures, etc. Are you surprised? I doubt it. At the end, the two tell us, IBM Credit replaced its specialists with generalists, slashed its turnaround time from six days to four hours, and a smaller number of workers were now able to process *100 times* more requests. This is impressive any way you look at it, and I am not about to suggest otherwise.

The IBM Credit problem was a process that was designed with a *hidden assumption* that every request for finance was unique and difficult. Once this assumption was exposed and eliminated, the process became much simpler. As the paradigm holds, "Companies can reengineer only processes, not the administrative organizations that have evolved to accomplish them."[163] I concur completely: The secret of rejuvenation is indeed in reengineering *processes.* Processes are the heart of the organization. In attacking restructuring, the authors of *Reengineering the Corporation* claim; "Overlaying a new organization on top of an old process is pouring soured wine into new bottles." Well, I chose the moving-the-terminal-patient-into-a-new-room analogy, but the idea is the same.

> **"Restructuring is similar to moving a terminal patient into a new room in the hospital."**

Why am I not happy with the new paradigm? Because what its advocates reengineer, the assumptions they attack, center on the old myth: productivity. Reengineering raises the productivity of old processes, sometimes dramatically. So here we go again: Top management, being blind to fundamental changes in market realities, including the real strengths and weaknesses of their own organization, can relax—all they need to do is look for ways to improve productivity in their old processes. The consumer can switch to discounters, but all Sears needed to do was improve its inventory processing time?

Reengineering does solve some blindspots, especially old assumptions underlying *operational* processes. It should be adopted by every manager looking for ways to rejuvenate his or her organization. The exercise of asking "why do we do what we do this way" in itself is a wonderful exercise. However, it does not go to the heart of the problem of successful companies: the strategic myths, taboos, and assumptions developed by their *top* managers. Overlaying new processes on top of an old guard who lost touch with reality is giving an adrenaline shot to a horse who broke its legs. How far can it run with the new and improved procedure to process credit requests? One process—the most critical process: charting the strategy of the corporation—is typically outside the charter of the reengineering consultants. Does the CEO, along with his or her lieutenants, use an effective process? Is it still appropriate to our global competition? Is it based on competitive learning or are they wallowing in the same old rut?

One of the greatest limitations of reengineering is that it is focused *inward*. Companies must learn to learn from their environment. Recall the essence of competitive intelligence: deciphering early signals from the competitive arena. If IBM Credit's executives listened to their customers, they would have found out very quickly that waiting six days for approval was not the high point of their week. If IBM Credit had an effective competitive intelligence process, customers' preferences would have been transmitted to them. Companies and executives must learn to listen to signals coming from *the outside*.

Finally, as most corporate middle managers know, if top management was truly interested in reengineering, all it had to do was ask. The people who carry out the ineffective and inefficient routines know exactly what is wrong with the process, but no one asks them. When they suggest improvements, or complain about the irrational nature of some of their tasks, they are whipped into silence very quickly by their immediate bosses who know better. Though badly designed processes are undoubtedly a problem in most companies, the more basic problem is senior managers who, merely by virtue of becoming senior, have developed blinders *they themselves are not aware of wearing*. Take away their blinders, design a process *specifically* aimed at reducing *their* blindspots, and reengineering will be a breeze.

Think of it: How did IBM Credit come to realize its credit approval process was overdesigned? Two senior managers had a "brainstorm." Where were these two executives until then? Why didn't they see the problem earlier, if it was so obvious? Could reengineering have changed the blindspots of IBM's former chairmen Carey and Akers regarding mainframes? Would they have ever turned the technique on themselves, or is reengineering good for middle managers and credit clerks only?

Companies can reengineer themselves to death, but even if they gain infinite productivity they will shrivel and die without an effective (not an efficient!) process of learning from the market. The emphasis in the '90s is shifting outside. Thus, as much as reengineering is similar in its basic tenet to what this book proposes, it does not go far enough.

An Ancient and Venerable Tool

Unlike restructuring and reengineering, competitive intelligence is not a new thing. It has been around for as long as traders needed information on business opportunities to expand their trade—i.e., thousands of years. The Phoenicians used it to expand trade in the Mediterranean; the city-states in Italy used it to bring about the end of the Dark Ages; and the Neanderthal traders used it to exchange skins with their neighbors. (The intelligence function? Next cave on the left!) Companies have been gathering, communicating, and using competitive information for ages. Yet only recently has competitive intelligence come into its own as a respectable and essential tool of strategy and operation. In its new light, competitive information is seen as the fluid that oils both the day-to-day drive to sell the product and the overall jostling for competitive position.

It should be clear by now what my belief is: To fight competitive sclerosis, a company needs an effective immune system. An effective competitive intelligence process is one such immune system. In the following sections I will describe, in great detail, an intelligence process that my experience with corporations in the United States, Europe, Israel, and Japan leads me to believe is an effective tool for competitive learning.

The principles of the process I will outline shortly are universal. They hold true for each and every company. They have held true since the days of Joshua. What is not universal, what I cannot predict, is the extent to which top management commits to and uses the process. Joshua listened to his scouts and led the Israelites to the promised land.

For some companies, there is no process and no cure for blindspots. There are always stubborn, arrogant, closed-minded executives who will not listen to anything or anyone. For them, and their companies, the only hope is a quick decline.

But for the many executives who are genuinely interested in learning, the intelligence process I describe will do the job, and do it well. *However, in order to understand the role and objectives of the intelligence process in a company, the reader must keep the following points in mind at all times.*

A. Against popular belief, the competitive intelligence process's primary role is not to prevent surprises. Few intelligence processes can do that well, as numerous examples from history can prove beyond a shred of a doubt. Just think of Pearl Harbor, Yom Kippur, Sadam Hussein, and the

Shah of Iran. An effective competitive intelligence process attempts to decipher trends and changes in the direction of the market *as well in advance as possible*. This is the early warning function of intelligence that experts talk about so often. Typically, however, it cannot prevent the surprise of a new product introduction by competitors, an entry of a new player to the industry, an acquisition, or other strategic moves that are well concealed from the public. Since the intelligence process does not use espionage, it is ridiculous to expect it to accurately predict specific acts of specific competitors, potential competitors, or other players. The process's outcomes may be a "guesstimate" of intentions, goals, make-sense-type moves, etc., but not actual actions. This is not a drawback to the process: It is simply not aimed at predicting *specific* moves. It is aimed at putting together the puzzle of the competitive environment and the company's position in it. The performance of companies such as USX, Procter & Gamble, Boeing, Jaguar, Macy's, Du Pont, Pirelli, Volkswagen, Southland, Travelers, Kmart, and many, many others would not have been improved in the '90s by an intelligence process that could have predicted a competitor's specific new product. *It could have been improved by a process that would have continually examined their own thinking and practices against the competitive reality by patiently collecting, deciphering, and actually learning from market signals.*

One of the more significant breakthroughs in how companies handle their intelligence activities occurs when executives stop viewing the intelligence process as an alarm system (which entails the typical-next-morning-question: "How come we did not know about it?") and start treating it as an organizational learning process ("What can we learn from this move?"). Beyond merely adjusting executives' expectations of the process, the difference in the two views translates operationally into an emphasis on one modus operandi versus another.

Anyone familiar with the information flows in a typical corporation knows that news about a "hot" surprise (new product, takeover bid, executive shakeup, etc.) reaches top management long *before* it is known to most other members of the organization. Ties with security analysts, a tip from the sales vice president that goes directly to the president, a friendly golf game with another executive vice president, and other channels make it almost impossible for an intelligence function to learn about a new development before top management. (In contrast, blindspots make it almost impossible for top management to learn about slow and gradual developments before anyone else.)

In regard to hot developments, the relationship between executives' own information networks and the intelligence function is analogous to the relationship between local police and a SWAT team. When a crime occurs, the local police are the first to be notified through the 911 system. This is similar to the informal and personal networks that inform top executives of hot developments almost instantly. *If the situation warrants it*, the local police calls upon the SWAT team to intervene. The team then "takes it from there." The intelligence function takes it *from there* as well. It should be asked to investigate this hot development as to the details, future possibilities, background understanding, fit with the total strategic picture, and action implications to the company. The intelligence function is the company's SWAT team for another reason: It uses a network of experts I term "So What" experts, or, in short, SWAT experts.[164]

For the strategic purist wondering how the pursuit of hot developments can be consistent with the blindspots-busting role of the intelligence function, here is an example: In one company with which I worked closely, the entry to the market of a new competitor resulted in a whole discussion of capacity planning at that company, risk taking as to investment in capacity, and the time it took (way too long) to install capital equipment. Tactical may turn strategic in the blink of an eye.

B. "Who's the Boss?" is not only a sitcom, it's a serious question.

While effective intelligence process can achieve maximum exposure to the competitive reality, *it should not be expected or encouraged to formulate strategies*. It can point to possible outcomes of a choice, it can serve to check reactions to a move, but it cannot replace the strategist. The choice of strategy and actions to take is and always will be up to the strategic shrewdness of the CEO and the president.

C. Competitive intelligence is human intelligence.

I know I am stepping on some very sensitive toes with this statement. Vendors of published information such as data bases and firms specializing in data-base searches may react in a storm of protest. They should not. Data bases, newspapers, magazines, trade publications, and so on are extremely important as providers of *background* information. However, they almost never provide competitive intelligence the way it has been defined repeatedly in this book: deciphered early signals from the competitive arena that tell the CEO on the corporate level and the president on the business unit level if their organization is still competitive; information that exposes blinders. *For competitive intelligence, a company must have a powerful and systematic process that relies primarily, if not exclusively, on human sources.* The background data based on annual reports and articles from *Business Week* or *Ad Week* or *Chemical Week* or Dialog's wealth of secondary sources should come from your library. The competitive intelligence process should be a human intelligence process. *You cannot gain any competitive advantage by reading outdated and equally shared information.* If you think you can rely on secondary sources to plan strategic moves, go help the Pentagon determine the effectiveness of Desert Storm's bombing attacks.

The Four Principles Underlying the CI Process

With the above three very important qualifying statements in mind, this section deals with the competitive intelligence process itself. The competitive intelligence *process* is very simple. Think of it as a network of neurons running through a transparent model of the body, and you get the basic idea. Behind an effective process lie four basic principles that, if adhered to, will deliver maximum results. I am not being facetious: The process is basic and easy to grasp. There is nothing in it that requires the application of complex statistical tools, surveys, and matrices that give the appearance of sophisticated methodology and are therefore so popular with the big consulting firms.

Principle 1: **The process should (and could) be made simple and cheap.** This principle will not endear me to most managers heading competitive intelligence units. Sorry, guys. I am your most ardent supporter; I just think your companies are going about you all wrong. Costly large departments with numerous analysts, costly equipment, costly software, and enormous data bases not only *guarantee* future cuts but are simply unnecessary. The competitive intelligence process should rely on the voluntary effort of many people. People are the heart and soul of intelligence. Published information, data bases, clipping services are the background. The process should be designed to maximize reliance on people—those who are the existing information sources and those who can be recruited. Good intelligence networks are always simple, basic, *people*-oriented. They require the understanding of human nature and the ability to persuade *people* and to listen to *people*. The more complex the process becomes, the less beneficial it will be. *Save the money to help your internal sources gain better access to external information (such as sending them on as many trips and to as many conferences and trade shows as humanly feasible) and to hire outside sources of knowledge.* This is where you should never count your change!

Principle 2: **The organization's culture is the most influential factor in the success—or failure—of the competitive intelligence process. It must be reckoned with.** The competitive intelligence process is a people process. Every organization's culture is different, but in many companies the dominant atmosphere is that of do your job, do it well, and stay out of trouble. The corporate spirit is that of execution; most managers and employees simply execute decisions and strategies handed down by top management. They are not typically concerned about competitive developments unless they directly impact their job. They are not typically aware that information they possess, or can easily get hold of, may have a significant impact on the strategy of the company. They are not typically encouraged to question top management's ideas, myths, taboos, or assumptions. They are not typically encouraged to question anything. More often than not, they are told to trust top management, which already possesses most of the information needed to make good decisions. Therefore, Principle 2 of the competitive intelligence process states that people in the organization *must*:

- understand the process.
- approve of it.
- be convinced that top management puts a lot of faith in it.
- believe it will do their careers good to take part in it.
- believe it will not *hurt* their careers.
- identify personally with its main goal—fighting blindspots.
- regard it as more than just one more of top management's whimsical projects.
- have an initial enthusiasm regarding its potential.
- be willing to give it a chance.
- not see it as an additional chore.

At least *some* people in the organization—the intelligence gatekeepers—*must*:

- see it as a way to advance their beliefs.
- believe they can have an impact through it.
- be willing to put in the extra time required to contribute to it.

In short, the competitive intelligence process cannot be imposed on an organization. Unless a company is willing to imitate the Korean or Japanese way of putting pressure on employees to deliver competitive data through promotion and/or explicit job descriptions, the competitive intelligence process is going to be based *solely* on volunteers. Ignoring the corporate culture is one sure way to ensure that the process will be squashed before it is even started by a 300-pound gorilla. *That does not mean that one has to accept the existing cultural norms*. If one always did, there would be no hope for IBM or AT&T. The emphasis is on designing the process with the culture in mind: At times the culture must be fought head-on; at times, circumvented; and sometimes the process can rely on existing cultural norms. In some companies, it may be enough for the CEO or the division president to come forward and declare, "We view the new competitive intelligence process as an immune system, our main defense against decline. Please help us out." In other companies, the subculture may be so strong that no top executive can truly affect attitudes. In this case, the process should rely on what the employees actually perceive as their worst fears or best motivators. For example, scientists, who typically loath collecting and transmitting competitive information, nevertheless regard travel to scientific gatherings as their most treasured privilege. Tying their reimbursement to a trip report or a pre/post-trip briefing may do the trick, even if a message from the R&D director or the CEO does not. Salespeople are a prime source of competitive *rumors*. They typically regard their "slush" fund (a discretionary amount they can spend to give merchants additional discounts) as a prime competitive weapon. Tying the size of the fund to information flows can accomplish what a mere message from the top may not. Sounds devious? It is more devious to leave well enough alone and then fire thousands of people because top management, wearing its normal blinders, was not made painfully aware of changes in the market or weaknesses at home.

Principle 3: **Don't confuse technological toys with intelligence capability.** One of the basic elements of an intelligence *system* serving the intelligence *process*, which I will discuss later on in this chapter, is the competitive data base. The need to establish a data base brings with it a whole array of computer and information technology "toys." How can anyone object to the latest in (labor-saving) technology? Shouldn't the company strive to have the best software for storing, communicating, and analyzing information?

Yes, it should. Fax machines, voice message technology, e-mail, electronic bulletin boards, and automatic distribution by predetermined interest profiles are among the most helpful tools in an effective intelligence process. But so is the old, reliable, underused . . . telephone.

The problem with technology is that too many intelligence professionals, or more typically their bosses, confuse it with intelligence capability. Competitive intelligence is a *people process*. It requires the understanding of human nature and the ability to persuade and listen to *people*. Technology that helps meet these requirements, does not cost much, and does not take over is good technology. When an intelligence professional tells me about the latest ultrasophisticated software he or she installed that can almost analyze a strategic situation on its own, can retrieve obscure details in a flash, can store and classify and sort and categorize and cross-reference and whatnot, I know that person does not understand the purpose of the competitive intelligence process or the essence of competitive intelligence—deciphering early signals from the competitive arena to fight the onset of blind-spots. Very often, the best corporate analysts have only one significant "technological" resource: a Rolodex—maybe even an electronic one—with hundreds of names they have accumulated over the years. Don't spend most of the budget on computers and computer-related services. Let me repeat: *Save the money to help your internal sources gain better access to external information, and to hire outside sources of knowledge.*

This is the place where you should never count your change!

Principle 4: **The competitive intelligence process is a tool to achieve the only empowerment possible in a corporate environment.** Second to *leadership*, the word *empowerment* is the most overused word in the corporate vocabulary. I often wonder how workers and managers avoid laughing, sitting through corporate communication meetings listening to their esteemed leaders (here I go again) tell them that they want more empowerment. Well, I guess the need to pay a hefty mortgage can help reduce the humor in any situation.

No executive in his or her right mind would voluntarily let go of decision power. Nor should executives desire to do so. Empowerment is non-sense invented by liberal intellectuals who never ran a corporation or any other organization. In a capitalistic world, the people at the top make decisions, take responsibility for them, and, if they consistently fail to make profit for the shareholders, are eventually forced to retire to their country clubs. That is the only way to run a company. Democracy is good for governments, because governments can print money.

Don't misunderstand me: I am very much for empowerment, as long as no one pretends employees are going to have power over any decision that may actually have some significance to bottom-line performance. The most they will be asked to handle will be minor decisions, and very soon even that will be chipped at by worried next-level managers who want to be sure the work is done according to what their bosses expect, and so on. Decision empowerment is the biggest fraud in corporate America.

> **❝Empowerment is nonsense invented by liberal intellectuals who never ran a corporation or any other organization.❞**

Empowerment should not be confused with decentralized control. In a decentralized corporation, a division, SBU, or subsidiary is given autonomous decision power over its business-level strategy. But as long as profit drives the business, *within* the division, the president and the executive vice presidents are going to make the decisions.

If decision empowerment is an empty slogan (one can only wonder at the proximity of the verb *empower* to the adjective *empty* in the dictionary), what empowerment is feasible within most companies?

"Democracy is good for governments, because governments can print money."

The answer many executives overlook is *information empowerment.* Knowledge is a truly powerful tool in creating the feeling of empowerment, of control over one's destiny. And while I never believed in giving top decision makers' decision power away, I have constantly urged companies to share information with their employees.

It is amazing how little information American companies share with their employees. The phenomenon often borders on paranoia. The explanations given for the fact that the overwhelming majority of managers and employees don't have the slightest idea of their own company's strategy, expected strategic moves, detailed performance, or strategic concerns range from security issues (completely misplaced) to a paternalistic attitude that "they don't need to know" (completely wrong) to "it is not practical" (completely outdated).

I am not talking about the corporate cheerleading information "shared" with employees during annual sales meetings or biannual company meetings. I am talking about real numbers, real concerns, real strategic debates at the top. Many progressive executives, especially those who have recently read the appropriate guru or have listened to the latest Executive MBA nonsense on "mission statements and visions" in some prestigious university, point out to me proudly how their companies have gone out of their way to instill a "shared vision" throughout the company. The little plastic cards on which they print the vision in short, succinct, catchy phrases always remind me of China's Mao Tze Tung's little red book. It might be necessary, it might be effective, it might perform miracles, but it has nothing to do with sharing real information and giving employees a real sense of empowerment. The Chinese people under Mao did not feel particularly empowered.

There are a few companies, such as Goodyear under Stanley Gault, that believe the more employees know the more they can contribute. But to accept this fact, executives must overcome the greatest obstacle of all: Information is power; therefore, sharing information might dilute their power. No one can deny the simple fact of life: *Exclusivity* in the possession of truly important information bestows status.

This is, unfortunately, a rational line of reasoning. Information privilege is one of the most coveted privileges of becoming a senior executive. *The price a company pays is so high, though, that executives should take a very serious look at changing their assumptions on this issue.* It causes all the information bottlenecks and feelings of powerlessness and loss of involvement and cynicism and lack of trust—and I can continue with many more typical corporate malaises—often ascribed to ambiguous "culture."

Executives should make decisions. That is what they are paid for. They should not feel guilty for not sharing that power. But they *should* share information. The change I am advocating is not just quantitative: Though *more* information should be shared, *different* information must be shared. Employees should become privy to the true P&L data of their division (something they *cannot* read in the annual report) or to the details behind the annual consolidated statements. Cost figures, markups, overhead, expenses by categories, and profit should all be communicated to employees, bad news and good. Strategic issues—what management is talking about, what areas of knowledge are missing, why management is interested in particular areas, what alternative courses of actions are available, why some alternatives are favored by the top, why the company does certain things, such as advertising, in certain ways (remember reengineering? it should start from the top)—should all be shared with employees.

I am far from naive enough to believe that an attitude change of this magnitude can happen overnight. Overcoming American executives' long-held beliefs about what subordinates should or should not know amounts to attempting a revolution in managerial thinking far more ambitious than restructuring or reengineering ever attempted. The best way to start, though, is through the competitive intelligence process. *In this process, information must flow from the top to the bottom to create an effective flow from the bottom up.*

But first, executives must accept three tenets:

1. A knowledgeable employee is an empowered employee.

2. The best way to fight blindspots is to expose them to everybody inside the company.

3. The best way to make employees more competitive is to make them aware of competitive information.

I know it sounds basic, but how well is it implemented in your company?

The Competitive Intelligence Process

Finally, we are about to take a look at the new old competitive intelligence process. Silence in the theater, please!

Look how simple the new model of the old competitive intelligence process is:

1. One central location for convergence of bits and pieces of data from all over the organization
2. A distributed force of collectors and analysts (dechiperers)
3. A system capable of storing information so as to enable easy retrieval and communication

You can't tell me the design of this process requires a multimillion-dollar contract with a consulting firm. I can tell you it requires vision and commitment.

1. The Convergence Point

Chapter 13 is devoted to talking about the specific location, organization, and structure of the convergence point for all data from around the company. At this point, let me state that unless there is one place where all data converge to, it is impossible to compose the strategic puzzle. Many executives understand this point intuitively but do not understand the requirement it imposes on *them*: they have to share *their* data with the organizational entity that is designated as a convergence point. This sharing has two aspects:

First, top executives have to share the extremely important bits and pieces they get through their daily contacts with such outsiders as security analysts and peers during golf games, leadership seminars, roundtables, board meetings, etc.

Second, and most important—they must learn to share the daily inflow of competitive data from *insiders*—the constant flow of news communicated to them by loyal (or less loyal but ambitious) subordinates who know that "the boss likes to hear it first."

Since the process of competitive intelligence is not designed to replace any of the informal flows and is not aimed at tactical responses, executives should not discourage their managers from reporting "hot news" to them. Au contraire. All that is required is that *the top executive who receives the hot news flashes transmits the information to the convergence point, just like everybody else in the company.*

This is not an easy requirement to implement, and even less easy to maintain. It is up to the CEO at the corporate level and the president at the unit level to demonstrate their commitment to this feature of the process. Few who understand the benefits resist this change: The executive input can be added to a growing puzzle, placed into a long-term competitive memory (e.g., a data base), and analyzed as part of a *total* strategic picture. The difference between a competitive intelligence process and the often-practiced marketing intelligence flow (from subordinates to the top) is that *top executives no longer serve as the last stop in the flow of competitively important information.* Their limited immediate processing of the information, therefore, is no longer the last processing the information receives in the organization. The phenomenon of "black holes" sucking up all the light is no longer an inevitable part of the organizational life. As simple as this feature of the process is, it represents a breakthrough in most corporate cultures—a signal of priority and a foundation for a tremendously improved decision process. If the CEO and president keep adhering to it, it eventually becomes second nature for everyone.

2. Distributed Collection and Analysis

In our 1988 book on the subject, *The Business Intelligence System*, my coauthor and I elaborated at length on the element of a *distributed* intelligence collection through a network of employees. The concept was revolutionary: Most companies that experimented with a competitive intelligence unit in the 1980s started by going the easy route—relying almost exclusively on data-base searches and other published information. As our model spread throughout corporate America, more and more units began turning to internal networks. Today, one will not hear a presentation by a corporate practitioner that does not emphasize the critical importance of an internal network of loyal employees who pitch in with the task of collecting competitive data.

Distributing the tasks of identifying and deciphering market signals among a wide and encompassing network of managers and employees remains the most celebrated element of the model. But, as proud as this development made me, I have slowly begun to wonder about its effectiveness (blindspot?). The problem was that over time, networks began to deteriorate. Maintaining enthusiasm is a challenging job. We in the West do not have the luxury of ingrained cultural values that keep the spirit of employee contribution toward a collective goal alive at all times. We have to work at it. This is easier said than done.

For that reason, my concept of a "collection network" has gone through a refinement. In recent years, I have implemented a distinction between a wide-reaching network of sporadic collectors, to which *all* employees are encouraged to belong, and a limited, focused, structured network of *competitive experts*.

The Competitive Experts Ring

Do you remember why I previously referred to the competitive intelligence unit as the company's SWAT team? One reason was the "so what" question answered by internal competitive experts. The competitive expert is an employee of any rank, color, sex, age, or religion who possesses one quality: When she (or he) sees competitive data, she will be able to answer the question "So what?"

Sounds rather stupid, doesn't it? The question posed to the expert is, "SO WHAT does it mean to us, here, at company X?" It forces the expert to decide what effect the bit of data can have on the way the company conducts its business. Data can be interpreted as pointing to a competitor's advantage, in which case the company should learn from the competitor. Data can point to a practice or process used elsewhere in the world that may give the company an advantage. In this case, the company should learn from "best practices." Data can point to a threat, an opportunity, or a weakness. Most important of all, data can point to a blindspot. "We have been doing it that way for the past 25 years. The data suggest we might need to change." Or, data can lead nowhere, be nice to know but have no real impact, be irrelevant like 99.99 percent of all data. In this case the expert discards them.

> **"It is much easier to train a technical expert in the fundamentals of competition than it is to turn a business expert into a technical expert."**

The competitive expert performs the deciphering of early signals from the competitive arena. Therefore, he or she should possess the technical skills required to understand and comment on an early signal in his or her area of expertise. But the expert should possess more than just a narrow technical knowledge; we are all familiar with the great scientist who can't see beyond his nose. The competitive expert should understand competition: what affects the company's competitive position, and *how*. If that sounds like an impossible combination of skills, don't despair: *It is much easier to train a technical expert in the fundamentals of competition than it is to turn a business expert into a technical expert.* I should know; I train business students all the time. Therefore, if your company is short on business-oriented experts, take your brightest, most energetic, most inquisitive, least cynical *technical* experts and train them intensively for a few days to understand the principles of competitive strategy. It shouldn't take more than a few days—we don't really know that much about competitive strategy.

The Role of Competitive Experts

Competitive experts are the few, the chosen, the proud *core* of intelligence analysts in the company. They are the Marines *before* the married-couples directive. They can also wear the hat of collectors (sources) of information, local coordinators, and other roles that are part of the entire competitive intelligence process. Their main task, however, is to receive competitive *data* from various sources across the company and to turn out competitive *information*—deciphered signals that then converge to one place to be assembled into a strategic puzzle.

Competitive experts, together with the local coordinators (to be discussed later), are the best first step in sharing information within the organization. The sharing of information proceeds along three routes: upward from the experts, lateral across experts, and downward to the experts.

Upward sharing. The upward portion is the easiest to see. The comments and evaluations of the competitive experts will eventually, in a properly designed intelligence process, make their way to top management.

Lateral sharing. The lateral sharing results from two distinct activities. First, competitive experts from various areas meet periodically to discuss competitive data and reach conclusions. This is part of the process. Second, within an electronic environment, competitive experts can be exposed to every comment and evaluation made by every other competitive expert by simply accessing the data base or bulletin board. Thus, in a second-stage intelligence process, where a computerized system is added to the infrastructure, a piece of competitive data will travel throughout the organization, accumulating comments and evaluations, promoting learning in its course, or dropping out for lack of interest or relevance. Such processes already exist in progressive organizations around the world.

Downward sharing. Downward sharing, from top management downward to the experts, is the one in which I have the most interest as a tool to create empowerment. Given the ambiguity of many senior executives in regard to sharing information with their employees, the downward sharing with the core of experts represents a less intimidating start. The reason for the sharing is so clear, it is hard for even the most paranoid executive to object: In order for competitive experts to be able to perform their task—evaluating the inflow of competitive data for the "so what" relevance to the firm—they *must* be informed of strategic issues with which management is grappling, alternative strategic directions being considered by the top, areas of opportunity under search, and issues that management considers potentially threatening. While I realize that logic and corporate reality are sometime incompatible, I did see senior managers taking the competitive experts core seriously. The switch, I believe, came about once they assimilated the notion that the core of experts is *their* front line of defense against blinders. They then regarded the sharing of information with the network as giving their "soldiers" ammunition for the battle.

> **❝Overcoming American executives' long-held beliefs about what subordinates should or should not know amounts to attempting a revolution in managerial thinking far more ambitious than restructuring or reengineering ever attempted.❞**

While there are several mechanisms for sharing information, not all of them can be included in this book, which tries to remain at the more universal level. However, here are two examples: In one company, a senior manager (each time a different one) joins a regular meeting of the experts to make a quick presentation, discuss concerns, and answer questions. In another company, top management invites specific individuals from the competitive expert ring to join intelligence briefing sessions that touch upon their areas of expertise or uses some of their comments on the data. In the better-designed processes, both techniques will be used as well as a host of other creative, company-specific routines. It is always amusing to see the response of some relatively junior-level experts who find themselves in a joint session with the CEO. It is even *more* amusing, however, to watch the reaction of some top executives who suddenly discover the hidden talents in their own organizations—hidden, that is, because most senior managers do not have the time to get in touch with the vast majority of the company's employees, except for the brief and impersonal duration of the grand annual meeting. Ironically, most senior managers truly enjoy the encounters made possible by the intelligence process. The reverse is less clear.

Not All Companies Are Born Equal

The intelligence process relies so heavily on the competitive experts core that no company can expect to progress toward an intelligence capability without it. Yet it is impossible to prescribe one mode of forming and motivating and rewarding this core to all companies. I don't say it so as to leave room for consulting assignments (the usual reason for refusing to recommend universal principles). I say it because after working with a diverse group of companies in many different industries and of many different sizes, I became a great believer in local solutions, originating from local *political* experts, and relying on local cultures. It is one thing to come up with a terrific concept of a SWAT team, and another to make it work for you and your company. The purpose of all local solutions, though, should remain focused on one goal: making the experts' ring a *status symbol* to which everyone aspires to belong. I personally can't think of a more status-imparting activity than having periodic meetings between competitive experts and top strategy makers to demonstrate that the top listens to, considers, and implements the ring's ideas and comments. By implication, I can't think of a more devastating blow to the ring than failing to provide feedback.

3. The Storage System

In *The Business Intelligence System*, my coauthor wrote a chapter about computers and their role in the intelligence function. In the 1992 Hebrew edition of the book, that chapter had to be augmented with a completely new addendum written by another expert to bring it up to date with new technologies and software. As a Computer Ignoratium (a specie of the Homo sapiens which does not find a discussion of RAM interesting), I stayed on the sidelines watching the experts discuss—at times fight about—which release of this or that package offered more bang for the meager intelligence bucks.

I guess this is exactly the problem. If Western companies invested one-tenth of what the Japanese invest in competitive learning, I would have been a much more vocal supporter of information technology and its role in intelligence. There is little doubt in my mind that information technology can be a tremendous tool in gathering, communicating, manipulating, and reporting intelligence. But, given the miserable investment in learning, where should the dollars go?

An information system to support the intelligence process is a *must*. The bits and pieces converging on one place must be categorized, stored, retrieved on demand, analyzed along a time dimension, and sent to several rings (experts, collectors) to decipher the weak signals. There are several amazing programs that can do just that in ways that would have left Cardinal Richelieu (Louis XIII's chief minister and a master of intelligence, 1585-1642) dumbfounded. Yet Richelieu, without hardware, and with pigeons as communication technology, could teach our generation of techies a lesson or two about strategic information and keeping close to the market. If there is no money for a trip to inspect a competitor's plant, or travel to an association's meeting, or for *retired* employees to make some phone calls for you to find out about an interesting development, or for outside consultants who can shed light on the character of a new entrant to your industry, or for a competitive "war game" (see Chapter 13), then all the information technology in the world will not produce competitive intelligence for your company. Of course, a computer memory is superior to what paper files can store. But at the end, it is the "decoder," the intelligence manager, with his or her address book and his or her phone who makes the difference. This is why I leave the in-depth discussion of an information system to the zillion books about information systems. In the end, you are going to spend millions on it anyway, but at least my conscience will be clear.

In Summary

In this chapter I began to introduce the new competitive intelligence process—a revised version of the old process (or collection of activities) that all companies employed informally since 3000 B.C. The main points: The process is not an alarm system; it starts, continues, and ends with people; it has "rings" or networks of people playing a variety of roles; and it changes in a fundamental way the sharing of information in a company—not only upward, but downward and laterally as well. Now that I believe I have foiled every opportunity you may have had to misunderstand the process in any possible way, the next chapter, at last, presents the whole model from start to finish. If you are a senior executive who is not interested in the technical details, skip to Chapter 14. If you are a middle manager who was summoned by the vice president of marketing yesterday and told to build an intelligence function, you might want to read the chapter carefully—then resign.

CHAPTER THIRTEEN

The Five Rings Model

I have carefully outlined the role the strategic intelligence process should play in the corporation. I have outlined the universal principles underlying any successful intelligence process, be it in an American, European, or Japanese company, be it in a small, medium, or large company, be it a blue, red, or yellow company. It is now time to bring the elements together and describe the structure of the whole process.

Figure 13-1 is a schema of the intelligence process. It is composed of five "rings" and one "center." Beginning at the bottom, the rings are:

1. A collection ring
2. A layer of competitive experts ring
3. An overlay ring of local coordinators
4. A ring of outside sources
5. A top ring of decision makers termed the "Strategy Kitchen."

In the middle is a competitive deciphering "center" (from the root *central*, not from the root "many MBAs").

Business Unit or Corporate?

Before I describe the structure in some detail, let me put to rest one question that is often raised at this point. The Five Rings Model is a *decentralized* model of intelligence *suitable for a business unit. A business unit is where I firmly believe the intelligence process should take place.* As Michael Porter pointed out, corporations do not compete, business units do. It is not that they don't need competitive intelligence up there at the corporate headquar-

Figure 13-1
The Five Rings Model (Divisional)

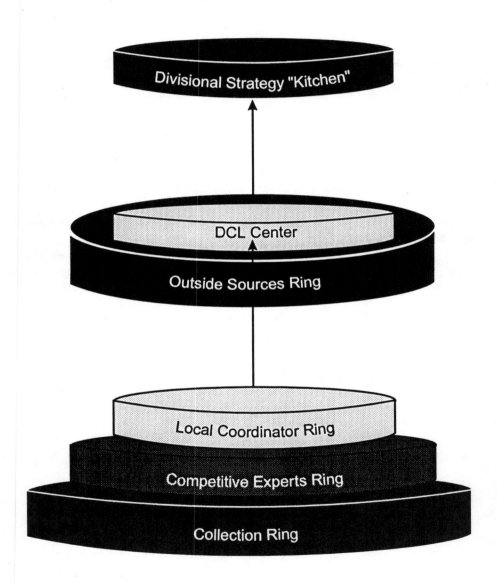

ters. Rather, it is that down there at the business unit, *they almost certainly do*. Competitive intelligence supports business strategy. The decision maker who has to fight the competitive battle, *the division's president*, needs, and deserves, strategic intelligence support more than anyone else in the corporate structure. This statement is always true. Whether or not a CEO needs an intelligence function depends on the type of corporate strategy followed and the type of CEO in charge.

The issue of a *corporate* intelligence function is the issue of whether *corporations* (i.e., the parent companies) suffer from blindspots. The examples in this book, Chrysler, IBM, Sears, and General Motors point to a definite positive answer. Yet the examples also have to do mostly with corporations dominated by one main line of related businesses—either computers, cars, or retailing—or with CEOs whose management style is "hands on" (e.g., Lego at Westinghouse). In short, if the CEO makes *competitive* decisions and requires a clear understanding of the market(s) and their major players, or if he regards his role as the keeper of the corporation's overall competitiveness (this concept will have meaning only in a corporation composed of *related* businesses), having a corporate intelligence process makes strong sense. A CEO whose management style is that of a portfolio manager has very little to do with real competition. He moves money around like an investor, can hardly be said to understand *in depth* any of the markets in which his units compete, and has to rely on autonomous business units. For this type of CEO, what would a corporate-level intelligence process do? Almost nothing that I can think of. This CEO's main blindspot may be related to the wisdom of using a portfolio approach after a decade of unshakable proof that it does not work.

The Five Rings Model's version for the corporate level is presented in Figure 13-2.

It is easy to see the extension into a corporate model. The local coordinator's ring is now an SBU's ring rather than a departmental ring. In other words, instead of a local coordinator in every major department in a business unit (see page 181), a coordinator for the entire business unit—that division's intelligence manager—represents this unit in the corporate intelligence process. The collection ring is made up of the various collection rings of the business units, although this can and should be augmented by the corporation's own outside (and perhaps inside) experts and collectors. The need for augmentation depends on the strength of the relationships between the corporate "center" and the businesses' intelligence processes. Despite the songs of praise one tends to hear about these relationships, I remain a strong skeptic. Unless a fraternity of intelligence professionals emerges in the corporation, with some loyalty to the *discipline*, the first and only alli-

Figure 13-2
Corporate Model

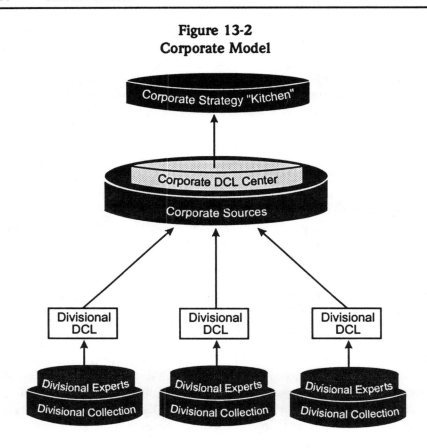

ance of the divisional staff will be to the division. As a result, the intelligence furnished to the CEO will be so biased and watered down that its value should be highly questionable.

Boards and Intelligence

Another issue is that of intelligence for the board of directors. With boards becoming more independent, at least in theory, the need to be informed of their company's competitive position, industry global competitive developments, and future competitive prospects should grow exponentially. How can the board be informed *independently* of the rosy picture painted by the insiders? Should a board establish its own intelligence process or risk being blinded?

As farfetched as the idea sounds at first, it may become the wave of the future. *This is especially true of companies whose divisions do not adopt a sophisticated intelligence process of their own.* For these companies, the board may be the only watch dog or immune system against a slow but certain decline. It then needs to take decisive action and appoint its own intelligence adviser. The organization of such a process should not be extraordinarily difficult. The basic structure is the same as the Five Rings Model presented here. The politics of such a move are still to be tested and require boards that go beyond rubber stamps or SCORE (an agency of retired executives who give friendly advice to companies).

The Structure of the Intelligence Process

Because of its essential role in the deciphering process, the expert's ring was already discussed in Chapter 12. Now I will explain the other four rings in order of their significance to the intelligence process.

Local Coordinators

I firmly believe that an intelligence program that has more than one full-time employee and a secretary is a program bound for eventual extinction, or at least severe cuts, under the lean-and-mean philosophy of the '90s. I also firmly believe that one does not *need* more than one very bright expert at the helm of the process. The model is built around the idea that the actual collection and deciphering of intelligence will be supervised by a network of *volunteer local coordinators*, not by an intelligence "unit." Therefore, an intelligence unit, per se, is not necessary. Instead, one manager of the entire process—the Director of Competitive Learning (DCL)—is enough. Local coordinators are responsible for transmitting the data collected from the collection ring to the competitive expert's ring, and from there information flows to the DCL. The local coordinators are also responsible for maintaining the *opposite* flow, from the DCL to the outring of internal sources (see Chapter 15 for details on the two flows, or modi operandi, of the intelligence process).

In a business unit, local coordinators come from major departments, functions, or areas, depending on how the organization is structured. Examples include a coordinator for the sales area, one for the R&D area, one for the marketing area, one for the finance area, one for the human resource area, etc. There is no limit on the number of coordinators who should participate in the process, although for practical reasons, since all coordinators are often run by one manager, the DCL, their number cannot be exceedingly large.

The coordinator's system is like the pyramid selling schemes so popular in the '50s, but with no scam or bubble to burst. Each local coordinator is responsible for identifying and recruiting competitive experts (see Chapter 12) from his or her own area. Each coordinator is also responsible for communicating collection targets and issues of current concern to the collection network. In addition, local coordinators are expected to identify sources within the area who might have good access to external information, appropriate to the changing needs of top management. For example, if the competitor is about to open a new plant in Yourtown, Some State, U.S.A., the coordinator will be called upon to identify within his or her area the employee whose second cousin happens to live in Yourtown and may even be on the local zoning board (yes, this is an actual example!). Or the employee who has good, and regular, contact with the vendor who will, in all probability, provide some of the equipment to the new plant.

The coordinator, in short, is a *gatekeeper*—he or she should know *people*. Not surprising, since as we all agreed, the intelligence process is a people process.

The coordinator is a voluntary role taken on by an individual within a given area, as an addition to a particular position that is located in a gatekeeping juncture, depending on (1) who is the best person for the job, and (2) the corporate culture. The advantage of attaching the coordinator role to a position is that of ensuring continuity. The advantage of attaching it to an individual is that of ensuring the best person for the job. Examples of gatekeeping positions include the quality engineer who spends many hours walking the plants and talking to workers and vendors; the manager of sales support who converses regularly with the sales divisions and field force; or the manager of financial reporting, with whom many finance and accounting personnel frequently interact.

The most important aspect of ringing the company with local coordinators is that *their managers are not going to like it*. This is almost guaranteed, since the coordinator role is time-consuming and will have to be done in addition to regular duties. Moreover, the task can often become fascinating, allowing the coordinator to interact with other members of the organization and with top executives who otherwise were invisible to him or her. Breaching departmental borders, conversing with senior executives, being at the center of intelligence operations—I would hate to be a coordinator's boss!

There are several ways to tackle the problem. One solution that I favor is to incorporate the intelligence tasks explicitly into the job descriptions of both the coordinator and his or her immediate supervisor. Beyond job descriptions, it is choosing the right people (who then deal with their bosses themselves) and the clear understanding that "top management truly favors this new role" that make the voluntary process happen. Creative solutions, however, could hardly be more appropriate than in this touchy area.

To summarize: The local coordinator layer is the channel through which the Director of Competitive Learning interacts with the companywide rings of collectors and experts. It is important to correctly understand the role of the coordinators: They are motivators, recruiters, transmitters of information, *but not filters.* Local coordinators are not supposed to add or subtract their own biases to the data coming through. They are supposed to identify the best competitive experts to send the data to, or the best sources to obtain the data from. They can add their own input at the monthly meeting with the DCL. They and their departments should be judged, and perhaps compensated, on the *volume* and *quality* of intelligence produced in their areas. But they are not, and should not be allowed to become, an added filter on the tortuous path information has to travel on its way to and from the president. Choosing the right coordinators, with the emphasis on people skills, makes it feasible to talk about the entire company rallying to help top management achieve maximum exposure to competitive realities. It makes it possible to activate huge networks of eyes and ears and brains, which replace costly and often less effective central intelligence units with their hordes of expensive analysts or expensive outside consulting firms. The choice of local coordinators is second in importance only to the choice of the Director of Competitive Learning.

> **❝The most important aspect of ringing the company with local coordinators is that** *their managers are not going to like it.***❞**

The Collection Ring

So much has been written in recent years (including the original chapters in my 1988 book) about internal sources of information and the need to recruit employees to collect competitive information, that I do not feel obliged to expand on the topic here. Every employee in the company should be encouraged to become a source of competitive data, a collector of bits and pieces that deal with the issue of competitiveness. The collection ring is the net of eyes and ears a company spreads around in the hope of identifying weak signals early on *through the regular interaction of employees with the outside world.* Selected portions of this ring are then also used to track data in a deliberate, top-directed collection effort.

I will further expand on the difference between the free flow of intelligence and the deliberate, or planned, intelligence projects in the next two chapters. For those who will not get that far, here is an insight: The free-flow mode is the old suggestion box, *but with teeth.*

Take for example the following real-life scenario. An employee in the engineering department spots a competitor's patent that seems to indicate an opening of a new category. He sends it in to his boss. The boss is busy or just lacks imagination. The employee's action goes unnoticed: no one responds. If he insists on sending in his pieces or his opinions, he soon becomes a corporate pest.

Now consider the same event under the new intelligence process. The employee's report goes to the local coordinator, who is a people person, not an interested (or rather uninterested) party. The coordinator floats it to several engineering experts, but also sends it to the local sales coordinator to see if her people noticed any competitive moves in this area, and to the manufacturing coordinator to check about related activity in the competitor's plants. They, in turn, activate some of their experts. In addition, if indeed there is some competitor activity related to the patent, perhaps a few salespeople or plant workers may report relevant data to their coordinators. In a monthly meeting (or before), the pieces come together. Some experts comment on the significance of the patent, or on the opportunity it opens to the company even if the competitor does not follow its own discovery (which often happens). Some discard it as unimportant. The debate brings together experts from various functions. Assuming the conclusion reached supports the original engineer's report, it goes upstairs as an analysis *backed by the opinions and additional data from sales, marketing, manufacturing, R&D, and other experts.* Which route is more effective in bringing competitive reality to the attention of top management?

The ring of internal collectors is easier to conceptualize than implement. It can work if—and only if—the company puts serious effort into education and training. Otherwise, it lasts for about six months (or until my consulting contract expires).

Education and Training

This is a painful subject—by all estimates, the Achilles' heel of American corporations. We do not invest in training. As simple as that.

There is only one way to establish a wide network of internal sources, or collectors: Make people understand that they must do it for the sake of their mortgages. If they want to rely blindly on top management staying in touch with the competitive reality, they should not be surprised, nor should they complain, when the next cost-cutting drive leaves them on the street.

There is nothing more frustrating to an employee than trying to improve a process within his or her department, shutter a taboo or a myth about the way things should be done, open superiors' eyes to changes in the market, just to be labeled a troublemaker or a nag. Yet the alternative is to see the job disappear because top management wore blinders and no one tried to poke a hole in them.

No less frustrating is to be the new CEO or president in a company that does not remember how to—or maybe never had to—compete. Don't envy Allen of AT&T, Gerstner of IBM, or Gault of Goodyear. How do you turn a self-centered cadre of managers and employees into fighting marines?

The answer is education and training. Boring answer. Long-term investment. Unmeasurable results. Costly. Anyone interested?

There is no substitute for plowing through the organization and preaching the message: You have to help us fight blindspots. You have to help us identify early market signals. You have to help us learn. Naturally, management has to believe in these words, in learning, in blasting blindspots. How many Jack Welches (GE's CEO) have risen through the corporate ranks in the last decade?

Welch is one of the great believers in training and education. His GE University program is more popular, and definitely more effective, than Harvard's. Other companies now believe in training their employees, and competitive awareness has become high on the agenda.

There are many ways to educate a work force about the need for, and methods of, identifying early signals from the competitive arena. General awareness briefings, video presentations of "war stories," and intelligence techniques workshops are among the methods my colleagues and I have used successfully in the past. But without a doubt, my personal favorite of all time is the one known as "war game."

The War Game. This simple exercise is relatively new to the managerial seminars' circle. Not too many experts are yet familiar with running a war game, but once the expertise grows, it is safe to predict that every training firm will offer the game as a regular feature in its color brochure.

This war game is not—I repeat, not—the laboratory computer decision simulation games that became popular in the '80s (and are much less popular today). The war game is an in-house, Red Team, Blue Team-type exercise. It is a two-round, presentation-based battle between interfunctional teams of managers and employees representing the company and its main competitors. In the first round, each team presents its answers to four assigned questions related to strategic options facing the company. They then break for a short time to prepare a competitive *response*, taking into account the range of projections presented by the teams representing their rivals. This is not professional wrestling, where the outcome is known in advance; I've seen a few knockouts by underdogs.

The war game sounds simple; it is simple, yet it requires meticulous preparation for its success. The teams must have access to rooms full of data long before the game and must plan their line of attack over several weeks. Rules of engagement must be clearly specified. Choices of who will be on which team are extremely important. Team leaders must be carefully debriefed lest the game quickly deteriorate into a political mess. The results, though, are simply amazing *and* long lasting. Aside from the obvious benefit of raising sensitivity to competitive intelligence issues, which is the explicit objective of the game, it may bring together managers and employees who otherwise had no interaction whatsoever, even though they were just across the hall and could have used one another's expertise in carrying out their daily tasks. Moreover, the long-lasting effect manifests itself in the formation of groups of employees who, in preparing for the "fight," became interested in their assigned competitor, and retained the interest long after the game was over. They then follow the competitor to find out if their projections were correct, keep a small data base or a file with clippings, participate in task forces and "shadow marketing" teams organized by the DCL, and so on. As a way of getting employees and managers to interact in concert to fight blindspots, and as a way to get top management to listen to their subordinates' ideas without the formal management presentation framework, and as a safe way for employees to expose blindspots without "naming names," the war game is an old, underused organizational invention with enormous, if subtle, long-term effects. Try it.

Outside Sources

The director of the intelligence process has two parallel rings at his disposal for collection of information: the inside collection ring and the outside sources ring. The outside sources include industry experts, vendors, consultants, people in the know, professors, government officials, information vendors, free-lance reporters, former employees, competitors' former employees, and so on. They can be kept on retainer, work for fun, or be the DCL's personal friends. The only requirement is that they have ethical and legal access to competitive information.

Once the DCL goes after a particular competitive question, both networks of inside and outside sources will be simultaneously activated. The ability of the DCL to develop a wide-reaching ring of knowledgeable outside sources is directly related to two factors: (1) his or her social skills and (2) his or her company-sanctioned network opportunities. The second is probably the more crucial one, as so many companies regard travel to conferences, seminars, and trade shows as a waste of precious resources.

Reading about the way a Japanese corporation sends teams of its employees to gather information at trade shows, and how its engineers take every opportunity for plant tours, and how its executives may spend months travelling in a foreign country collecting information, and how its representatives will be placed in undeveloped markets years before the actual market penetration takes place, one realizes how backward we are in giving our employees opportunities to form networks of information sources. That mistake, if applied to the *intelligence* function as well, is so costly, only truly blinded corporations can do it and actually not understand the consequence.

The DCL must go himself, or send someone from the four rings—a coordinator, an internal expert, or an internal or external source—to all the events in which industry issues are to be discussed and all the events in which competitors may be present. The travel budget of the intelligence process should be as large as feasible and should not exclude Paris or Miami, if that is where the contacts are. No cost cutting can be applied to this budget, since it is exactly during bad times that the company needs to identify market signals as fast as possible. Just ask Honda. It is much cheaper, and several times more effective, to let the DCL or her agents travel in search of information contacts than it is to bring in a large consulting company whose people do the travel, charge you by the nanosecond, and take their expertise and contacts with them when the job is done. And I am not even touching upon the issue of who does the better job!

At the core of the intelligence process is a person with a telephone and a Rolodex. If the Rolodex is not allowed to mushroom by the hundreds every year, when the time comes and top management desperately needs strategic intelligence, it may find it cannot get it at any cost.

The Strategy Kitchen

The outer rings of sources, competitive experts, and local coordinators are the competitive intelligence process' *infrastructure*. This entire, massive effort is, and should be, geared toward *one and only one* objective: to support the small, top ring of the "Strategy Kitchen."

The Kitchen is a term credited to a short list of close advisers that surrounded the late prime minister of Israel, Golda Meir. Born in Milwaukee, Meir was among the most influential leaders in the short history of Israel. Rising through the ranks of the Labor Party to become the party leader and Israel's prime minister during the famous Yom Kippur war, she was known to meet with her trusted advisers and selected cabinet ministers in her apartment's kitchen. It was the warmest place in the apartment, and in a country short on heating oil, the best place for early morning meetings.

The term *Kitchen* became synonymous with the closest political circle around a leader.

In a business context, I use "Kitchen" to signify the coalition of decision makers who actually run the company. Although it changes from one company to another, in most companies the kitchen includes the CEO (on the corporate level) and the five or six executives he uses as his closest advisers, and the president or head of a division and the five or six people he uses as his closest advisers. Sometimes the kitchen is the Policy Committee or Management Committee, sometimes it has no official title, sometimes it does not include officers whose titles sound important but who have no political power, and sometimes some of its members may not appear to the public, at least, as central players (e.g., the corporate lawyer, a trusted veteran sales manager, etc).

> ❝ Top executives are the people who need competitive intelligence the most, because if they become blindsided, the company is doomed, *regardless of how competitively aware other members of the organization are!* ❞

At GM, the Kitchen is the President's Council, known as the Gang of Five: CEO Smith, Chief Financial Officer Richard Wagoner, Chief Counsel Harry Pearce, Executive Vice President William Hoglund and GM Europe's chief, Lou Hughes.[165] At AT&T, an Operation Committee composed of the chief financial officer and four group executives is the team responsible for running day-to-day business, while Allen, the CEO, has his own Kitchen, including a chief strategist, Richard Bodman.[166] The essence of the Kitchen, or "executive team," as it is called by management academics, is not titles but *raw power to affect the direction of the organization.* These are the people who need competitive intelligence the most, because if they become blindsided, the company is doomed, *regardless of how competitively aware other members of the organization are!*

The kitchen is an appropriate term for many reasons, not the least of which is the fact that strategy does not come about with a single insight and a quick decisive action. Strategy emerges from a long series of decisions, debates, studies, realizations, trial and error—a slow-building consensus. It "cooks" or "simmers" for months at a time. It gets molded through pressures and compromises and setbacks and internal negotiations. All these activities take place within the Kitchen. Academics may use the term executive teams, but Strategy Kitchen is a much more *accurate* term.

The competitive intelligence process serves the corporate or divisional Strategy Kitchen, is created for the corporate or divisional Strategy Kitchen, is located near or inside the corporate or divisional Strategy Kitchen, is accountable only to the corporate or divisional Strategy Kitchen, is meaningless without the corporate or divisional Strategy Kitchen. Was I repetitive? Perhaps I was not clear though, so here it is again:

If the competitive intelligence process does not serve the Strategy Kitchen, and it only, the money invested in it should be placed in a big manila envelope and mailed to the following address: Ben Gilad, c/o Probus Publishing Co., 1925 N. Clybourn Ave., Chicago, IL 60614. Thank you in advance. No corporate checks, please.

There are no compromises, no buts, and no "maybe later on when the atmosphere is a little more receptive to such an idea." You cannot fight sclerosis by changing people at the bottom. Would you like additional cliches á la management gurus? Be my guest: "Competitive learning starts at the top or it does not start." Competitive intelligence is the imperative input to the top executives who constitute the Strategy Kitchen. Those at the Strategy Kitchen who do not understand it will not be there for long in today's competitive pressure-cooker.

The reason the competitive intelligence process is made to serve the Strategy Kitchen rather than the CEO or the president alone is that in most organizations, even the power of the chief executive will not be enough to introduce such an influential "outside" factor into the strategy formation process. If the process becomes threatening to other top executives, its life span will be shorter than that of a dragonfly. If, on the other hand, the process is made to serve all members of the Strategy Kitchen, they may actually lend a lot of support and help.

The Director of Competitive Learning (DCL)

Finally, at the center of the competitive intelligence process is the Decoder—the chief competitive expert of the organization. In succumbing to corporate realities, I will use the more corporate term of Director of Competitive Learning (DCL), though my heart is with the Decoder. After all, this manager is responsible for *decoding* vague, weak, ambiguous signals from the competitive arena before they become as loud as Heavy Metal. I prefer this title to the more common Director of Competitive Analysis or Manager—Competitive Research, since I would like to distinguish the process I am describing from current practices. Analysis is fine, but if the company does not learn from it, it is an empty intellectual exercise. Research is fine, but too often it stands for a bulky report, based on a comprehensive search of the literature, that no executive ever reads. Learning is what enables companies to survive: learning from competitors, from suppliers, from customers, from other companies, and from one's own internal experts.

The DCL is responsible for breathing life into the large infrastructure—the four network rings, and for keeping the other ring, the top executives in the Strategy Kitchen, tuned to reality. *For such a tall order, companies should designate their brightest, most fearless, least "corrupted" person as the Decoder.*

I am often asked what are the specific qualifications of a good DCL. My answer is that if the company can lure away a *Business Week* or *Fortune* reporter or editor, they have found the perfect candidate. If they could lure away a reporter from the *Economist*, they should simply close up shop for a day of celebrations. Why these magazines? Because I am partial to their *irreverent* attitude toward powerful companies and executives. They not only get most of the facts in a situation, but also bring a critical approach to these facts. They don't fall for corporate-speak. They don't shy away from confrontation, although they always check their facts before doing battle. They know HUMINT—human intelligence. They are the masters of HUMINT. Of course, it is easier for them: They are big enough and powerful enough to make everybody, or almost everybody, talk to them. To generalize from the skills of these people, the most important assets one can bring to the job of the Decoder in any organization are:

1. Curiosity (some will call it "nosiness")

2. Irreverence (willing to commit corporate blasphemy)

3. Good memory (for the little details that make the large difference)

4. Tenacity (never takes no for an answer even if he does not know the question)

5. A slight paranoia won't hurt (the opposite will)

6. Never satisfied, never content, never at peace (a happy person, in short)

7. As much as feasible: low need for power (saves on utility bills)

The Director of Competitive Learning does not have to possess an MBA, although a business background is nice. I am convinced, however, after some recent experience, that the DCL must be fluent in the technical aspects of the business so that the engineers, and the manufacturing types, and the R&D lifers won't be able to shout him down. The strategy aspects, the competitive analysis aspects, the financial aspects—all these and more the DCL can pick up in one semester or less. The technical understanding cannot be acquired that quickly.

The DCL does not need to have intelligence experience, although it definitely would not hurt. The problem is to find someone who combines a deep understanding of the business side of the enterprise with the art of intelligence. The bottom line, so to speak, is that comprehension of the economics and the technical aspects of the industry are more important than the ability to obtain the hottest news. Remember, the DCL does not collect the information alone. There are rings of sources and experts to support him or her. And while the DCL does not analyze the information alone, either, it is his or her strategic insight and instincts that decide what goes into the puzzle and what does not. The few I know who possess *both* an expertise in intelligence from their former life and an understanding of profits and losses are *exceptionally* good.

In some corporations, the influence of financial types is exceptionally strong. Some executives are inclined to manage by numbers and respect a bottom-line, P&L-type impact analysis more than anything else. In these companies, the temptation to place a finance person—a former security analyst, a banker, a development expert, or just someone who is "good with numbers"—is strong. I never object to putting a well-qualified person in this spot, be it a finance, marketing, philosophy, or nuclear physics person. However, one must always keep in mind that competitive intelligence is based on *human* intelligence. It is often soft, regularly based on early rumors, qualitative much more than quantitative, and, most important, geared at identifying early market signals and fighting the onset of *strategic* blindspots, not financial blindspots. When financial impact analysis accompanies intelligence reports of competitive moves and presentation of strategic alternatives, it adds credibility and depth to the intelligence process. When it becomes the *focus* of intelligence, it can easily rob it of most of its decoding early signals value.

> In summary, my view of the best DCL is simple. *He or she is Hillary Clinton with a cheaper haircut and no political agenda.* If you can't immediately think of one, what does it say about your organization's supply of talent?

China Breaking and the Office of the President

At last, it is time to present the spiritual foundation of the model. The infrastructure is there, championed and supported throughout by the Strategy Kitchen's inhabitants. The education process motivated many employees to join the drive to increase competitive learning. The information technology enables the Decoder to extend tentacles and gather tidbits from all over the company. He or she can now start compiling data into strategic puzzles; decipher early signals; provide situation updates, hypotheses, and alternatives; and guesstimates of trends and moves. In short, the process can deliver the vital deciphered signals from the competitive arena early enough to keep the company successful. And yet the most important step in the process has not been mentioned at all.

What is to be done with all this wonderful information?

This final step in implementing the process requires the most courageous, decisive act of management, and the most politically sensitive one. The question of how a company uses its competitive intelligence is, in my opinion, the most crucial question of all. I therefore devote the entire next chapter to it. If you read nothing but the next chapter, you might still create an immune system for your company that might save it from slow death.

Chapter Fourteen

China Breaking and the Office of the President

The final step in establishing a competitive intelligence process is to anchor it in the organization's structure. This is also the most difficult step, requiring top executives to make some risky decisions. Naturally, most top executives prefer not to rock the boat, and whenever possible go for solutions that face the least resistance. Unfortunately, in this case it will not work. My advice to decision makers: Either do it right or don't do it at all. At least with the latter the disappointment is smaller.

This chapter borrows from two institutional innovations, one American and one from Japan, to propose a new organizational structure that will help companies to keep the fighting spirit alive. The proposed structure for the competitive intelligence process defines both the character of the DCL and to whom he or she should report. The proposed solution may sound either too simple to affect long-term decline or too politically radical to be implemented. It is neither.

The first organizational innovation I would like to borrow is the concept of a China Breaker. As mentioned earlier in this book, Lou Gerstner, formerly of RJR and now IBM's CEO, is credited with inventing this term to describe "mavericks with unconventional ideas, who don't think linearly and who *challenge everything.*"[167] (emphasis added) Gerstner has been known to place china breakers throughout the organization to promote change.

I would like to adopt the china breaker concept as a way to define the *character* of the task of the Director of Competitive Learning. *I regard the Director of Competitive Learning, the chief competitive expert, the decoder of the early market signals, as a companywide, unofficial china breaker.*

Moreover, as will become clearer later in the chapter, this companywide, unofficial china breaker should be regarded by the top executive as his or her Vizier of ancient times,[168] the confidential adviser, the counselor, all rolled into one.

By encouraging the intelligence process to assume the role of a companywide, continuous purveyor of signals pointing at areas where china may need to be broken, the process is made to serve its true objectives: fostering competitive learning, exposing blindspots, informing the division's president and the CEO of opportunities to become more competitive and threats to the company's competitive position. *Without this broad managerial perspective on the role of competitive intelligence, the tendency for even the best intelligence processes is to degenerate into a "nice-to-know" operation where the intelligence product is served mainly to educate rather than to become a "must act" effort.* The intelligence product must actually transform the company in line with a changing competitive reality.

To better understand this perspective, let us look at instances of official china breaking and their effect on the organizations involved. Not surprisingly, official china breakers are often visionary executives.

Shining Like a Neon

Robert P. Marcell, the head of Chrysler's small-car team, is the father of its new small car, the Neon. If he had given up at any stage of the process, Neon would never have seen the light (sorry—could not resist!).

American companies had not been able to produce a small car profitably for decades. General Motors had turned to Toyota and Isuzu for small cars. Ford was selling the Escort at a loss and looking to Mazda for help. Lee Iacocca, Chrysler's CEO at the time, was no different. He was looking to Fiat and other potential partners for help in the small-car arena. But under his nose, with the backing of Robert Lutz, Chrysler's president, Marcell began planning the Neon, Chrysler's first entry into the subcompact market since 1987.

From the beginning, Marcell declared, "If we dare to be different, we could be the reason the U.S. auto industry survives."[169] He then borrowed freely from the competition: The team drove the Honda Civic and the Ford Escort, and then tore them apart to find out what costs they would have to beat. The team borrowed management techniques such as Quality Function Deployment from the Japanese. Because of the break with Chrysler's traditional culture, blue-collar workers got more responsibility in the Neon program than in any other program at Chrysler. Marcell enlisted the UAW union, bringing assembly workers to Detroit to help assemble the first production prototype and to suggest improvements in production methods at an early stage.

The team then actually talked to the final consumer—small-car buyers—to get a feel for what they expected from a small car.

Then Marcell broke more china: relationships with suppliers. He and his team, together with suppliers' teams, agreed on *fixed cost and performance targets*, "in stark contrast to the typical U.S. new-car program, where countless small changes inflate the price."[170]

In another break with Detroit's practices, Marcell accepted higher cost for his parts, as long as it lowered the overall cost of the car, such as a rear seat that was made more complex but simplified final assembly.

Finally, by the time the first models appear in the showroom, Marcell's team will have test-driven them 4.7 million miles. The china breaker made an unprecedented decision to allow production workers at the Belvidere (Illinois) plant to test-drive the car to get personal experience with the products they manufacture, identify weak spots, and make improvement suggestions. So far, workers logged 4,000 suggestions, many of which have been adopted.

None of Marcell's activities can be classified as corporate-sanctioned routines. Every time he broke with tradition, he was going outside the accepted doctrine of developing cars at Chrysler. What was especially amazing about Marcell is that he was an example of a china breaker who was outside the top corporate power structure.

A Baby IBM[171]

More often than not, it is easier for a *top* executive to break the china. One such executive was James Cannavino of IBM. In December of 1988 he was named president of the Entry System Division, which was responsible for the IBM PC. Cannavino, a maverick, had been waiting in the shade for a chance to change the IBM culture. As early as 1990, when PCs were still making a lot of money ($3 billion, to be exact), he realized the operation needed a shakeup. He did not stand a chance. IBM's top corporate executives, the symbol of blindspots, did not want to "tamper with success." If it ain't broke, don't fix it. What the hell are you doing breaking this china?

Cannavino took his top executives to Tokyo to plan for an overhaul. The plan called for bringing control of R&D under the division. IBM succumbed but kept a tight lead on most other decisions, including pricing. The division's performance continued to slide against much faster competitors. Cannavino pushed for complete autonomy, something IBM's top executives regarded as sacrilege. By 1992, with disaster looming, management relented. The PC Company was created, with full control of its manufacturing, marketing, research, advertising, and distribution. Cannavino chose another china breaker to head the new company—Robert Corrigan. Corrigan's first move? A radical change from IBM's functional structure to brand teams, with each team controlling its pricing, brand development, manufacturing, and marketing. By fall 1992, the liberated company had produced 89 new products in two months and priced them only 30 percent above mail order (instead of the traditional 88 percent). To complete the breaking of the china, Corrigan was said to be considering a move from PC Company's typical IBM-type headquarters in New York to a cheaper place, away from the parent company. A CEO of a small start-up dealing with PC Co. remarked: "These guys aren't like the old IBM."[172] Yet these were IBM's people! The secret was to give them the freedom to break the china.

Turning Around a Goliath[173]

When it comes to breaking china, no challenge is greater than AT&T's. Though size in itself is *never* a reason for lack of competitiveness, many years of complete dominance of an industry definitely are. When Robert Allen took over AT&T in 1988, his task of breaking china was more on a scale of breaking China.

As of 1993, the signs indicated that he was succeeding. One of his most effective tools? Promoting china breakers throughout AT&T. One example: Jerre Stead.

An AT&T executive who does not shut his office door? Had the lock removed? Asks his employees to call him "coach"? Ridiculous. Yet Stead, the new head of AT&T's NCR business, is the new type of executive AT&T's CEO Allen promotes.

Listen to what this new type has to say:

I say if you're in a meeting, any meeting, for 15 minutes, and we're not talking about customers or competitors, raise your hand and ask why. If it goes on for half an hour, leave! Leave the meeting![174]

Anyone familiar with the old AT&T recognizes the revolution that enabled this quote.

Allen himself is a china breaker. He created a new Kitchen to run AT&T's day-to-day operations, replacing the traditional corporate president. He recruited executives from the outside, such as Jerre Stead (an unheard-of act at AT&T), and aggressively promoted openness. Just his way of fighting blindspots: "One of our challenges is to be sure that our network does not become the mainframe business of the future . . . IBM simply did not recognize the fragility of the market. We can't be comforted by the fact that our network is strong."[175]

These are the words of someone committed to removing blinders. As additional ammunition, Allen appointed another outsider, Richard Bodman, a former merchant banker and a Comsat executive, as his top strategist. Whatever else Bodman was, he did not have the blinders affecting the old AT&T strategy makers. Bodman's philosophy seems to place him in a china breaker's hall of fame: "The worst peril," he says, "is to think about things only one way."[176]

It is worthwhile noting that china breaker leaders appoint china breaker advisers. One may suspect the disease is contagious.

The Office of the President

The second organizational innovation I intend to borrow for the sake of the intelligence process is straight from Japan. To understand it, one needs to understand the organizational structure of a typical Japanese firm and the various titles used in Japan.[177]

The highest titles in a Japanese corporation are chairman, vice chairman, and president. The chairman is often a symbolic position that does not necessarily parallel the western CEO. It is given to a semiretired president, or as an honorary. The head of the organization is often the president. His second-in-command is a vice president. Then there are managing directors and senior managing directors that might or might not correspond to executive vice presidents in the United States.

> **❝The worst peril is to think about things only one way.❞**

In terms of decision making processes, there is the traditional board of directors, but also a supplemental decision forum called jomukai, which translates into "meeting of the managing directors." This meeting is chaired by the president and takes place once every week or two to discuss policy issues. Sometimes there is also an Executive Committee consisting of the chairman, president, vice president, and senior managing directors. This forum handles higher-level corporate policy issues than the jomukai and meets less frequently.

Within this power structure is the office of the president.

The office of the president is a unique institution found in many Japanese corporations. In most cases, the office of the president handles the so-called general staff activities. *The head of the office of the president is the chief of staff and usually reports to the president and chairman and other board members, advising them on many important corporate strategic matters.* Often, the head of such an office is a member of the board.[178] (emphasis added)

According to the author of the paper quoted here, the head of the office of the president is a managing director (corresponding to an executive vice president?).

Wonderful, you think to yourself, but what does it have to do with us Western companies?

Everything. I contend throughout this book that most division heads (business unit presidents) in the United States (and Europe as well) suffer from a remarkably low level of strategic support, *yet they are the ones who are supposed to make the strategic choices.* For many division presidents, the office of the president means an executive secretary and a typist.

I would be the last one to put down the executive secretary. On several occasions, the person in this role was the most knowledgeable intelligence source in the organization when it came to *internal* affairs. I often owed a lot of my success with corporations to the insights I gained through their astute and intuitive and remarkably perceptive executive secretaries. But as far as the office of the president is concerned, Japanese corporations seem to know better: An executive secretary is not *strategic* support.

*Now, take the two separate organizational innovations, the china-breaker perspective of organizational change and the concept of a powerful office of the president, and put them together with the new competitive intelligence process to create this synergy: **The Director of Competitive Learning, the decoder of early signals whose chief assignment is to gather information that will enable management to fight the onset of blindspots, must be the top level's china breaker and must be located in a reorganized Office of the President.***

This is not an easy concept to spring on Western firms. For whatever reason, from cost-consciousness to a distorted image of "lean and mean," to a feeling of "we have enough information," top executives regard line staffing as wholesome and strategic staffing as wasteful overhead. Almost uniformly, they react favorably to a suggestion to strengthen the intelligence support for their subordinates. *Yet the effect of better intelligence at these levels is minuscule compared to the effect of bad intelligence at the top.* Is there a valid reason that presidents and their top lieutenants acquiesce to making extremely difficult decisions in a relative vacuum with hardly any strategic intelligence support? Motorola's CEO Galvin, returning from a stint on Nixon's Foreign Advisory Board, created a Strategy Office reporting to him that *included an intelligence function*. He knew what he was doing, even if Nixon didn't.

The Japanese concept of the Office of the President, which includes a close confidential adviser, is simply common sense. It is a familiar concept in other places as well. For example, one of the most powerful executives in the Western world makes use of a similar structure. He is the President of the United States.

The NEC

They must love acronyms that include an *N* and a *C* in Washington, D.C. Harry Truman created the NSC (National Security Council) to fight the Cold War, so Bill Clinton created NEC, the National Economic Council, to fight the Economic War. The NEC is a "policymaking body of cabinet-level economic advisers."[179] Its chairman is the president himself. It is run by a point man—Robert Rubin, a former chairman of Goldman Sachs. From this book's point of view, it is interesting that the NEC was created based on a key campaign promise: to reinvent the government (i.e., fight its blind-spots!). Even more interesting is the philosophy behind NEC's operating mode, as expressed by its deputy director: "The government is organized vertically, but the solutions to our problems—from the budget deficit to underinvestment in education, training, and technology—cut across agencies."[180] Replace agencies with departments (or divisions) and you have the classic strategic business problem that underlies the use of the cross-functional collection and expert's rings in this book's model of competitive intelligence. One needs to bring marketing, manufacturing, technology, financial, and other perspectives together to come up with *strategic* intelligence.

The NEC is Clinton's economic Kitchen, and Rubin is his decoder. In the NEC, Clinton shapes out his economic plans, just like division presidents do in their strategy kitchens. Rubin's role is very much in line with that of the Director of Competitive Learning in this book. For example, Rubin's Council must analyze proposals made by Hillary Clinton's health reform task force and provide the president with "a crucial economic *reality check*" before he takes them to Congress.[181]

The NEC, like a typical Strategy Kitchen, includes all high-level members of the president's team: Vice President Gore, Treasury Secretary Bentsen, Budget Director Panetta, Commerce Secretary Brown, Council of Economic Advisers Chairwoman Tyson, Secretary of Labor Reich, and others.

But it is the role Rubin plays that is crucial to the proposed corporate structure of the Office of the President. "Clinton was very conscientious about wanting an honest broker, not an advocate, managing the NEC," says a high Treasury official. As an honest broker, Rubin stays away from politics: "We are trying to analyze the issues, to understand them better."[182] Just like a DCL should help the divisional strategy kitchen *understand* the major players in the competitive arena, staying away from politics.

To become a point man for the president, one needs the president's ear. Rubin gets 15 minutes a day with Clinton, to "set the NEC agenda and offer counsel." Since he works for Clinton's Economic Kitchen as a whole, senior cabinet members do not see him as a rival. This is the perfect setting: Report to the president, work for the entire Strategy Kitchen. Ultimately, says an article, the NEC may become "the forum for developing domestic strategies to increase competitiveness."[183]

This is exactly what a Strategy Kitchen is supposed to do, with the DCL as its honest broker.

The Five Rings Model Completed

With the perspective of a DCL china-breaking function reporting to the top strategy maker, the model is completed. The main thrust of this book has been the need to systematically, continually, and effectively identify and decipher market signals early enough to fight the onset of blindspots that lead to competitive sclerosis ("complacency," "sluggishness," or other buzz-words), which leads to decline. To do it, this book sketched a grassroots, companywide network of eyes and ears ready to learn from the competitive environment, making learning a competitive weapon. In order to carry out this task with any hope for success, the process was placed under the umbrella of the Office of the President, with its head, the Director of Competitive Learning, reporting directly to the division's president (and in a corporate setting, to the CEO).

Whether or not Western companies would eventually adopt a role similar to Japan's powerful Chief of Staff, and whether the DCL evolves into that type of a role (which might be a natural extension of his or her duties) is left to be seen. Not every Japanese management structure or technique worked well in the West. Those that did, though, revolutionized the organizations that adopted them.

The competitive learning process six commandments

Thou shalt give thy DCL:

1. *Open* access to the president (CEO for corporate-level intelligence)

2. *Regular* access to the president (CEO)

3. Physical proximity to the president (CEO)

4. Physical presence in every high-level discussion involving competit*ive* issues

5. Physical presence in every high-level discussion involving competi*tor* issues

6. Ability to set or affect the agenda for periodic or ad hoc meetings of the Strategy Kitchen pertaining to issues of competitiveness, blindspots, and strategy.

And thou shalt have a fighting chance in this global pressure-cooker.

Strategic Planning, Strategy, and the Intelligence Process

The relationship between the intelligence process proposed here, the Director of Competitive Learning, and the process of *planning* can easily become a sore spot. It should be clear that what I am talking about is not just another twist on the old and controversial role of the strategic planner. Whether a company believes in a *function* of strategic planning, in managers doing their own planning, or in no orderly planning at all, competitive intelligence is still essential for the actual strategic debates and actions that take place at the top. *Unless the top management of the division, business unit, operating company, and/or corporation completely surrenders its role as direction setter for the company*, it needs competitive intelligence to tell it whether or not the company is still competitive and how to fight the signs of sclerosis.

Placing the intelligence process in a planning organization poses the same disadvantages as placing it in marketing or business development: One cannot ensure that top management reads the deciphered signals early on unless one reports to the president and serves the entire Strategy Kitchen equally well. For me, the planning vice president, *if* part of the Kitchen, is then just another *user* of intelligence. Even when the strategic planner role becomes that of a strategic adviser to the president or CEO, such as Bodman at AT&T, and the adviser is a trusted Vizier rather than a paper shuffler, the intelligence function should not report to that position. *Any* filter between intelligence (reality) and the decision maker (strategy) is a potential for disaster. Planning should be based on intelligence and not vice versa! Intelligence should always be a *disinterested, objective* party in the strategy formulation process.

The argument I am advancing is simple, if unfamiliar or even uncomfortable for many business managers: *The ultimate user of intelligence is always the person at the top of the pyramid.* It is counterproductive to place a filter between the flow of intelligence regarding the competitiveness of the business unit and the person ultimately responsible for that competitiveness. The president is the one who pays with his job if competitiveness declines. He is the one ultimately responsible for the strategy of the unit. While he surrounds himself with trusted lieutenants, from a marketing vice president to a finance director to a planning vice president, these are often *advocates* rather than "honest brokers"—and there is nothing wrong with this situation. Yet the president needs an objective view of reality *regardless* of the strategy adopted, the strategy implemented, or the strategy considered by him and his strategic planners.

66 Intelligence should never be confused with strategy. 99

An intelligence adviser is one of the closest advisers to top decision makers everywhere on the national level, from the President of the United States to the Prime Minister of Britain to the Sultan of Borneo to the clan leader in Somalia. There is a reason that decision makers at that level prefer to get intelligence reports directly rather than after the Defense, Foreign, or Commerce department reviews and approves them. *It is not a matter of trust at all.* After all, if a president does not trust his top executives, how can he trust their strategic advice? Rather it is a matter of natural *bias and access.* In every corporation, filters exist in the channels of human information that rise up through the marketing, operations, planning, and other departments. These are not merely political filters aimed at protecting turf; they are also access filters. Marketing personnel typically notice marketing intelligence. Manufacturing engineers visit manufacturing trade shows. Planners notice signals favorable to their recommended strategy. For the bits and pieces to be put together by an intelligence coordinator placed in a marketing or planning department, he or she will have to overcome departmental barriers and subtle, or not so subtle, bias from above. If these pieces are not put together, one does not get strategic competitive intelligence; one gets marketing intelligence or academic studies. Placing the DCL—the convergence point for the HUMINT—away from the chief decision maker's office defeats its very purpose.

Finally, a word of caution: *Intelligence should never be confused with strategy.* To keep the honest broker honest, plaster these words on every wall in his or her office:

It is up to the intelligence users—the president and the Strategy Kitchen—to formulate the strategy.

It is up to the DCL to provide a reality check.

CHAPTER FIFTEEN

Napoleon's Mistake

This chapter was written for the eyes of the division president and the corporate CEO. If you are not yet there, make a copy of these pages and slip them into the top man's or top woman's "must read on plane" basket. You might just save your company and, more important, your job.

The last chapter ended with a stern warning: Do not confuse intelligence with strategy. The message is clear: Decision makers make decisions, competitive intelligence provides deciphered market picture. But this distinction makes two implicit assumptions:

1. Top management makes decisions, and
2. Top managers are interested in receiving competitive intelligence against which to check their decisions.

Which assumption is incorrect in your company?

The effectiveness of the competitive intelligence process hinges on the use of its output. This is why I insist on placing the process squarely in the middle of an Office of the President, and always at the operating company/division level. However, if the top executive avoids making decisions, or does not want to be confused with facts, the intelligence process in your company will go the way quality circles went in most American firms.

The Napoleons

On Thursday, May 6, 1993, Jack Smith, the new president of General Motors, nominated Robert Purcell, 40, to the *new* post of chief of corporate strategy development. This was a remarkable event. First, GM never had such a post, and Roger Smith would never have thought it was needed. GM's strategy was fine; the consumer was lousy.

Second, Purcell is very young, by any corporate standard, to be named chief strategist and one of the GM president's inner circle. Young blood at the top was never a strong preference of GM's old hands. You had to learn the corporate ropes to get into the exclusive club. In other words, you had to become as blind as everyone else.

Jack Smith's act was indeed revolutionary. The question is, will he listen to his adviser? This is a strange question. Of course he will. Otherwise, why nominate one? But consider the case of Napoleon.

Napoleon was a genius strategist—at least in the short run. But he had one bad quality that eventually did him in: He did not like to listen to his intelligence advisers. He believed in formulating his strategies alone. What was worse, though, in terms of the eventual *reality* of his plans, was that he believed only in his *personally* collected intelligence.

In the battle for Acre, an important port city in Israel, Napoleon suffered his first military defeat. In preparing his attack on the city, he sent for intelligence estimates of the strength of the fortification. The intelligence reports failed to reach him in time for his self-imposed morning deadline for the attack on March 28, 1799. Instead of waiting for the competitive experts to furnish facts and analysis, Napoleon relied on his own estimates, attacked, and was beaten back.

You would think he would have learned his lesson. He did not. His fatal march on Russia was carried out against the advice of his intelligence officers who warned him of the harsh climate and difficult-to-defend supply lines. This attack led to his eventual downfall.

It is not that Napoleon did not have an appreciation for intelligence. On the contrary: He had too much appreciation. He cultivated the famous "Black Bureau," the intelligence arm founded by the Dominican priest, Father Joseph, for Cardinal Richelieu. He had another intelligence arm in his own military headquarters, headed by a colonel. He just didn't listen nor trust the professionally collected, patiently analyzed intelligence. He trusted only his *own* intelligence collection and operated a personal network, often without coordination with the professional bodies. *Many top executives make exactly the same mistake.* Most will not end up deported to a small island, but then early retirement on the golf course can be boring, too.

Competitive intelligence that is not used is worthless. Competitive intelligence that is good only for the *lower* echelons has insignificant effect in the long run.

A division president or a CEO who, as a rule, prefers to rely on personal sources rather than on a companywide network providing him or her with facts and analyses would tend not to understand or appreciate the crucial benefit that can be derived from a professional, focused, systematic deciphering of early signals.

The issue of use depends heavily on who is the decision maker, how open-minded he is in fighting his own blindspots, and what type of relationship he is going to develop with his chief intelligence adviser. This personal aspect of intelligence can explain why some of the more traditional pharmaceutical firms, facing growing competitive pressures, *cut* the budgets and personnel of their existing intelligence operations, while Dick Jenrette, the miracle maker who pulled Equitable out of a sure demise, bolstered its intelligence activities despite a sweeping cost-cutting drive. At these pharmaceutical giants, sheltered from tough competitive pressures for many years, the operating presidents never felt the need to rely on competitive intelligence to support their judgment calls. The typical attitude had been that competitive intelligence was good mainly for the *middle* managers and salespeople. Little wonder that the people at the top hardly ever felt the benefits or were able to lean on the intelligence adviser for help. So as now in 1993 times become tough, it makes sense to cut the "overhead." *The fact that these managers at the top are going to need all the competitive intelligence and learning help they can get in the coming, very tough, years is a moot point at this time. Just watch what is happening with Merck.*

It is interesting to compare the behavior of these managers in the pharmaceutical industry with Japanese managers. An expert on Japanese business recently reported her research showing that top managers in Japanese companies rely mainly on information and research and much less on intuition. They use internal reporting as the prime source of knowledge and do not attempt to bypass the routine collection and analysis carried out in the organization by turning to their own personal network.[184] Several pharmaceutical top executives need to take these findings to heart before they find themselves selling generic drugs door-to-door to keep their country club membership.

Snow White's Stepmother and the Mirror

To better understand the interplay between the leader and the intelligence adviser, and why some division heads or CEOs will never use competitive intelligence properly (or at all), I will borrow from the personal experience of some very successful intelligence advisers. Despite my considerable effort to distance this book and the competitive learning process from the world of espionage and military intelligence, the interplay between reality and decisions is the same interplay, regardless of the methods used to obtain information or the goals pursued. Therefore, I like to make use of a little-known (outside Israel) book of collected essays, *Intelligence and National Security*, edited by Lt. Col. (Res.) Zvi Offer and Maj. Avi Kober, and published by Maarachot (1987), the official Israeli Defense Ministry publishing arm. I took some liberties in translating the text from Hebrew to English, but did not make any significant departures from the original text.

❝Several pharmaceutical top executives need to take these findings to heart before they find themselves selling generic drugs door-to-door to keep their country club membership.❞

My choice of the Israeli experience was not coincidental. While the United States has never faced an actual danger of annihilation, and could put a lower or higher priority on intelligence depending on the times and presidents involved, Israel always depended on intelligence for its sheer survival. The Israeli experience of decision makers and their intelligence advisers is, therefore, more pertinent to the business world: Corporations today are fighting for survival.

The first insight is the issue of *intelligence needs*. What is the most common complaint of competitive intelligence professionals in the business world? They do not know what top management needs in terms of competitive input. The most common reason intelligence budgets are cut and personnel dispersed and the "process" is considered a flop is that division heads do not get any meaningful benefit from it. *A very significant reason is that the vast majority of these functions in Western corporations are several steps removed from top management.* Mary in room 238A on the left does not typically have breakfast with the president. That would *never* be remedied by periodic questionnaires or interviews in which intelligence experts ask top management to share its concerns. Strategic concerns are dynamic. Strategic questions emerge on the plane, in meetings, at night. (John Sculley, for example, never actually sleeps.) No one waits for the intelligence manager to show up two months later with a questionnaire. The structural change proposed in this book, in which the DCL is placed *at the center* of strategic discussions, is a way to solve these problems. You probably do not believe me. OK, listen to the voice of experience.

In his essay, "The Relationship Between the Intelligence Function and Decision Makers," Yehoshafat Harechavi, former head of Israeli military intelligence and a respectable professor of International Relations, says the primary role of the intelligence function is that of providing *answers*. It is the responsibility of *decision makers* (in his case, it was the prime minister) to present the intelligence functions with questions, he says, and *if they do not ask, they should not expect the intelligence support to materialize automatically.* This support should enter the decision process twice: the first time to provide situational assessments to serve as a basis for strategy, and the second time, *after* the decision/strategy has been formulated, to estimate the response of the other side and the potential for the strategy to achieve its own objectives.

This view of top management *actively directing* the intelligence process is shared by another former head of Israeli military intelligence, Shlomo Gazit. He observes:

> The decision maker must understand that he is *responsible* for directing the activities of the intelligence system. The intelligence system can not operate in a vacuum; *it must be told* what to look for, what interests the decision maker and what he needs.[185] (emphasis added) . . . It is very important that the intelligence professional participates in all meetings leading to a decision . . . No discussion at the governmental level on the subject [of national security] should be carried out without a representative from the intelligence function.[186]

Compare this description to the typical corporate experience: "Why don't we ask Bob to join us for the meeting?" "Where is he located?" "Isn't he in room 238A?" "No, accounting is there now." "Then where is he?" "Somebody saw him in Building D last week." "What? They moved competitive intelligence again?" "Oh, so that's what he is. I always thought he was logistics." Do you see a difference?

According to Gazit, the representative of the intelligence function contributes to the decision process in two ways: Decision meetings should *open* with an intelligence presentation of the situation vis-á-vis the project/decision, and the intelligence function's representative should provide answers to questions arising during the discussion.

Keep these views in mind. Together with my own experience with corporations, the experts' observations will serve as a foundation for the following discussion of the modus operandi of the competitive intelligence process. The two modes were mentioned briefly earlier, and were treated as equally important. No longer.

The two ways to run the intelligence process are:

1. "Free flow"
2. The magnifying glass approach

Both are important for different reasons. However, one is critical.

The Eyes That Never Sleep

My original 1988 conception of the collection ring was based on the conviction that companies can derive great benefits from the organization and channeling of all the bits and pieces of competitive information floating in the organization into one central location. Indeed, this aspect of the competitive intelligence process proved more successful than I could ever have imagined. The essence of this collection has always been a relatively undirected *upward* flow, from the field and the "trenches" to the president and the Strategy Kitchen (naturally, with appropriate *downward feedback* flow). In Figure 15-1, this spontaneous upward flow is represented on the righthand side.

Figure 15-1
The CI Process Modus Operandi

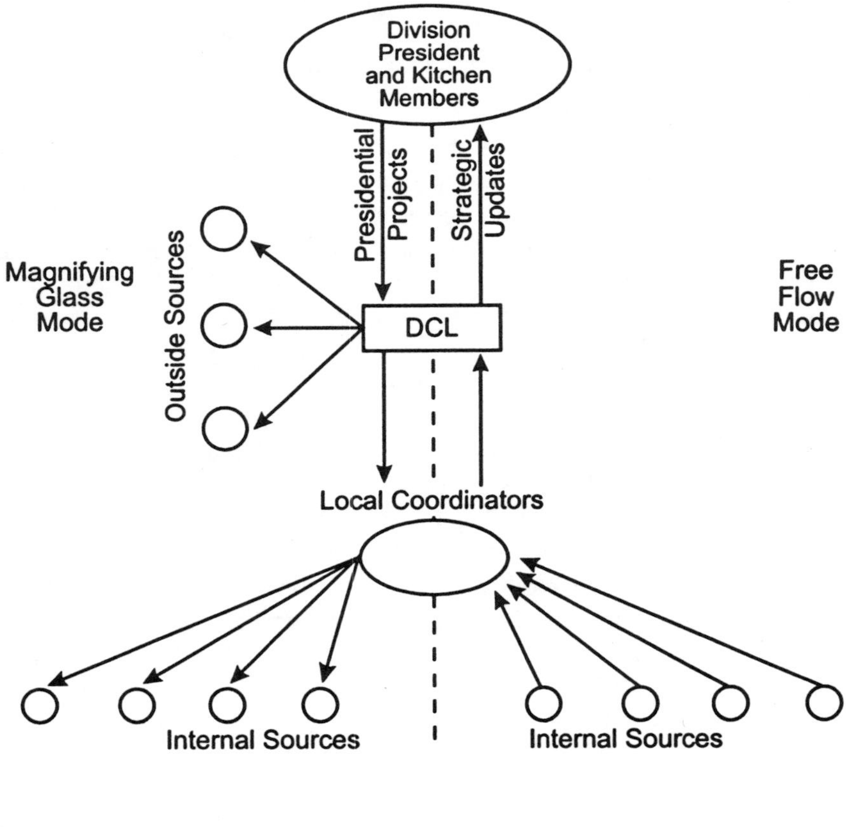

The upward flow should be tuned to shifting company concerns, though in practice this is rather difficult to accomplish with the wide ring of collectors participating in this effort. It requires the communication of changing strategic concerns at the top to the *entire* collection network at sales meetings, annual communication meetings, departmental meetings, and plant gatherings. At the same time, top management does not want to intervene in the upward flow to the extent that such direction will prevent the flow of data deemed important by the collector. Too much direction of the spontaneous daily collection can defeat the purpose of identifying early signals from the competitive arena to fight the onset of blindspots. It is also counterproductive to the empowerment given to all employees to decide what is and is not important to the company. Therefore, the only *specific* direction should come in the form of training: training for asking questions, going actively after information, listening to sources, recognizing competitive sources, and so on. The emphasis should focus on tapping human sources: vendors, service people, customers, competitors, relatives, friends, friends of friends. The free flow collection should never cease.

The importance of the free flow notwithstanding, over the years I have concluded that this free flow of intelligence might not be sufficient to support top management in rigorously competitive environments. Another, parallel process, driven by demand, must take place.

The Magnifying Glass

The left side of the figure shows the downward flow to the intelligence process. This is the magnifying glass—the other modus operandi of the intelligence process. This is where one finds the true *focus power* of the intelligence process. This power should be released to the service of the executive who does the battle: the division's president. To unleash the power, the routine direction of the intelligence effort must come in the form of *presidential projects*.

Presidential projects are those requested by the division's president (or the CEO on the corporate level) and the few selected aides in his or her Strategy Kitchen. They can be as small as a quick competitor profile, a personal profile of an executive with whom the president is about to meet, a delicate mission into an acquisition target, or negotiation that the president would like to initiate with his trusted expert intelligence adviser as the lead. Or, they can be large projects, such as strategic compilation and analysis of a very detailed and accurate competitor's financial performance, situation analysis of competitive moves in the marketplace, competitive process-benchmarking (as compared with competitive performance-benchmarking), supplier analysis, or foreign intelligence (for a global company). Most units' presidents understand the difference between tactical concerns—such as a competitor's promotional move, price policy, or new product introduction—for which one should call the vice president of sales or vice president of marketing and request immediate information (or data), and competitive intelligence projects that carry far higher significance to the future of the firm.

The competitive intelligence process should be activated and harvested to answer questions from the president of the division (or SBU or operating company), and, by proxy, the members of his Strategy Kitchen. This is why the Director of Competitive Learning must report directly to the president, sit next to his office (even if it means a cubicle!), be present in all his meetings with the Strategy Kitchen, and have at least 15 minutes per day with him. These conditions are not required for the sake of the competitive intelligence process, or the prestige of its chief; they are required for the sake of the president!

The Demand/Supply Balance

The intelligence activities directed by the president and his or her Strategy Kitchen should not be confused with project-based intelligence programs recommended by some experts. In this latter approach, the entire intelligence activity is organized around various ad hoc, task force-type projects that may be initiated by any manager in the company. *That is not the magnifying glass approach.* The magnifying glass flow, furthermore, is not a substitute for the free flow of deciphered early signals from the competitive environment. My experience shows that companies need and desire both. However, sometimes, a choice must be made as to which takes precedence over time and resources. Most of us are familiar with the term *demand and supply.* When it comes to running the intelligence process, one must at times choose between demand-driven or supply-driven. The free upward flow of competitive information coming through the individual efforts of an all-encompassing ring of employees/collectors is a *supply*-driven process. Whatever the human ring can pick up through daily interaction with the environment (big fish, small fish, blue fish, or all fish, as Dr. Suess would say) is eventually supplied to the top.

When the intelligence process executes presidential projects, it is demand-driven. By designing the whole process so that the rings of sources can be tapped quickly and efficiently to answer the president's competitive questions, the process is geared to provide the president (and his very close aides) with a magnifying glass focused on outside developments. A demand-driven process may give the president more than he wants—i.e., expose blindspots—but never *less*. In contrast, and this is political reality, a supply-driven process might take a long time to hit the bull's-eye—sometimes too long for impatient top executives. The combination of both flows is therefore the optimal mix, with priority given to the president's initiated projects.

Presidents who understand the tremendous benefit they can derive from the deployment, at will, of a close, trusted, expert handler of a large human network of competitive information will use the process the way General Harechavi described it above.

This is why any compromise as to *where* in the organization the DCL should be placed is a wasteful effort. Presidents who let the DCL report to anyone else—a planning function, for example—should not be surprised if they get little benefit from the intelligence expertise. Even if the decoding is not subject to political or other filtering, it is impossible for the DCL to know what the president needs in real time, if he or she is hidden two or three levels below. Unless the president calls the DCL regularly into his office, drops a note on his desk, gets him on the car phone, leaves a message on his voice-message center, and brings him into official *and* unofficial meetings with the Strategy Kitchen, the benefit to the president, *and therefore to the entire company*, will be rather haphazard. *Intelligence experts in a planning department do not get close enough to the president.* It is simply not the correct protocol.

Work on demand is straightforward. As the DCL is called in, he or she activates two rings simultaneously: outside sources and coordinators. The coordinators send the word to the best collectors (internal sources) in their respective areas, explaining what is needed and why. For small projects that require a quick turnaround time, either competitive files or a few selected sources or coordinators can be used. The magnifying glass must be portable.

Top Executives As Their Own Intelligence Experts

But what about those executives who are especially good at collecting their own competitive information? Do they need an *additional* function just to keep them abreast of competitive developments? Don't they have sufficient knowledge of what is actually happening out there?

No. Sorry, they don't have sufficient knowledge of what is actually happening out there, although invariably they think they do. The view of intelligence as providing expertise for top decision makers to support their decisions is shared by almost all researchers and practitioners in the field of national security. The interface of the two groups—policymakers and intelligence professionals—is described as *asymmetric*: the "meeting of expertise without authority and authority without expertise."[187] This seems to be an apt description of the state of large parent companies, where the CEO and the board of directors are in control of multiple business units. However, even at the division level, the concept of the expert ring in this book is consistent with the view that the *person at the top of the business unit (division) can never know as much as the collective expertise of a well-run network.*

This is especially true when it comes to identifying and deciphering large amounts of weak signals pertaining to early developments. Most executives are too busy, too insulated, and too involved in their own strategic concepts to identify early signals regarding change. They receive their information when the signals are strong enough and late enough to have been identified by security analysts or newspaper reporters. No competitive advantage can result from identifying loud signals. My own experience is that a competitive intelligence session that brings together a DCL, his or her coordinators, and competitive experts from various ranks and departments in the company to thrash out a particular set of competitive questions produces more knowledge and better analysis in two hours than any top-level meeting ever could in a month of disjointed deliberations. If you haven't seen this unleashing of tremendous competitive knowledge and expertise hidden in the various corners of the organization, you may never appreciate its full effect on the competitiveness of a company.

Finally, it is interesting to compare the intelligence professionals' view of the role of intelligence support for people at the top with that of the decision makers themselves. Haim Barlev, former chief of staff of the Israeli Defense Force and a cabinet member in several Israeli governments, suggests that the decision maker should get not only estimates from the intelligence function, but all the important facts/data that led to the development of the estimates. The intelligence function's role is to present the facts and to suggest several possible scenarios. The role of the decision maker is to estimate which of the possible scenarios is more likely and make a decision.[188]

> 66 The person at the top of the business unit (division) can never know as much as the collective expertise of a well-run network. 99

In another essay, Gen. Peled, a field commander and a user of intelligence, adds that the continuous exchange between the decision maker and the intelligence professional regarding the correct intelligence estimate of the situation is an important factor in the close relationship between the two functions.[189] It is indeed a far cry from the business model, where the battle is more for survival of the intelligence function than for the accurate assessment of the situation. In a world of uncertainty, the give and take between the intelligence function and the decision maker is an *enriching* exercise that creates a better understanding of what strategy to adopt, and what effect strategic moves might actually have. Corporate leaders who make decisions without a continuous and intimate support from an intelligence expert are being deprived of an important source of uncertainty reduction.

Serving Top Management: Can I Help You, Sir?

A DCL in the service of an operating division's president must adjust his products and services to the needs of this unique client or quickly lose his place. Several rules of thumb might help the intelligence adviser *and* his boss to unleash the power.

The Time Factor

Top managers have no time. Long papers and detailed studies will not be read. *It is that simple*—and it is unchangeable. Short notes, one-page memos, or verbal debriefings will have an impact. That does not mean serious analyses are worthless; it means that they will never be fully communicated. But their bottom-line essence should be. To the DCLs, for whom, like most of us, *all* insights are indispensable, my advice is: Learn to dispense. Don't fall in love with your own analysis; think of what the customer really needs to know to *do* something about the situation.

The details behind the short note must be ready for the question-and-answer period, if one takes place. Also, some top executives (definitely not the majority) like to see the data later on to make their own judgments.

Often, when top managers need answers, they need them fast. The ability to quickly tap sources inside and outside the company is a real asset.

Strategic Advice? No Thanks

Intelligence advisers who are tempted to give strategic advice should remember the following: The reason so many large American corporations have fallen from grace over the past two decades was not lack of strategic advice. Strategic advice was available, and supplied, in large quantities by the prestigious consulting firms (for hefty sums but few results).

Top management must chart strategy. To chart strategy, top executives need to listen to the low whispers from competitors, customers, consumers, suppliers, and other market forces—and, most important, their own *internal* experts. Top management can do that effectively through the intelligence process. Thus, *the DCL paints the pictures, but does not advise which scene is nicer!*

Should the DCL offer strategic *alternatives?* If he can think of some, sure. The more important aspect of his or her job, though, is to bring to the attention of the president deciphered early signals that point to the need to do *something.* It is up to the chief and his Strategy Kitchen to determine the creative and brilliant action to take.

The necessity to stay away from becoming another strategic adviser who takes sides and stakes his reputation on the success of one strategy should not be interpreted as anti-action. On the contrary. The only way to measure the DCL's effectiveness is to tally action—the *president's action.*

The Search for "Satisfaction"

Several intelligence functions in large American companies have developed a whole array of market research tools to measure the unmeasurable: their benefits to the company. Since the benefit of the intelligence product cannot be measured *directly* (what is the value of knowledge?), they contrived to mail a customer-satisfaction survey to main users on a periodic basis.

If the function serves many users on all levels of the organization, this might be the only way to measure its value. However, I do not regard such a function as useful, or its product as true competitive intelligence. Being part of the Office of the President means that satisfaction questionnaires are out. Instead, there is a much more powerful performance measure: *What has been done with the intelligence?* It is up to the president, the CEO, and their Strategy Kitchens to take action. It is up to the DCL to provide the impetus for action. The measure of benefits should follow directly from this simple philosophical distinction.

No Questions Asked

In serving the president or the CEO and his or her Strategy Kitchen, a delicate balance must be struck between working directly for the president, but still helping the other members of the Kitchen.

Without the active support of the other top executives in the division (or corporation), an intelligence adviser may find his collection efforts severely hampered by turf issues and his credibility brought into question. Most top executives intuitively support the new kid on the block, since the benefits are so obvious. But they need to know that they, and their organizations, can benefit from it too without jeopardizing their standing in the Strategy Kitchen.

If a Kitchen member calls on the DCL to answer a competitive question the DCL should always oblige. He or she should also be aware that sometimes the executive may not want the president to know the question asked of the DCL. The DCL should *never* leak this information. Trust must be established at all costs for the good of the company. The cost of betraying the trust will exceed its temporary benefit several times over.

Let me expand on this point. The intelligence process might not identify truly important early signals for months or years. But when it does, the entire future of the company may be changed. I am talking survival in a changing market, not a quick saving of a few million dollars. When markets change and executives do not, the consequences are not temporary lower revenues but a disastrous, sometimes irreversible, decline. One hundred and fifty thousand IBMers and 100,000 AT&Ters and who knows how many auto industry workers can testify to that. *Before tinkering with the effectiveness of the process that is the only systematic mechanism that can identify weak signals early enough to make a difference, a unit's president should think twice, and maybe even three times. It is better to let the decoder move freely and confidentially among the top ranks than to risk the top ranks moving against the company's only immune system.*

- ## Chapter Sixteen

Is It Good for Our Country? And What About Ethics?

This will be a very short chapter. The main issues mentioned in the heading have been addressed elsewhere in the book. However, since the topic of ethics is sensitive, and some critics may complain about its "casual" treatment in a book on competitive intelligence, let me devote a whole chapter to it.

This book recommends, based on experience, that every corporation should adopt a well-organized, well-deployed, well-supported intelligence process as its best defense against competitive decline. Yet I can hear the purists: This might be bad advice. What about antitrust? What about ethical questions?

Yes, what about them? Let me start with antitrust. As an economist by training, I know the flimsy assumptions underlying the models supporting antitrust legislation. Neoclassical models of an imaginary "perfectly competitive" market combined with a hypothetical state of equilibrium brought the United States to adopt a harmful, naive, and often silly policy against business cooperation. A mythical consumer "surplus," long criticized as an abstract geometrical representation of reality, substituted for common sense when the Chicago-trained, government-paid economic advisers won political support for their ideas. Antitrust, as practiced by the American government, is really anti-sense—and even if it was a rational policy, it has nothing to do with competitive intelligence. Competitive intelligence activities are not collusion with competitors on prices. By deploying a serious competitive intelligence process, no one intends to *restrict* competition—only to win it; and only a few inexperienced DCLs will try to get any information by directly contacting competitors. These managers will find out quickly that they can get much more by going the indirect route.

But even if competitive intelligence is not in conflict with antitrust regulations, is competitive intelligence good for the consumer, i.e., society at large, i.e., the country?

Yes, with a capital *Y*. Competitive awareness means corporations can minimize the waste of resources duplicating efforts in R&D, capital investment, and product marketing. Instead, with better knowledge of what the consumer actually wants and what others offer or intend to offer to satisfy these needs, corporations can make competitively better offerings to their customers. Thus they can advance *real* consumer welfare, not the static, meaningless consumer welfare imagined by academic economists. With better competitive intelligence, entrepreneurs, which in *real* life operate in continually *dis*-equilibrated markets, can move faster to exploit profit opportunities, creating wealth and employment.

Competitive intelligence is good for any country. The Japanese have known it since 1945.

OK, but what about the legal aspect of collecting competitive intelligence? And what about ethics?

When I first started to teach corporations to fight, I expected a lot of grief from their legal departments. To my surprise, I found corporate lawyers to be among the best sources of competitive advice, and among the brightest analysts of competitive information. Not only were they forthcoming with extremely useful competitive bits and pieces glimpsed from court cases, but also with gossip and rumors from government agencies, opinions and suggestions about consumers trends, and so forth. Naturally, they also offered help in safeguarding against breaches of ethics in the collection and distribution of intelligence, and help they meant. Not once have I encountered a legal counsel who advised against being more competitively aware!

Of course, this is *my* experience. But it is always a worthwhile effort to try to bring the lawyers into the networks. Not because the competitive intelligence process is legally sensitive—it should not be—but because lawyers are bright, inquisitive, and subject matter experts. Check out Tom Cruise in "The Firm," for example.

For those who still believe that competitive intelligence is a questionable activity, legally or ethically, all I can offer is, go back and actually *read* this book. Most of those beliefs are based on incorrect assumptions about the nature of competitive intelligence. Competitive data are obtained from open sources—published or human. The information is out there; it crosses employees desks every day. Trade secrets and protected information have little strategic value; and the important point is being alert to what is around you, not what is under the mattress. *In short, competitive intelligence is raising the goose, not stealing the golden egg.*

If a corporation disguises industrial espionage as competitive intelligence, we have a simple case of theft of information covered by lofty corporate-speak. Ever since a team of schlemiel thieves disguised themselves as plumbers and attempted to steal political information from a building in Washington D.C., most legal systems know how to deal with this issue.

Finally, what about counterintelligence? Shouldn't corporations be concerned with preventing information leaks that can be exploited by their competitors?

Yes, they should. Interestingly enough, by educating employees about the importance of *gathering* competitive data, the awareness of the necessity of preventing leaks of competitive data rises significantly. It is a by-product, a "halo" effect, or just common sense. Moreover, ask yourself the following question: Do you know what your company's top management is up to? Do you know what your colleagues across the hall are doing? Counterintelligence may be your company's last problem.

If your company doesn't act on this book's advice, summarized A to Z in the next and last chapter, counterintelligence may be *your* last problem as well. Just ask John Doe, *formerly* with Procter & Gamble (or IBM, or DuPont, or . . .).

CHAPTER SEVENTEEN

Just Do It
(Before It's Too Late)

Whether you went the distance or merely read the introduction and summary chapters, this final chapter will crystallize the more important lessons I have learned over the years working with corporations on three continents and summarize the significant points I make in this book. Naturally, it reflects my subjective opinion as to what the important points are. You are free to disagree and welcome to open my (blinded?) eyes.

So here it is, the A to Z of blindspots, sclerosis, and decline—and how to fight them.

A. In most industries, companies can be divided into those who dictate the pace and those who feel the game has remained the same and they basically know its rules. The latter may suffer from competitive sclerosis. In industry after industry, agile competitors prove that there is no such thing as "this is the way you do things in our industry." At times, it takes executives with *no* industry experience to show the industry players with a lot of industry experience that conventional wisdom is conventional, but not necessarily wisdom. Stanley Gault, of Goodyear, is one such outsider; Mike Walsh, of Tenneco, another.

B. One can talk up a storm about the need for corporations to develop competencies and capabilities and the need for leaders to push empowerment and decentralization. The bottom line is that if top management wears blinders, if the president or the CEO prefers not to learn from the competitive environment, the most competent company is doomed, and no extent of empowerment will change that. Examples abound.

What is needed is a voice inside the corporation persistent enough, and accessible enough, to bring about change *at the top*. As Ford's experience with trucks showed, a slowly built, powerful consensus of experts across a firm could sway even blinded top managers. Building a "grass-roots" movement of competitive awareness and transmitting its findings laterally and, eventually, upward is the principle underlying my model of the competitive intelligence process.

C. When a company on the decline decides at the eleventh hour to learn from the competitive environment, it can still achieve competitive excellence. Just ask post-Iacocca Chrysler.

D. The conditions under which strategic commitments are made are so perfect for information filtering, that one can only wonder why more executives did not end up like the leaders of IBM and Sears. To keep them constantly tuned to a changing reality, to prevent them from falling into the comfortable and human and natural state of wearing blinders, executives need all the help they can get. No doubt about it. Those who can't see even this much are beyond hope and are bound to become the theme of a future documentary.

E. The tool I propose to fight competitive sclerosis—the competitive intelligence process—is just one of many ways to combat blindspots. Its great advantage is that it is a *proactive* measure, a preventive medicine. Its purpose is to identify and decipher weak signals from the competitive arena early enough to make a difference. Its greatest disadvantage is that it requires that top executives use it continually, *in good times as well as bad*. Sam Walton knew how to use this tool. If top management is remiss in its commitment to the process, the only remedy might be the more radical after-the-fact change strategies used by change masters such as Walsh or Pfeiffer: leaders who are brought into the organization from outside, or from remote divisions, to fight the rot that has already spread.

F. Fighting a competitor whose leader wears strong blinders is the best thing that one can ask for. This leader is not going to wake up too soon: Does a horse *know* what's happening outside its blinders? However, beware; your company may be harboring as many blindspots as the competition. Identifying your own and your competitors' blindspots is one project you can only hope your company does not delay.

G. Newswire: "BusinessDoctors Inc. reports its introduction of Blindspotchecker 5.1. The software diagnosing business blindpots in corporate America will be available at a price of . . . ."

No such luck. All tests of blindspots are qualitative and require a lot of listening and a truly open-minded division head or CEO. Pretense at open-mindness won't do it. The tests themselves are less important than the perspective of "china breaking." As Thomas J. Watson, Sr. of IBM admitted, "It is harder to keep a business great than it is to build it."[190] If his successor, Akers, had had an unofficial china breaker by his side, and a systematic process of bringing in weak signals from the market, he may have fared much better.

H. As an academic, I could not have avoided developing *some* methodology to study and identify blindspots. The method presented in Chapter 8 is simple and subjective, and most probably biased. Its importance is not in its rigor or accuracy but in the fact that if we, a group of outsiders, were able to find so much blindness so quickly, imagine what a bright insider can do armed with this or some other diagnostic tool, and *top management blessing.*

I. Competitive intelligence is deciphered early signals from the market that tell top management if the organization is, or is not, still competitive. Competitive intelligence is *strategic:* a composition of the bits and pieces of data that only *together* can become a useful puzzle. That presents a paradox: The bits and pieces are available only to employees who interact daily with the outside world; however, the total picture must be available to top executives if the company is to survive. Top executives are too few and too busy to systematically identify all the relevant weak, ambiguous signals and then decipher them early enough to make a difference. A patient and powerful organizational learning process is needed to ensure that the relevant bits and pieces come together and are interpreted with patience, and that the puzzle has an effect on the decisions and discussions at the top of the organization. Competitiveness does not require espionage; Sears and American Express and Schwinn could have broken into Wal-Mart's and Visa's and Specialized Bicycle Components' vaults at midnight and stolen all the five-year plans they could have laid their hands on, and they still would have gained no insight into the changing realties of their markets. The information about change was all around—available from open sources—but the executives wore blinders.

J. Experiments with intelligence programs and units flourished in the United States in the 1980s but did not produce unequivocal enthusiasm. The reason was not lack of proven successes or lack of substantial investment. Instead, it has always been the lack of direct relevance to top executives that did them in. Foreign firms, especially trading firms from the Far East, have been more consistent and much more successful with their approach, which has always been short on formalities and long on culture. However, their network of thousands of loyal collectors and other organizational mechanisms cannot be easily duplicated in the West. Moreover, they themselves seem to recognize the benefit of a more *formalized* intelligence process.

K. CEOs or division presidents who can't let go of the need to be their own intelligence officers are better than those who don't care to hear any voice but their own. In the long run, however, the reliance on limited, personal sources at the top, rather than a focused and patient organizationwide learning process, is detrimental to the company's health. The Japanese, for example, rely on systematic intelligence, not on executives' intuition. Maybe that's why they eat sushi for lunch rather than a chock-full-of-cholesterol meat patty.

L. If you believe in Jack Welch's (of GE) definition of management as "Looking reality straight in the eye and then acting upon it with as much speed as you can,"[191] you realize that precious few of the intelligence operations of American firms can do what Welch's definition *commands* them to do: Make sure management looks reality straight in the eye. A radical change in approach is needed.

M. The new competitive intelligence process is a company's SWAT team: It is charged by management with fighting competitive blindness and exploring competitive developments throughout the market. Like a SWAT team, it does not write traffic tickets.

The intelligence process is politically neutral. It simply presents a picture of reality obtained primarily from networks of human sources who identify and decipher early signals. The emphasis on human networks and human intelligence (HUMINT) is one lesson from Japan: The speed of information passing through a human network, as well as its richness, is crucial to the competitiveness of Japanese firms. Data bases and publications are good for academics who can wait for the information to be obsolete.

N. The intelligence process is a companywide weapon: In the process of keeping top management constantly updated with strategic developments, employees at all levels and all organizations inside the company become more competitively aware. In some companies, where downward or lateral information sharing is minimal, this may be as important a benefit as the primary role of management's SWAT team. I call this side benefit *"information empowerment."*

O. At the intelligence-process' heart is one manager, one telephone, and a PC. The rest is nice.

P. The model for the process, which I term the Five Rings Model, is based on an infrastructure of human networks and a convergence point—the "center of analysis"—serving a top circle of influential decision makers. The process is modeled on a business unit. A corporate-level intelligence process must rely on business units' processes to be effective (efficiency in intelligence is much, much less crucial).

Q. Boards of directors whose corporations lag in collecting and analyzing competitive intelligence may want to consider appointing their own independent intelligence analyst, or double their liability insurance.

R. The fastest and most effective way to turn whole units toward the subject of competitive awareness, Red Team/Blue Team-type war games, are superb competitive tools. These are not the academic, computer-based simulation of decisions; these are the real thing. Get some help mediating them.

S. The most crucial issue in regard to the intelligence process is: What is *done* with the wonderful intelligence collected by all and provided to the few? The Director of Competitive Learning (DCL)—or, as I term this position, the Decoder—can provide the message; top executives provide the action. If they don't, they have only themselves to blame.

T. The intelligence process' best chance to radically affect the competitiveness of the company and fight blindspots depends on its being recognized for what it is: a formal, focused, professional, and systematic, ever-alert, china-breaking process aimed at the top. Its place is in the Office of the President, a concept borrowed from Japanese companies. This Japanese import does not require calisthenics in the morning or abolishing reserved parking for executives, but does require the company's leader, the SBU's president or the corporate CEO, to take seriously his *or her responsibility* to keep the organization attuned to the competitive environment.

U. Intelligence and planning are two related, but not equivalent, processes. Intelligence is neutral, planning is not. Intelligence is reality, planning is a structure imposed on reality. When strategic intelligence becomes the way to affirm current or planned strategy, it loses its relevance. In other words, the strategic planning function is just one more user of intelligence, not its owner. Companies that place their intelligence operations in a planning department rather than next to the

CEO/president will see benefits as unattainable as Niagara Falls is to a thirsty man in the Sahara.

V. Japanese managers rely on the orderly collection and analysis of competitive information carried out by all levels in their organization as a basis for strategy formation. The typical Western executive uses intuition, experience, and personal networks of sources as the basis for his or her strategic call. The difference is obvious in the field. In other words, Western executives who believe they are well plugged into their markets without a systematic process of updating are setting themselves up for blindspots. This statement is true regardless of how good the executive is in tapping his own personal network and how good his sources are. Napoleon proved that.

W. I am sometimes asked by top executives for examples of information that a process can provide that they cannot get themselves. I tell them: Let me gather a few experts from around the company in one room for two hours and see who knows more, you or the collective *them*. I even venture to select the experts at random by shooting darts at the organizational chart. By the time executives receive the market signals from their own highly placed sources, the signals are strong enough to be heard by the deaf. The trick for survival is early detection.

And this is just the beginning. What the inside experts learn from *one another* in the process of collectively identifying and deciphering early signals is amazing.

X. If top management is out of touch, it will not help that middle management or the salespeople are in touch. In other words, tactical (marketing?) intelligence is not a substitute for strategic intelligence. If the intelligence process is not an integral "shadow" accompanying the executives in their daily routine, it will never be able to keep top management in touch. However, the intelligence function down in Market Planning *can* keep middle management ahead of top management, and give the salespeople the best clips of competitive newsprint around, and publish quarterly newsletters. Welcome to IBM.

Y. What is the benefit of the competitive intelligence process? Can you measure it? No problem. Just show me how the intelligence was used at the top (not the middle and not the bottom) and the question becomes moot in an instant. Competitive intelligence that is used by the president and his or her Strategy Kitchen determines the fate of the company, no more and no less. And while the process of identifying and deciphering market signals continually benefits the entire organization in terms of empowerment, education, competitive awareness, and improvement in ongoing decisions, it can take a year or two, or three or four! until the process pays off in a big way. *It is enough that the process deciphers one significant early signal from the competitive arena, and influences one decision at the top related to that decoded message from the market, to save the company from "missing the moment" and ending up as a sorry example in a book such as this one.* Schwinn and the mountain bike is a perfect example.

Z.   Are you the president of an operating company? Do you have a competitive question you would like answered—e.g., how does the P&L of the competing division of a large parent company look, or how do other companies compensate their labor force with stocks, or what structural changes encourage more risk taking among managerial ranks, or what are the weaknesses in your engineering organization and philosophy compared to an innovative competitor's? Do not turn to the marketing vice president or the finance vice president or the Labor Relations Department and ask the executive in charge to follow up on this issue. The best you will get is what his or her ad hoc, almost "amateurish" intelligence activity can provide on short notice. The median response will be a filtered answer distorted by internal politics. The absolute worst you will get is what you want to hear. Do not turn to expensive outside consulting firms, either. The most they can do will not come close to what your own best people can. Turn to the professional: Call your blindspot-buster. Set the SWAT team to work. You need an intelligence adviser—and *your organization **depends** on you to get one.*

Conclusion

Put the following on a laminated plastic card and take it to the next companywide annual meeting:

Identifying and deciphering weak, ambiguous signals from the competitive arena early on can save a company from decline. A company that does not have a powerful process to do just that may find itself unprepared for a changing reality, and defenseless against the onset of Business Blindspots.

Endnotes

Chapter 1

1 "The New Computer Revolution." *Fortune,* June 14, 1993, p. 68.
2 Ibid.
3 *Business Week,* Jan. 20, 1992, p. 58.
4 *Fortune,* May 3, 1993, p. 40.
5 *Fortune,* Feb. 8, 1993, p. 122.
6 *Fortune,* May 3, 1993, p. 39.
7 *Fortune,* May 17, 1993, p. 83.
8 Facts and quotes are from "Companies That Service You Best," by Patricia Sellers. *Fortune,* May 31, 1993, pp. 73–88.
9 *Fortune,* May 31, 1993, p. 63.
10 Ross Perot, formerly a GM director, was known to pester GM executives whom he considered too insulated from reality. General Motors bought his share for this amount and pushed him out.
11 *Business Week,* May 31, 1993, p. 93.

Chapter 2

12 W. Weitzel and E. Jonsson. "Reversing the Downward Spiral: Lessons from W. T. Grant and Sears Roebuck." *Academy of Management Executive,* Vol. 5, No. 3, 1991, pp. 7–22.
13 *The Economist,* Sept. 28, 1991, p. 94.

Chapter 3

14 "Reinventing the Wheel." *The Economist,* Aug. 1, 1992, pp. 61–62.
15 *Fortune,* Sept. 21, 1992, p. 81.
16 Ibid.
17 This anecdote is from "The Decline and Fall of Westinghouse's Paul Lego," *Business Week,* March 8, 1993, pp. 68–70.
18 Michael Porter. *Cases in Competitive Strategy.* The Free Press, 1983, pp. 31–48.
19 Peter Nulty. "The Bounce is Back at Goodyear." *Fortune,* Sept. 7, 1992, pp. 70–72.
20 This anecdote is from "Compaq," *Business Week,* Nov. 2, 1992, pp 146–151.
21 *The Economist,* Oct. 10, 1992, p. 83.
22 *Business Week,* Dec. 16, 1991, p. 38, and Nov. 23, 1992, p. 96.
23 *Business Week,* Dec. 16, 1991, p. 41.
24 This anecdote is from "What Price Glory," *The Economist,* Aug. 24, 1991, pp. 57–58.
25 *USA Today,* Oct. 28, 1992, p. 2B.

26 *Business Week,* Dec. 16, 1991, p. 38.

27 *Business Week,* Nov. 23, 1992, p. 92.

28 *Business Week,* Nov. 23, 1992, p. 96.

29 Unless otherwise noted, facts and quotes are from "U.S. Cars Come Back," by Alex Taylor III. *Fortune,* Nov. 16, 1992, pp. 52–85.

30 It is also illuminating that eventually, when the spell of the blindspots was broken, GM's board elected John Smale as chairman. He came from Procter & Gamble, and his main strength was his reputation as an advocate of market research and listening to customers. See *The New York Times,* Oct. 27, 1992, p. D7.

31 *The Economist,* Aug. 10, 1991, p. 62.

32 *The Economist,* Aug. 10, 1991, p. 62.

33 This anecdote further supports the value of Personality Intelligence—predicting competitors' strategies by digging into their leaders' past. This topic will be discussed later in this book.

34 Ibid., p. 63.

35 Ibid.

36 Taylor III, "U.S. Cars . . . ," *Fortune,* Nov. 16, op. cit.

Chapter 4

37 This chapter is based on two articles: (1) B. Gilad, S. Kaish, and P. D. Loeb. "Cognitive Dissonance and Utility Maximization," *Journal of Economic Behavior and Organization,* Vol. 8, 1987, pp. 61–73; and (2) B. Gilad, S. Kaish, and P. D. Loeb, "A Theory of Surprise and Business Failure," *Journal of Behavioral Economics,* Vol. 14, Winter 1985, pp. 35–55.

38 See D. Kahneman, and A. Tversky, "Prospect Theory: An Analysis of Decision Under Risk." *Econometrica* 47, 1979, pp. 263–291, and D. Kahneman, P. Slovic, and A. Tversky, *Judgment Under Uncertainty: Heuristics and Biases.* Cambridge University Press, 1982.

39 Israel M. Kirzner. *Perception, Opportunity and Profit.* Chicago: University of Chicago Press, 1979. Kirzner, a nontraditional economist, explains the unique quality of entrepreneurs—their ability to see what other people, staring at the same facts, just don't see!

40 F. V. Fox and B. M. Straw. "The Trapped Administrator: Effects of Job Insecurity and Policy Resistance upon Commitment to a Course of Action." *Administrative Science Quarterly,* Vol. 24, 1979, pp. 449–471. As a rule I don't recommend this type of academic journal to anyone over the age of 18 or with a heart condition, but this particular article, despite its moronic title, is a good one.

41 Much of the research on which this section is based is reported in R. A. Wicklund and J. W. Brehm, *Perspective in Cognitive Dissonance.* Hillsdale, N.J.: Lawrence, Elbaum Associates, 1976.

42 *Business Week,* Sept. 13, 1982.

43 *Fortune,* Aug. 8, 1983.

44 See, for example, I. D. Dunhaim, "Influences on the Divestment Decisions of Large Diversified Firms." Ph.D. Diss., University of Pittsburgh, 1981.

45 R. M. Cyert and J. G. March. *A Behavioral Theory of the Firm.* Englewood Cliffs, N.J.: Prentice Hall, 1963.

Chapter 5

46 *The Economist,* Aug. 17, 1991, p. 65.

47 *Business Week,* Oct. 14, 1991, p. 62 D-E.

48 *Fortune,* Sept. 23, 1991, p. 50.

49 *Business Week,* Oct. 14, p. 62 D-E.

50 "Boxing Clever." *The Economist,* Nov. 2, 1991, p. 69–70.

51 "How Packard Bell Broke Out of the Pack." *Business Week,* Jan. 27, 1992, p. 45.

52 *Business Week,* Oct. 19, 1992, p. 52.

53 "The Age of Consolidation." *Business Week,* Oct. 14, 1991, pp. 44–45.

54 *The Economist,* Sept. 21, 1991, p. 100.

55 *Fortune,* Dec. 14, 1992, p. 81.

56 Ibid.

57 *Fortune,* Dec. 14, 1992, p. 110.

58 Ibid.

59 Ibid.

60 Quotes and facts in the next few paragraphs are from "Managing in the Midst of Chaos," by John Huey. *Fortune,* April 5, 1993, pp. 38–48.

61 *Fortune,* Dec. 14, 1992, p. 88.

62. Quotes and facts are from "Deconstructing the Computer Industry," *Business Week,* Nov. 23, 1992, pp. 90–100.

63 *Business Week,* Nov. 23, 1992, p. 96.

64 *Business Week,* Nov. 23, 1992, p. 75.

65 Quotes about Microsoft are from "Bill Gates's Next Challenge," by Alan Deutschman. *Fortune,* Dec. 28, 1992, P. 30–41.

66 *The Economist,* Aug. 7, 1982.

Chapter 6

67 Reverse engineering is the practice of taking apart competitors' products to learn as much as possible about them. Whirlpool, for example, rips apart any product that ranks higher than its own in a mail survey of 180,000 households (see *Fortune,* Jan. 11, 1993, p. 77). Quality Function Deployment is the practice of measuring competing products against consumers' ranking of desired attributes at the design stage of a new product.

68 The description of the battle at Gaugamela is based on A. Livesey, *Battle of the Great Commanders.* London: Michael Joseph, 1987, pp. 14–18.

69 *Business Week,* Aug. 10, 1992, p. 67.

70 The description of the battle at Cannae is based on R. E. Dupuy and T. N. Dupuy, *Encyclopedia of Military History*, Rev. Ed. Harper & Row, 1970.

71 *The Economist*, Sept. 14, 1991, pp. 79–80.

72 A. Livesey. *Battles . . .* , p. 24–25.

73 See *Fortune*, Sept. 21, 1992, and Nov. 30, 1992, pp. 82 and 98, respectively.

74 For IBM's attempts at shattering its blindspots, see *Business Week*, Dec. 16, 1991, pp. 36–39.

75 B. Quinn, et al. *The Strategy Process*. N.J.: Prentice Hall, 198 , pp. 750–778.

Chapter 7

76 *Forbes*, April 12, 1993, p. 47.

77 Ibid., p. 48.

78 *Fortune*, April 19, 1993, p. 64.

79 Our team at Rutgers did try to develop a quantitative index, knowing academic referees' fascination with numbers. The result is presented in B. Gilad, G. Gordon, and F. Sudit, "Competitive Intelligence and Strategic Group Decisions: A New Diagnostic Tool." *Group Decisions and Negotiations*, Vol. 1, 1992, pp. 5–25. In my judgment, the qualitative tests prescribed here are superior.

80 See *Business Week*, Dec. 2, 1991, p. 28.

81 Many of the examples in this section are dated around 1988. They were collected as part of the final assignment by my students in two Competitive Intelligence courses conducted at Rutgers and New York universities in 1988. The students did such a terrific job that I keep using their examples. My thanks to them.

82 The following facts and figures are from "Guess Who Lost," by Lisa M. Keefe. *Forbes*, Sept. 7, 1987.

83 *Forbes*, May 16, 1988, p. 40.

84 *Business Journal of New Jersey*, 1988 (exact date unknown), p. 16.

85 John Sculley. *Odyssey*. Harper & Row, 1987.

86 *Odyssey*, op. cit., p. 33.

87 The following is based on "King No More," by John H. Taylor. *Forbes*, April 18, 1988, pp. 37–38.

88 *ONline Access*, Sept./Oct. 1987, p. 25.

89 *Business Week*, May 2, 1986.

90 William M. McGrath, Jr. "Improving Competitor Intelligence's Value to Management." In John Prescott's (ed.) *Advances in Competitive Intelligence*. Vienna, Va.: Society of Competitor Intelligence Professionals, 1989, p. 177.

91 *Fortune*, April 18, 1993, p. 67.

92 "Stevens Cries Double-Cross." *Business Week*, May 2, 1988, pp. 35–36.

93 "Kraft, Minus Some Extra Baggage, Is Picking Up Speed." *Business Week*, March 9, 1987, pp. 74–75.

94 The following fairytale story is based on an article written by *Fortune* magazine's Carol Loomis for an Israeli newspaper, *Haaretz*.

Chapter 8

95 For an unnecessarily complicated but mathematically elegant exposition of the method, see B. Gilad, G. Gordon, and F. Sudit, "Competitive Intelligence and Strategic Group Decisions: A New Diagnostic Tool." *Group Decisions and Negotiations,* Vol. 1, 1992, pp. 5–25.

96 *Business Week,* April 26, 1993, p. 102.

97 Ibid.

98 Reprinted with permission from Pergamon Press Ltd., Headington Hill Hall, Oxford OX3 OBW, UK, "The Diagnosis and Treatment of Intelligence Gaps and Blindspots," to appear in *Long Range Planning,* Vol. 26, No. 6, Dec. 1993.

99 For example, see K. Davis, "Success of Chain of Command Oral Communication in a Manufacturing Management Group." *Academy of Management Journal,* Vol. 11, 1968, pp. 379–387, and K. Roberts and C. O'Reilly, "Measuring Organizational Communication," *Journal of Applied Psychology* 59, 1974, pp. 321–326.

Chapter 9

100 The Clinton saga is based on the excellent article "An Early Loss Cast Clinton as a Leader by Consensus," by Elizabeth Kolbert. *The New York Times,* Vol. CXLII, No. 49,103, Sept. 1992.

101 This insightful treatment of the subject appeared in "What the Competition Is Doing: Your Need to Know," by J. Wall. *Harvard Business Review,* Nov.–Dec. 1973, pp. 22–42. Since then, HBR has not published anything about the subject.

102 Based on "Our Competitive Advantage," by Zina Moukheiber. *Forbes,* April 12, 1993, pp. 59–61.

103 Ibid., p. 60.

104 Thomas A. Stewart. "Allied-Signal's Turnaround Blitz." *Fortune,* Nov. 30, 1992, pp. 72–76.

105 *Fortune,* Sept. 21, 1992, p. 81.

106 See his seminal article "From Competitive Advantage to Corporate Strategy," *Harvard Business Review,* May–June 1987, pp. 43–58.

107 B. Burrough and John Helyar. *Barbarians at the Gate.* Harper & Row, p. 301.

108 *Fortune,* Sept. 21, 1992, p. 77.

109 Ibid.

110 See Polaroid vs. Kodak in M. Porter's book, *Cases in Competitive Strategy.* The Free Press, 1983.

111 *Business Week,* Feb. 10, 1992, p. 40.

112 *The Economist,* Aug. 31, 1991, p. 62.

113 *Fortune,* Jan. 11, 1993, p. 77.

114 *Business Week,* Oct. 14, 1991, p. 62.

115 Ibid.

Chapter 10

116 "Keeping Tabs on Competitors." *The New York Times,* Oct. 28, 1985, p. D1.

117 "Competitor Intelligence: A Grapevine to Rivals' Secrets." *The Wall Street Journal,* April 17, 1989.

118 "Corporate Spies Snoop to Conquer." *Fortune,* Nov. 7, 1988.

119 Ibid., p. 69.

120 Ibid.

121 *Fortune,* Nov. 7, 1988, p. 76; *The New York Times,* Dec. 23, 1990.

122 "007 It's Not. But Intelligence is In." *The New York Times,* Dec. 23, 1990.

123 *The New York Times,* ibid.

124 "The New Race for Intelligence." *Fortune,* Nov. 2, 1992.

125 *Fortune,* Nov. 7, 1988, p. 76.

126 *The New York Times,* Oct. 28, 1985.

127 Anecdotes are taken from "'Competitor Intelligence': A Grapevine to Rivals' Secrets," *The Wall Street Journal,* April 17, 1989.

128 This section and its quotes are based on "Picking Japan's Research Brains," by Susan Moffat. *Fortune,* March 25, 1991, pp. 84–96.

129 Unless otherwise noted, this section including quotes is based on "The Realist," by Julie Pitta. *Forbes,* May 12, 1991, p. 116.

130 *The New York Times,* April 28, 1991, Sec. 3, p. 6.

131 *Forbes,* op. cit.

132 Sumantra Ghoshal. "Environmental Scanning: An Individual and Organizational Level Analysis." Ph.D Diss., MIT, 1985.

133 Perhaps one of the best accounts is the paper written by the "father" of modern-day business intelligence, Prof. Stevan Dedijer of Lund University in Sweden. The paper, "Development and Management by Intelligence: Japan," can be obtained by writing to the author at Lund University, Box 7080, S-220 07 Lund, Sweden. It contained an extensive bibliography of sources on the subject.

134 *Fortune,* Nov. 7, 1988, p. 68.

135 *Fortune,* Nov. 2, 1992.

136 Justin Martin and Michael Stedman. "Still a Distant Second." *Across the Board,* Nov. 1991, pp. 45–46.

137 *Forbes,* Nov. 12, 1990, p. 96.

138 *Across the Board,* p. 45.

139 *Forbes,* ibid.

140 Juro Nakagawa, "The Role of Japanese Trading Companies," a paper delivered at Alfred University, April 1988.

141 Juro Nakagawa, "Using Competitive Intelligence to Improve International Competitiveness," a talk delivered to SCIPAUST, Sydney, Australia, Feb. 1993.

142 *Fortune,* Nov. 7, 1988, p. 68.

143 *Forbes,* ibid.

144 *Across the Board,* p. 46.

145 *Across the Board,* ibid.

146 Patrice Duggan and Gale Emenstodt. "The New Face of Japanese Espionage." *Forbes,* Nov. 12, 1990, p. 96. The expert, Thomas Zengage, is a market researcher based in *Tokyo,* for a change.

147 For example, the author's first book, *The Business Intelligence System* (coauthored with Tamar Gilad, AMACOM, 1988) is about to be published in Japan.

148 From "Competitive Information as a Managerial Tool," an article in Hebrew by Shmuel Eyal from *Technologies—An Israeli Monthly for Advanced Technologies.* Eyal should know what he is talking about: He was Israeli Aircraft Industry's manager of business development at one of its largest divisions.

149 This anecdote is from *The Economist,* Dec. 8, 1990, p. 70.

Chapter 11

150 All the information about intelligence systems presented in this chapter is taken from public sources. Several surveys have been published in recent years about corporate intelligence programs, among them: H. Sutton's *Competitive Intelligence,* Conference Board Report # 913, 1988, and D. McGinty-Weston's *Best Practices in Competitive Analysis,* SRI Report # 80, 1991. In addition, some of the better firms make presentations and public speeches about their competitive analysis activities.

Since corporate attitudes toward the subject of competitive intelligence are notoriously unpredictable, the information might no longer be accurate. In fact, the companies discussed may have even dismantled the intelligence function, downgraded it, or transferred its duties to other "marketing"-type operations. This chapter provides you with a sketch of how companies tried to organize their activities rather than the most up-to-date state of affairs.

151 If you are a senior manager who hasn't yet read Michael Porter's seminal paper "From Competitive Advantage to Competitive Strategy" (*Harvard Business Review,* May –June 1987, pp. 43–59), this is the time to do it. If the sheer logic does not convince you, apparently you are still looking for the easy way to manage, popularized by such consulting firms as BCG.

152 D. Smith and J. Prescott. "Demystifying Competitive Analysis." *Planning Review,* Sept.–Oct. 1987, p. 13.

153 Information on the early days (to 1987) of the Motorola system was obtained from "Creating and Managing a Business Intelligence System," by J. Herring and T. Stone, a paper delivered at the International Conference of the Planning Forum, May 24, 1988.

154 Many professionals in the field of competitive intelligence make a strong case for the distinction between raw data and information, where the latter is data evaluated for relevance and reliability. For this book, this distinction is not critical. I believe a company has either strategic intelligence—blindspots-related information—or an undeciphered clutter.

155 I am referring, of course, to Philip Morris's surprising move, on what became known as Marlboro Friday, to cut its most profitable brand's price by 20 percent. For facts and figures, see *Fortune*, May 3, 1993, pp. 68–69.

156 Ibid., p. 69.

157 Carol Loomis. "Dinosaurs?" *Fortune*, May 3, 1993, pp. 36–42.

158 Herring and Stone, ibid.

159 This is not a criticism of other "intelligence gurus": I myself am guilty of popularizing business intelligence in similar ways in the 1980s.

160 *Fortune*, May 3, 1993, p. 39.

Chapter 12

161 See, for example, Carol Loomis's "Dinosaurs?" *Fortune*, May 3, 1993, pp. 36–42.

162 This account of the reengineering concept is taken from *Fortune's* book excerpt, *Reengineering the Corporation. Fortune*, May 3, 1993. pp. 94–96.

163 Ibid., p. 96.

164 I owe the term "So What experts" to Mr. John Hurdis.

Chapter 13

165 *Fortune*, May 17, 1993, p. 85.

166 *Fortune*, May 17, 1993, p. 56.

167 *Fortune*, April 19, 1993, p. 64.

168 The vizier, a "bearer of burden," was the minister of state in the Byzantine and Ottoman empires, the closest adviser to the sultan or emperor.

169 This and other quotes and facts are from "Chrysler's Neon," *Business Week*, May 3, 1993, pp. 117–126.

170 Ibid., p. 119.

171 The following is based on "The Freewheeling Youngster Named IBM," *Business Week*, May 3, 1993, pp 134–138.

172 Ibid., p. 134.

173 The following is based on "Could AT&T rule the world?" by David Kirkpatrick. *Fortune*, May 17, 1993, pp. 55–66.

174 Ibid., p. 55

175 Ibid., p. 56.

176 Ibid., p. 62.

177 The following discussion relies heavily on "A Guide to Japanese Business Practices" by Mayumi Otsubo, *Japanese Business*, Subhash Durlabhji and Norton Marks (eds.), State University of New York Press, 1993, pp. 221–238.

178 Ibid., p. 230.

179 This quote and the other in this section are taken from "Clinton's Point Man on the Economy," by Ann Reilly Dowd. *Fortune*, May 3, 1993, pp. 75–79.

180 Ibid., p. 75.

181 Ibid. Emphasis added.

182 Ibid., p. 79.

183 Ibid., p. 79.

Chapter 15

184 D. Grossman. "Why the Japanese Turtle Beats the Western Rabbit." *Status,* May 24, 1993, pp. 18–20 (in Hebrew).

185 S. Gazit. "Intelligence Estimates and the Decision Maker." *Intelligence . . .* , p. 459. (Translated from Hebrew, emphasis in the original.)

186 Gazit, op. cit., p. 461.

187 Harechavi, *Intelligence and National Security,* p. 442.

188 H. Barlev. "The Decision Maker and the Intelligence Function—The Decision Maker's Point of View." *Intelligence and National Security,* p. 489.

189 "Appendix: The Qualities of the Intelligence Officer—A Panel Discussion." *Intelligence and National Security,* p. 607.

Chapter 17

190 *Fortune,* May 3, 1993, p. 37.

191 *Fortune,* May 3, 1993, p. 39.

Index